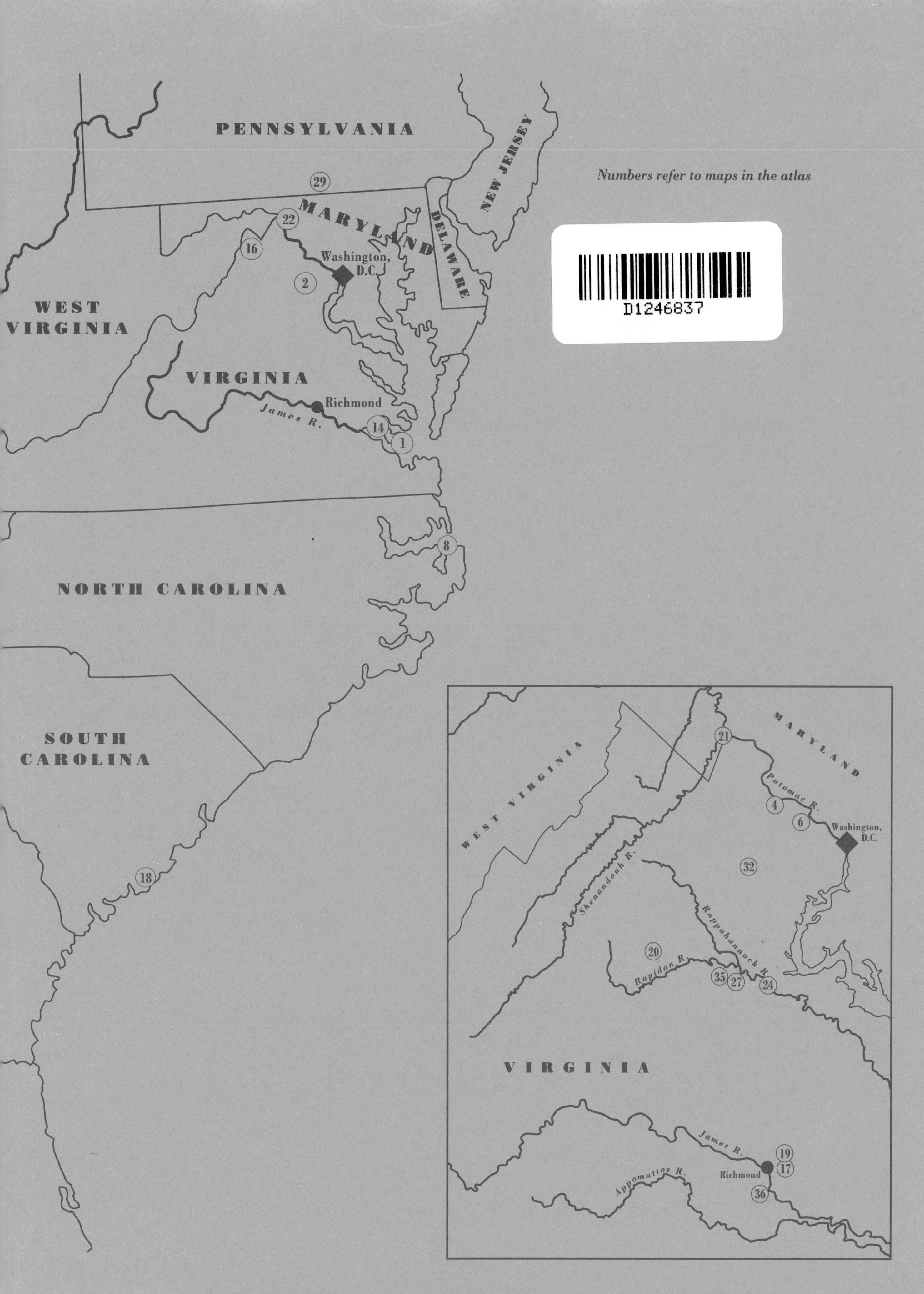

PENNSYLVANIA
NEW JERSEY
Numbers refer to maps in the atlas
29
MARYLAND
22
DELAWARE
16
Washington, D.C.
2
WEST VIRGINIA
VIRGINIA
Richmond
James R.
14
1
8
NORTH CAROLINA
SOUTH CAROLINA
18
MARYLAND
21
WEST VIRGINIA
Potomac R.
4
6
Washington, D.C.
32
Shenandoah R.
Rappahannock R.
20
Rapidan R.
35
27
24
VIRGINIA
James R.
19
17
Richmond
Appomattox R.
36

Civil War Newspaper Maps

A HISTORICAL ATLAS

CIVIL WAR
Newspaper Maps

David Bosse

The Johns Hopkins University Press • Baltimore and London

Printed in the United States of America on acid-free paper

The Johns Hopkins University Press
2715 North Charles Street
Baltimore, Maryland 21218-4319
The Johns Hopkins Press Ltd., London

LIBRARY OF CONGRESS CATALOGING-IN-PUBLICATION DATA

Bosse, David C.
Civil War newspaper maps : a historical atlas / David Bosse.
p. cm.
Includes an introd. on journalistic cartography.
Includes bibliographical references and index.
ISBN 0-8018-4553-X (alk. paper)
1. United States—History—Civil War, 1861–1865—Maps.
2. United States—History—Civil War, 1861–1865—Cartography.
3. Cartography—History —United States. I. Title: Newspaper maps.
G1201.S5B6 1992 G&M
973.7′022′3—dc20 92-33942 CIP
MAP

Text illustrations and maps are reprinted through the courtesy of the following:

Figures 1 and 12: Harlan Hatcher Library, University of Michigan, Ann Arbor. *Figures 2–5, 7–11, 13–27, 29, and 30:* William L. Clements Library, University of Michigan, Ann Arbor. *Figure 6:* James Gordon Bennett Papers, Manuscript Division, Library of Congress. *Figure 28:* Geography and Map Division, Library of Congress. *Figures 31 and 32:* Special Collections Department, William R. Perkins Library, Duke University.

Maps 1, 2a, 2b, 4, 6–8, 11a, 11b, 12b, and 13–39: William L. Clements Library, University of Michigan, Ann Arbor. *Maps 3 and 5:* American Antiquarian Society. *Maps 9 and 12a:* The Newberry Library. *Map 10:* Special Collections Department, William R. Perkins Library, Duke University. *Map 40:* Cincinnati Historical Society.

For Kathleen

Contents

Preface and Acknowledgments

THE AMERICAN CIVIL WAR HAS SUPPLIED MATERIAL FOR COUNTLESS BOOKS, ARTIcles, and films, all of them testifying to the interest still commanded by that fascinating chapter in our history. Yet among these riches, surprisingly little concerns Civil War maps and mapping. In the case of newspaper maps, the shortage of published bibliographies has fostered neglect. Discouraged by the prospect of sifting through thousands of issues, scholars and students of the war have largely ignored the many war-related maps printed in daily Northern newspapers between the attack on Fort Sumter and Lee's surrender four years later.

Intriguing and historically significant maps await those who brave the reams of densely printed Civil War newspapers. Eyewitness sketches by correspondents attached to armies in the field formed the basis of many such maps. Correspondents sent maps with all possible dispatch to their newspaper offices, where they were redrawn, engraved, and printed within days of a battle. In some cases newspapers provided the only published cartographic record of military operations, and they frequently printed military maps far in advance of the maps' official military publication. The urgency of Civil War journalistic cartography occasionally spawned inaccuracies, but most newspaper battle plans are remarkably reliable, and no other cartographic source rivals their immediacy.

This atlas of newspaper maps—grown out of the work of compiling a cartobibliography of all known maps in Northern dailies—illustrates celebrated and obscure battles and campaigns from Pennsylvania to Louisiana and Missouri to Georgia. For most battles, the map selected represents the first to appear in the daily press. (It should be noted that newspaper maps do not exist for all major battles.) A brief overview of the military event and commentary on the map itself accompany each map. For some battles an additional map is included to illustrate particularly significant differences in cartographic treatment. Also accompanying each reproduction are the following: references to additional reports about the battle, published in U.S. War Department, *The War of the Rebellion: A Compilation of the Official Records of the Union and Confederate Armies* (Washington, D.C.: Government Printing Office, 1880–91) and in U.S. Naval War Records Office, *Official Records of the Union and Confederate Navies in the War of the Rebellion* (Washington, D.C.: GPO, 1894–1922), and maps, published in U.S. War Department, *Atlas to Accompany the Official Records of the Union and Confederate Armies* (Washington, D.C.: GPO, 1891–95) and other daily Northern newspapers.

Much of the research for this book made use of the splendid collections at the William L. Clements Library of the University of Michigan, and the university's Harlan Hatcher Library. Elsewhere, James Flatness of the Library of Congress, Geography and Map Division, provided excellent reference assistance on numerous occasions. The author is indebted to John Bergen, James Flatness, Luke Gilliland-Swetland, Mary Pedley, Richard W. Stephenson, and Galen Wilson for their valuable comments on an early version of the manuscript. Robert J. Brugger of the Johns Hopkins University Press made many useful suggestions in the preparation of the manuscript. Special thanks go to John Dann, director of the Clements Library, who encouraged the research of this book in a number of ways, and to Robert W. Karrow, head of special collections at the Newberry Library, for his advice and moral support.

The author gratefully acknowledges the Office of the Vice President for Research, University of Michigan, for partially funding research in New York City and Washington, D.C., and the Hermon Dunlap Smith Center for the History of Cartography at the Newberry Library for fellowship support.

INTRODUCTION

The Development of Journalistic Cartography

CARTOGRAPHY HAS LONG BEEN AN ACCESSORY TO WARFARE, SO IT COMES AS NO surprise that during the Civil War government agencies, military personnel, and commercial publishers all produced maps pertaining to military operations. Plotting strategy required maps, as did recording and celebrating the war's military episodes. Thanks to advances in technology and frantic mapmaking engendered by the war, the quantity of Civil War cartography far surpassed that of any previous American war.[1]

A far different situation existed at the war's beginning. Generals quickly discovered that few maps of the scene of conflict met the requirements of military planning. In some instances the lack of adequate maps forced commanders to rely on commercial cartography. An 1862 letter from Gen. Henry W. Halleck, Lincoln's military advisor, to Gen. Don Carlos Buell testified to this situation. Halleck conceded that he possessed no maps of Kentucky with which to plan a campaign other than "general ones in book stores."[2] The opposing armies soon began creating their own map supply, and the shortage of suitable maps was to a large extent alleviated.

If commercial cartography lost favor with the military, it gained an enormous public audience with an abiding interest in the war. Most Americans eagerly followed the war's progress and in doing so valued maps for reference. Northern and, to a far lesser extent, Southern publishers exploited this market by issuing a multitude of sheet maps covering battles and the various theaters of war.[3] The impressive production of commercial cartographers did not, however, keep pace with the war maps printed in newspapers.

Although American journalistic cartography originated in the early eighteenth century, newspaper maps were rare before the Civil War.[4] To a large extent the development of illustrated journalism in the 1850s foreshadowed the frequent publication of newspaper maps during the war. By the mid-nineteenth century, increasing literacy and new technology had combined to create a thriving market in books and periodicals, many of them illustrated. "Embellished with numerous engravings" became a stock phrase on the title page of novels, poetry, scientific works, and even copies of the Bible in the two decades preceding the Civil War. The first pictorial newspapers catered directly to the public's growing taste for illustrated works by offering credible illustrations in an inexpensive format.[5] Pictorial newspapers featured portraits, views, and representations of current events, adding an exciting dimension to prose description. As early as 1853, one editor argued that text alone inadequately conveyed news and also failed to satisfy the desires of the public.[6]

Publications like *Harper's Weekly* and *Frank Leslie's Illustrated Newspaper* courted this growing news market by pioneering a new form of journalism, which treated graphics as a legitimate source of information rather than simply as entertainment. *Leslie's* "swill milk campaign" of 1858 set the tone in a series of explicit drawings exposing the practice in the New York City area of selling adulterated milk from diseased cows (see Fig. 1). These images, perhaps the first use of illustrations in investigative reporting, helped create a public outcry that eventually forced dairies to improve health standards.[7]

Figure 1. Engraving parodying the "method of milking a sick cow," from *Frank Leslie's Illustrated Newspaper*, June 26, 1858.

Champions of illustrated journalism explicitly distinguished the genre from the contents of the typical "pictorial" newspaper: "The pictorial paper is merely the medium of presenting to the public pictures, whose merits consist in their abstract attractiveness, without regard to the passing events of the day. An illustrated newspaper, on the contrary, not only furnishes its weekly gallery of art, but gives the current news, thus bringing the genius of the pencil and the pen promptly to illustrate the recorded event."[8]

Timeliness played a role in the public's acceptance of illustrated journalism. The first American illustrated newspapers often portrayed "news" several weeks after the fact, thereby diminishing public interest in these papers and contributing to the failure of some.[9] In the 1850s, a shortage of commercial artists and wood engravers was the primary cause of this delay. In the North the demand for artisans was met largely through immigration, but a lack of competent workers plagued Southern publishers. After the war began the situation in places like Richmond and Charleston worsened. Plaintive

The New-York Times.

VOL. XI.—NO. 3103. NEW-YORK, MONDAY, SEPTEMBER 2, 1861. PRICE TWO CENTS.

THE GREAT REBELLION.

HIGHLY IMPORTANT NEWS

A Great National Success at Hatteras Inlet.

Capture of Forts Hatteras and Clark.

Upwards of Seven Hundred Rebels Taken Prisoners.

Twenty-five Cannon, a Thousand Stand of Arms, and a Quantity of Munitions and Stores.

Three Vessels, One Loaded with Cotton, Made Prizes.

A Number of Rebels Killed and Wounded.

"NOBODY HURT" ON OUR SIDE.

A SERIOUS CHECK TO PRIVATEERS.

The Minnesota Coming to New-York with the Prisoners.

THE HARRIET LANE AGROUND.

A BRILLIANT VICTORY.

CAPTURE OF THE FORTS AT HATTERAS INLET.

GEN. WOOL'S ANNOUNCEMENT OF THE VICTORY.

IMPORTANT RESULTS OF THE EXPEDITION.

THE HARRIET LANE.

OFFICIAL REPORTS OF THE ENGAGEMENT.

[Continued on Eighth Page.]

Figure 2. The format of newspapers from this period was considerably different from that of their modern equivalent. This is a typical front page of the *New York Times* in 1861. The addition of illustrations relieved the denseness of the text.

advertisements for engravers that ran in July 1863 in the short-lived Richmond *Southern Illustrated News* attested to the need for skilled labor. Other Confederate newspapers experienced a crippling lack of press operators, printers, and correspondents, as well as printing materials.[10] The Southern press generally lacked either drawings or maps, which has made the study of Confederate journalistic cartography problematical. Although newspapers such as the *Charleston Mercury* and the *Augusta Constitutionalist* printed maps, they did so rarely.[11]

Despite the deficiencies in the Southern press, the Civil War firmly established illustrated journalism as a vital means of reporting news. Images of the war and news maps played to an enthusiastic audience of virtually national breadth. During 1861–62, circulation figures for *Leslie*'s and *Harper*'s reached 100,000 or more, exceeding all other newspapers except the weekly edition of the *New York Tribune*.[12] The apparent economic advantages of illustrated journalism spurred several urban daily newspapers to begin printing war-related maps at the onset of the conflict.

The common use of maps to illustrate news reports was one of several journalistic innovations occasioned by the Civil War.[13] Newspapers made extensive use of the telegraph, railroad, and steam-powered printing presses to gather and disseminate military intelligence for a public audience. As part of this expanded press coverage journalistic cartography suddenly became a familiar feature to many readers who had never before seen a map in a daily newspaper. Early in the war, editors recognized the unique ability of maps to portray spatial relationships, as demonstrated by this note accompanying a map in the *New York Herald*: "We have heretofore given a graphic description of the unsuccessful attack . . . but the map which we publish today will give our readers a clearer understanding of the position of the respective combatants than the most minute word picture could possible [*sic*] afford."[14] Maps added visual interest to the dense, unbroken text of Civil War–era newspapers and presumably attracted readers by focusing attention on a particular event. Most important, they helped readers interpret news of the war.

The Mapmakers

THE ADVENT OF THE AMERICAN WAR CORRESPONDENT GREATLY INFLUENCED THE disclosure of military operations during the Civil War.[15] To obtain the earliest news from the field the Northern press dispatched well over three hundred correspondents to cover practically every theater of combat.[16] These journalists formed a vital link between the war and the public, filing reports on everything from the boredom of camp life to the horrors of battle, and frequently sketching maps. Since few maps named their makers it is impossible to know the exact number that correspondents actually drew. Judging on the basis of cartographic content, however, it is likely that journalists in the field accounted for as many as one-third of all Civil War newspaper maps.

Commonly available cartographic sources usually served as the basis of small-scale newspaper maps compiled at the newspaper office. For this reason, distinctions among the general theater-of-war maps published by different papers reflected style rather than content. In contrast, large- and medium-scale maps, often based on correspondents' sketches, displayed unique cartographic features. These maps, drawn at the scene, contained a variety of details not to be found on much of the war's other mapping, whether commercial or military.

Daily newspapers had taken few steps to insure the success of journalistic cartography at the onset of the war. Although they did not provide for their training, editors encouraged correspondents to include maps when submitting written reports. The *New York Herald* specifically requested that its correspondents "send maps and plans with all descriptions of battles, though they may be but hastily and rudely drawn, they will be of great value. The *Herald* is designed to be a complete history of the war and nothing should be omitted by you."[17] Albert D. Richardson, a *New York Tribune* correspondent who early in the war coordinated that paper's western news-gathering activities in Cairo, Illinois, instructed correspondents to "write short frequent letters and in case of a great battle, or anything else of sufficient importance to justify it, to get up diagrams, collect the facts and go directly through to New York."[18]

Because editors believed that anonymity protected their correspondents from military reprisals, few published reports carried a by-line for the first years of the war.[19] Presumably for the same reason, most newspaper maps did not identify their maker. A correspondent's published letter might lay claim to authorship by referring to the "map I hereby enclose," but this simply established that the same person was responsible for

Figure 3. Mathew Brady photograph of a group of *New York Herald* correspondents in the field.

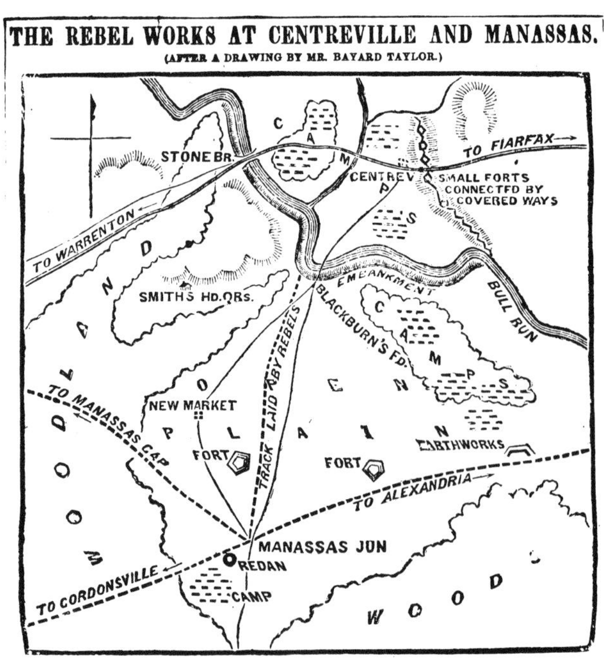

Figure 4. This map, published in the *New York Tribune* on March 17, 1862, is unusual in stating its authorship. Bayard Taylor was a well-known author of travel literature who had contributed many pieces to the *Tribune*. Because of his notoriety, the map was published under Taylor's name.

both. In an attempt to hold correspondents accountable for their statements, Gen. Joseph Hooker issued an order in the spring of 1863 requiring published letters from the Army of the Potomac to be signed.[20] Hooker's proclamation had little effect on newspaper mapping, which remained an anonymous venture.

Being a resourceful breed, correspondents seemed undaunted by their lack of drafting skills. Charles Carleton Coffin, correspondent of the *Boston Daily Journal*, may well have been the only reporter with any cartographic experience, having worked as a surveyor before the war.[21] Ironically, the *Journal* ran his maps (accompanying reports identified by the signature "Carleton") as single-column schematic diagrams composed of type and printers' rules, thereby losing the advantage of any drafting talent he possessed. Nearly all correspondents' maps were detailed, large-scale depictions of battles or military operations drawn on the spot.[22] Some map titles made explicit claims of cartographic accuracy, but prudent editors realized that correspondents normally worked under adverse conditions. Describing its map of Columbus, Kentucky, the *New York Tribune* assumed a guarded tone: "Of course it is not drawn with the precision of a practical engineer, but it is sufficiently accurate to present an intelligible idea of the place and its surroundings."[23] While journalists tended to be brash and self-confident, they, too, occasionally recognized their limitations. In the summer of 1861 an unidentified *New York Herald* correspondent noted the accuracy of the source of his map but added, "You can see that I am no draftsman, and I have no time to make it [the map] more full."[24]

George Alfred Townsend, a young writer in the employ of the *New York Herald*, wrote one of the few known accounts of a correspondent's mapping activity. Townsend witnessed the Battle of Cedar Mountain, Virginia, on August 9, 1862. Four days later the *Herald* published his description of the battle, illustrated with a map. Townsend's letter to the paper provides a glimpse of the map's creation not long after the fighting ceased:

> I rode across the brook to a knoll, and proceeded to sketch on the back of an envelope the locality of the battle ground. While thus engaged a man in a gray suit . . . trotted up the ascent and saluted me. "Are you making a sketch of our position?" said the General to me curtly. "Not for any military purpose, sir," I replied, "merely for reference." "Are you a reporter?" "Yes sir." "You may go on."[25]

The officer who questioned Townsend and approved of his sketching was Confederate general J.E.B. ("Jeb") Stuart.[26] Later that morning Townsend received permission to ride within the Confederate outer lines while watched over by a Lt. Charles M. Blackford, presumably taking the opportunity to improve his map.

The calm scene of civility at Cedar Mountain in no way typified the circumstances surrounding the creation of most newspaper maps. More often journalists contended

Figure 5. Engraving from *Harper's Weekly* of April 30, 1864, suggesting the difficulties correspondents faced in observing the field of battle.

with military chaos and conditions that hampered the transmission of news. Henry Villard, a correspondent for the *New York Herald*, and later the *New York Tribune*, was well acquainted with the dangers and rigors of war reporting. He believed that only through extraordinary mental and physical efforts could a battle be successfully reported. Correspondents had to depart from the battlefield "immediately after actions were over, in order to lose the least possible time in getting their reports through, riding whole nights and days through regions infested with the enemy's marauders, and jumping aboard steamboats or trains, devoting every available moment of the entire journey to the drawing of maps and writing out of notes."[27]

Ultimately the haggard correspondent reached the newspaper office where he turned his documents over to an editor. Although some editors claimed to be cognizant of the historical value of these maps, they evidently took little care to preserve them. A thorough search of numerous archives has yielded only one manuscript map done by a correspondent.[28] The lone example, a small sketch of the Union lines in Kentucky and Tennessee, is found in a letter from Thomas Knox to the *New York Herald*'s editor, James Gordon Bennett (see Fig. 6).[29] In contrast, many drawings made by Civil War artists to illustrate weekly papers survive in public and private collections.

Not all maps drawn in the field can be attributed to newspaper correspondents. Civilians not associated with the press played a minor role in Civil War newspaper cartography. For example, a "loyal spy" reputedly drew a map of Fort Pillow, Tennessee, published in the June 11, 1862, issue of the *World* (New York). According to the correspondent who included the map with his article, several officers examined the map and attested to its accuracy. Similarly, the *Chicago Daily Tribune* of January 24, 1862, featured a map of the Confederate defenses at Columbus, Kentucky, based on a sketch "drawn from memory by one who has been there and knows all about the place." Correspondents usually acted as intermediaries between such mapmakers and editors, but some maps, like that of the siege of Washington, North Carolina, by Chaplain H. S. White, Fifth Rhode Island Artillery, found their way directly to the newspaper office.[30] The *New York Tribune* published White's map on April 9, 1863, under the title "General Foster's Situation in North Carolina."

The notion of military secrecy did not prevent officers from drawing maps for publication during the war. Many officers, especially in the volunteer army, desired to advance their careers through public exposure and therefore freely cooperated with the press. Some went so far as to court the favor of correspondents in order to get their names into print.[31] Publicity was not always the reason officers shared their cartographic skills. Referring to a map of the siege of Corinth, Mississippi, published in the *New York Herald* of June 5, 1862, the paper's correspondent credited "the good nature of a friendly captain of topographers for a sketch of the Rebel position," without revealing the name of his source.

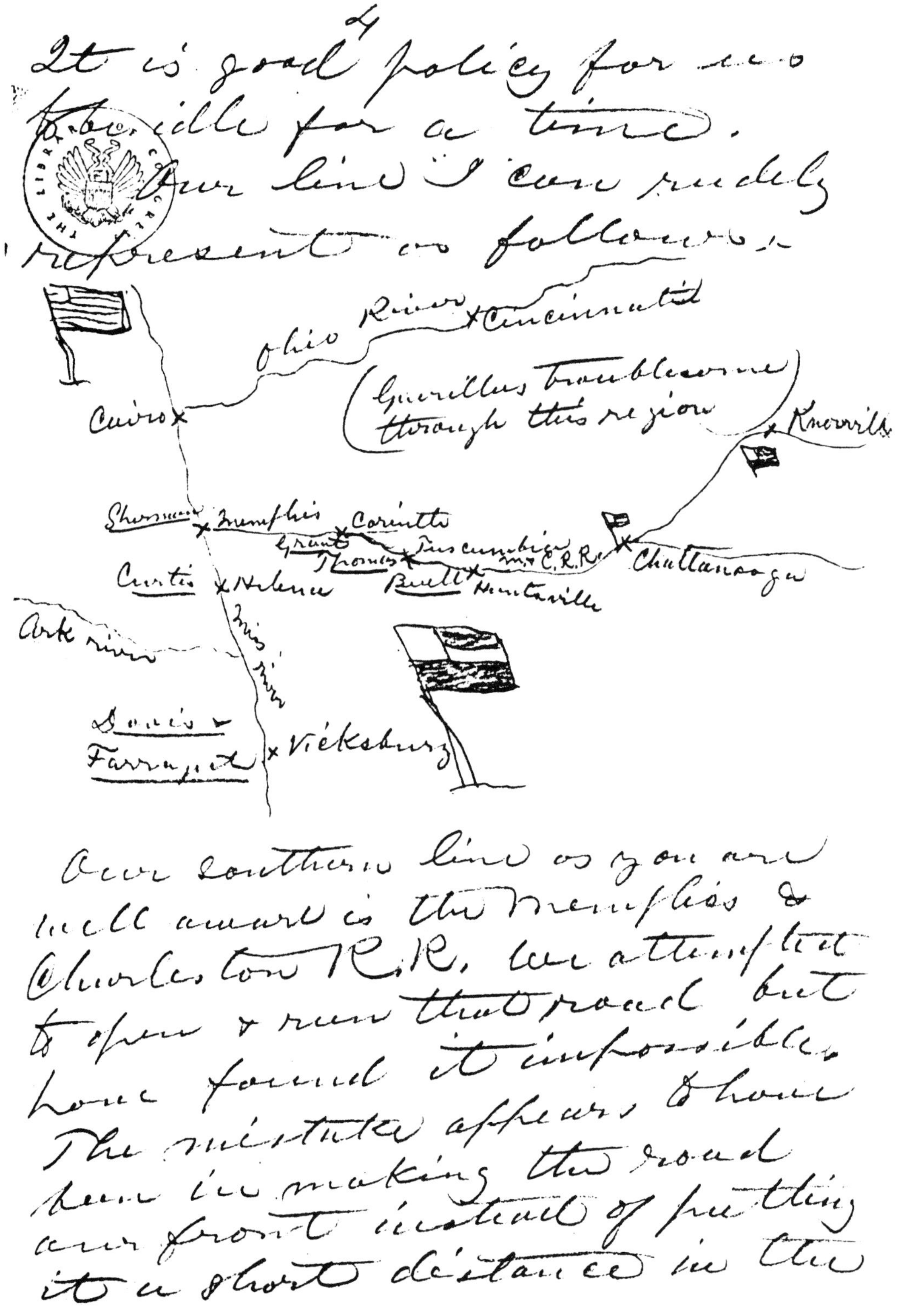

It is good policy for us to be idle for a time. Our line I can rudely represent as follows:

Our southern line as you are well aware is the Memphis & Charleston R.R. We attempted to open & run that road but have found it impossible. The mistake appears to have been in making the road our front instead of putting it a short distance in the

Figure 6. Sketch map drawn by Thomas Knox in a letter to his editor, James Gordon Bennett, dated June 28, 1862.

A St. Louis newspaper can claim the distinction of publishing the first map drawn by an officer for the daily press. On August 25, 1861, the *Daily Missouri Republican* featured a map of the Battle of Wilson's Creek, Missouri, by Frederick W. Reeder of the First U.S. Cavalry. The *Republican* rewarded Reeder's effort by prominently displaying his name in the map's title (see Map 3). The Battle of Carnifex Ferry, West Virginia, provided another notable occurrence in the history of Civil War cartographic journalism. The coverage of this relatively minor engagement marked the first time the daily press printed a military map prior to its official publication.[32] On September 18, 1861, the *Cincinnati Daily Commercial* and the *Cincinnati Daily Gazette* each included a map attributed to Capt. W. Angelo Powell, an officer on the staff of Gen. William Rosecrans, who commanded the Union forces. Powell's original map accompanied Rosecrans's report of the battle, later published in the *Atlas to Accompany the Official Records of the Union and Confederate Armies*. Whether Powell or Rosecrans made the map available to the press is undetermined.

Newspapers also obtained copies of military maps by means other than directly from military mapmakers. Gen. Irvin McDowell's official report and map of the first battle of Manassas, or Bull Run, Virginia (July 21, 1861), apparently falls into this category. The map's initial publication occurred in the August 16, 1861, issue of the *New York Herald*.[33] The *Herald* did not disclose its source but mentioned that the map and report had been "transmitted to the War Department," where some enterprising *Herald* agent presumably procured a copy.

More than any other newspaper, the *New York Herald* featured maps of military authorship. Its correspondents were particularly adept at securing copies of official military maps, which they immediately passed on to New York for publication in the pages of the *Herald*. Maps published this way included Gen. Egbert Viele's map of the assault on Fort Pulaski, Georgia, that he commanded (published May 20, 1862); a map of the siege of Chattanooga, Tennessee, from the surveys of William E. Merrill, chief of topographical engineers (September 8, 1863); a map of military operations on Brazos Island, Texas, by Capt. James T. Baker of the topographical engineers (November 17, 1863); and a map of the skirmish at Port Royal Ferry, South Carolina, by Lt. Col. James Fraser, an engineer with the Forty-seventh New York (January 11, 1862). One can only marvel at the availability of these and other authoritative maps for public dissemination.

Maps drawn at the scene by eyewitnesses and published within a short time of the events they depicted possessed a relevancy unequaled by any other mapping of the war available to the public. Within days of important battles or movements readers could consult maps of military operations for as little as two to five cents, the cost of a newspaper.[34] When considering the numerous difficulties attending the creation of newspaper maps, their efficiency and economy become all the more remarkable.

The Newspaper Map Enterprise

WAR CORRESPONDENTS ENJOYED REPUTATIONS AS EITHER HEROES OR SCOUNDRELS, depending upon the source, and in fact may have been something of each. Criticism of Civil War journalism dwells mostly on the correspondent, but Henry Villard defended his fellow "Bohemians" (as those vagabond writers dubbed themselves) by blaming their employers for the deficiencies in war coverage. Villard believed that editors encouraged correspondents to sacrifice accuracy for expediency. "To print the first, however incorrect and incomplete, intelligence," he accused in 1865, "was the height of their ambition."[35] While editors certainly do not deserve all of the blame, there is little doubt that the intense competition among papers influenced judgments made in newspaper offices as well as in the field.

Correspondents understood that their employers placed a premium on getting news first. The *New York Herald* made it clear that it must never be beaten by rivals, and a *Herald* correspondent noted that to fall behind another newspaper's coverage often meant dismissal.[36] Under these circumstances journalists might be inclined to leap to unsubstantiated conclusions. To gather reliable information, surpass rivals, and successfully transmit maps and dispatches under adverse conditions went beyond the ability of some correspondents. One journalist berated the tactics of certain of his colleagues, stating that as soon as a battle began they would "dash immediately for New York, and there portray a plan of the battlefield [they had] never seen, with all the worm fences and creeks running the wrong way."[37] This charge may not be as extravagant as it seems, for it is possible that some published letters described battles that the writer never witnessed.[38]

The only known case of fabricated journalistic cartography followed the Battle of Pea Ridge, Arkansas, fought March 7–8, 1862. Only two correspondents, Thomas Knox of the *New York Herald* and William Fayel of the *Daily Missouri Democrat*, accompanied Gen. Samuel Curtis's Union army into northwestern Arkansas. After the battle, Knox traveled some two hundred miles by horseback to Rolla, Missouri, where he mailed his report. Eventually Knox arrived in St. Louis, confident of an exclusive story, but instead found a copy of the *New York Tribune* with a map and full-page account of the battle.[39] Junius Browne, an otherwise reliable journalist who wrote for the *Cincinnati Daily Times* as well as the *Tribune*, authored the fraudulent description. Browne resourcefully concocted his letter from telegraph dispatches, rumors, and his own sense of military drama. Richard Colburn, representing the *World*, also described the battle from St. Louis, probably in concert with Browne.[40]

Several newspapers published dubious maps of the Pea Ridge battle. The first appeared in the March 17 issue of the *Cincinnati Daily Times*, "taken on the spot by our special correspondent," the sly Junius Browne. A map in the *Tribune*, differing in several particulars, followed on the twentieth (see Map 11b). On March 21, the *World* printed a map of Pea Ridge that it stated had been "received from our correspondent at Pea Ridge." It was also on the 21st that the *New York Herald* printed Knox's map. William Fayel's newspaper, the *Daily Missouri Democrat*, did not include a map of the battle.

Insufficient information, rather than journalistic duplicity, caused the greatest shortcomings of both maps and reports in newspapers. Rarely could correspondents view the entire field of battle; consequently their knowledge of incidents and positions suffered. If a newspaper had more than one correspondent at the scene, as sometimes happened, the chaotic conditions of battle still made unequivocal description nearly impossible. Other witnesses, including officers, found themselves in a similar position. Conflicting official reports and charges and countercharges made by commanders in postwar memoirs reflect the confusion of combat.[41] Newspaper reports might even surpass military accounts, as claimed by Union general Henry Boynton after comparing Whitelaw Reid's description of the Battle of Shiloh, written for the *Cincinnati Daily Gazette*, with passages in William T. Sherman's published memoirs.[42]

The challenge of combat reporting was revealed in a correspondent's admission that he had "labored vainly all day to get some idea of movements, but in the hurry, the din, and the confusion, nothing was clear."[43] Another correspondent recalled his predicament at the Battle of Wilson's Creek, Missouri:

> After I found a position beyond range of musketry, the artillery would insist upon searching me out. While I was seated under a small oak tree . . . and my pencil busy on my note-book, the tree above my head was cut by a shell. Moving from that spot, I had just resumed my writing, when a shot tore up the ground . . . and covered me with dirt. Even a remove to another quarter did not answer my purpose, and I finished my notes from the rear.[44]

Because combat physically limited one's ability to record information, correspondents relied on the statements of other observers and participants, although not without questioning their validity. In his account of the Battle of Logan's Cross Roads, Kentucky, the *New York Tribune*'s correspondent excused his letter with the following:

> Perhaps the most difficult task that can devolve upon a journalist is to describe correctly a battle. No two human eyes can overlook the whole, and observe every

The New-York Times.

VOL. XI...NO. 3183. NEW-YORK, WEDNESDAY, DECEMBER 4, 1861. PRICE TWO CENTS.

THE NATIONAL LINES BEFORE WASHINGTON.

A MAP EXHIBITING THE DEFENCES OF THE NATIONAL CAPITAL, AND POSITIONS OF THE SEVERAL DIVISIONS OF THE GRAND UNION ARMY.

...HE ARMY BEFORE WASHINGTON.

...he interest which attaches to the military ...perations of the National army on the line ...f the Potomac, has induced us to present the ...eaders of the TIMES with the above very ...mplete and accurate map of the impreg...able lines on the Virginia side of the National ...apital. These masterly defences sweep from ...he neighborhood of Great Falls, ten miles ...bove Washington, southward to the mouth of ...he Accotink Creek, 15 miles below the City; ...nd occupy the arc of a circle the outermost ...oint of which, in the direction of the main ...ody of the enemy at Manassas, may be fixed ...t Flint Hill. This territory is actually in ...ossession of our troops; the National pick...ts and reconnoitering parties frequently push...ng miles nearer the rebel host, but fully maintaining the ground embraced between the dotted line traced on the map, and the banks of the Potomac.

The principal permanent fortifications, which the rebels, if they attempt them, will find to be an impassable barrier to their ambitious designs upon the Capital, have been enumerated by title and position in the General Orders of Gen. McCLELLAN, but are, for the first time, located and named upon the present map. How perfect the circle they describe about the city and that of Alexandria, will be perceived at a glance. To state how heavy is the armament of these posts; how numerous the bodies of men detailed for their defence, and what skill in gunnery these new artillerists have already attained, would be a revelation more valuable to the enemy than instructive to the loyal reader. It is enough to say that officers of European armies, skilled in the latest results of military engineering, pronounce the works in front of Washington as absolutely impregnable against the largest assailing force, if held by no more than fifty thousand men.

Another novel and useful trait of our present map is its geographical definition of the territory occupied by each of the eight divisions constituting the grand defensive army. They are indicated by dotted lines extending from the river to the outer defensive lines, and distinguished by the Roman numerals, I, II III, &c.

POSITION OF THE SEVERAL DIVISIONS.

I..Gen. GEORGE A. MCCALL,
II..Gen. WILLIAM F. SMITH,
III..Gen. FITZ-JOHN PORTER,
IV..Gen. IRVIN MCDOWELL,
V..Gen. LOUIS BLENKER,
VI..Gen. WILLIAM B. FRANKLIN,
VII..Gen. SAMUEL P. HEINTZELMAN,
VIII..Gen. EDWIN V. SUMNER.

The force embraced in each of these divisions, is, it is needless to say, withheld from publication. It is only known that at the general review, on the 18th ult., seventy-six regiments of infantry, seventeen batteries of artillery, and seven regiments of cavalry, forming an aggregate of seventy-five thousand men, passed in line before Gen. MCCLELLAN; while it is also known that immense reserves, occupying the fortifications and the camps, and acting as redoubled picket-guards, made no appearance in that splendid parade. We reproduce from the columns of the TIMES, the following schedule of the several divisions, as represented on that occasion:

GEN. M'CALL'S DIVISION.
Twelve regiments of infantry.
Two batteries.
One regiment of cavalry.

GEN. SMITH'S DIVISION.
Ten regiments of infantry.
Two batteries.
One regiment of cavalry.

GEN. FITZ JOHN PORTER'S DIVISION.
Thirteen regiments of infantry.
Three batteries.
Two regiments of cavalry.

GEN. M'DOWELL'S DIVISION.
Eleven regiments of infantry.
Three batteries.
One regiment of cavalry.

GEN. BLENKER'S DIVISION.
Eleven regiments of infantry.
Two batteries.
Dickett's regiment of mounted riflemen.

GEN. FRANKLIN'S DIVISION.
Twelve regiments of infantry.
Three batteries.
One regiment of cavalry.

GEN. HEINTZELMAN'S DIVISION.
Seven regiments of infantry.
Two batteries.
One regiment of cavalry.

Gen. SUMNER, upon his return from California, was at once placed in command of an Eighth Division, assigned to the west bank of the Potomac, below Alexandria; and to constitute his command twelve regiments of infantry, with a corresponding strength of artillery and cavalry, have been drawn from the reserved force upon the Maryland side of the river. We have also reason to believe that Gen. ERASMUS D. KEYES has been ordered with a powerful body of troops to a point on the Orange and Alexandria Railroad, near Springfield, whence at the proper time a movement will no doubt be made to outflank the insurgent positions at Manassas Junction.

...PRESIDENT'S MESSAGE

...case, discarding all moral, social and treaty ... of the American people. The correspondence [illegible]

Figure 7. Union general George McClellan took exception with publication of this map, printed in the *New York Times*, December 4, 1861, complaining that it aided the enemy. Roman numerals vaguely show the location of Union divisions.

> noteworthy incident of one of these culminating episodes of war. And furthermore, the number of the actors engaged—their constant shifting of position—their inevitable excitement and comparative confusion during and after the action, render the immediate availability of sources of trustworthy information other than his own observations precarious to the chronicler.[45]

Beyond the restrictions imposed by the vicissitudes of battle lurked the suppression of information through censorship. Empowered to monitor telegraph dispatches and to open mail, government officials arbitrarily altered or deleted information deemed too sensitive or controversial for publication.[46] Given the nature of the information they contained, maps soon became an issue. On December 4, 1861, the *New York Times* provoked the wrath of Gen. George B. McClellan by printing a map of Washington, D.C., and northern Virginia showing the Union troop positions. McClellan immediately sent a copy of the newspaper to Secretary of War Simon Cameron demanding sanctions against the *Times* for aiding and abetting the enemy. Cameron declined to act but wrote to Henry Raymond, editor of the *Times*, enclosing a copy of McClellan's letter and advising Raymond to avoid a "similar inadvertency" in the future. Raymond countered that his map simply copied one printed in Washington and available to any purchaser.[47]

Military censors rarely took on editors directly, preferring instead to confiscate correspondents' letters and maps, as in the celebrated case of Thomas Knox of the *New York Herald.* Knox was one of several correspondents who accompanied the expedition of Gen. William T. Sherman that ended in the Battle of Chickasaw Bluffs, Mississippi, on December 29, 1862. Knox wrote a disparaging account of the costly Union repulse, complete with two maps, and put it on a mail boat bound for Cairo, Illinois. The next day he learned that his letter had gone no farther than Sherman's headquarters.[48] Sherman wished to try Knox on espionage charges and threatened him with hanging but settled for expelling the correspondent from the Union lines. From that point on, Knox operated in the eastern theater of war.

In a subsequent letter to the *Herald* describing the battle, Knox commented on his missing maps of Chickasaw Bluffs:

> Just as I am closing this account of the battle I have the pleasure of receiving the manuscript of my first letter, with a cool and refreshing note. . . . The letter is all right, but I fail to find two elaborate maps, drawn with great care. It is possible that General Sherman may need them for his instruction. Had he possessed them earlier it is possible that he would have taken Vicksburg.[49]

Throughout the war Sherman remained at odds with the press and continually sought to have its representatives banned from the army. Although his efforts never fully achieved their goal, they did have an impact on journalistic cartography, as witnessed by

Thomas Knox. Sherman restricted the press to an even greater extent during his Meridian campaign (February–March 1864), when he allowed only one correspondent to accompany him.[50] The single exception, De Benneville Keim of the *New York Herald*, also served as an aide-de-camp to Gen. James McPherson. Keim filed the only newspaper report of Sherman's raid through central Mississippi, but without a map. Some Chicago and Cincinnati newspapers published general, small-scale maps purporting to show the Meridian campaign, but Sherman's movements were so well concealed that on February 27 the *Chicago Daily Tribune* printed a map not of Mississippi but of Alabama with the caption "Sherman's Expedition."

In the East, censors busily attempted to control the flow of information from correspondents to their papers. Before the Peninsular campaign in Virginia (March–July 1862), the War Department established a voluntary parole system to prevent correspondents with the Army of the Potomac from communicating intelligence that included maps and pictorial representations of Union positions.[51] The War Department's threat to bring charges of treason and expulsion from the lines met with some success. Nonetheless, many published maps violated the regulation that news of battles must not discuss or indicate the position of Union forces.

The *New York Herald*'s cartographic coverage of the Peninsular campaign exceeded that of any other newspaper, and in many ways complied with War Department restrictions. Their full-page map of the siege of Yorktown, Virginia, published on April 22, 1862, illustrates the point (see Fig. 8). The map depicts Confederate earthworks and fortifications and even notes the number of their cannon, but in a show of great restraint indicates no Union positions. Referring to the map, a Cincinnati correspondent questioned the detailed portrayal of the Confederate defenses, arguing that if the Union command had to guess at the strength and disposition of the enemy, the *Herald* could do no better.[52]

In addition to censorship, factors far from the scene of war affected cartographic journalism. Once a map left the hands of its maker it was prey to both intentional and unintentional alteration. Editors, draftsmen, and engravers, each in their turn, transformed the sketch into its final form. Hurriedly working to meet deadlines they undoubtedly introduced some inadvertent changes into a correspondent's drawing, and because of time constraints or ignorance such changes escaped notice. The map's author might then take exception, as did George Alfred Townsend after the Battle of Cedar Mountain, Virginia. Returning to New York, Townsend delivered his report and map to Frederic Hudson, managing editor of the *New York Herald*, whose staff quickly executed both for the following day's edition. Townsend recalled his dismay upon seeing his efforts in print: "Next morning, to my astonishment, there was a map of the battle-field that had nothing intelligible about it, and my account was distributed in half a dozen places in the paper amongst a lot of rubbish by other persons and a good deal of it I could not find at

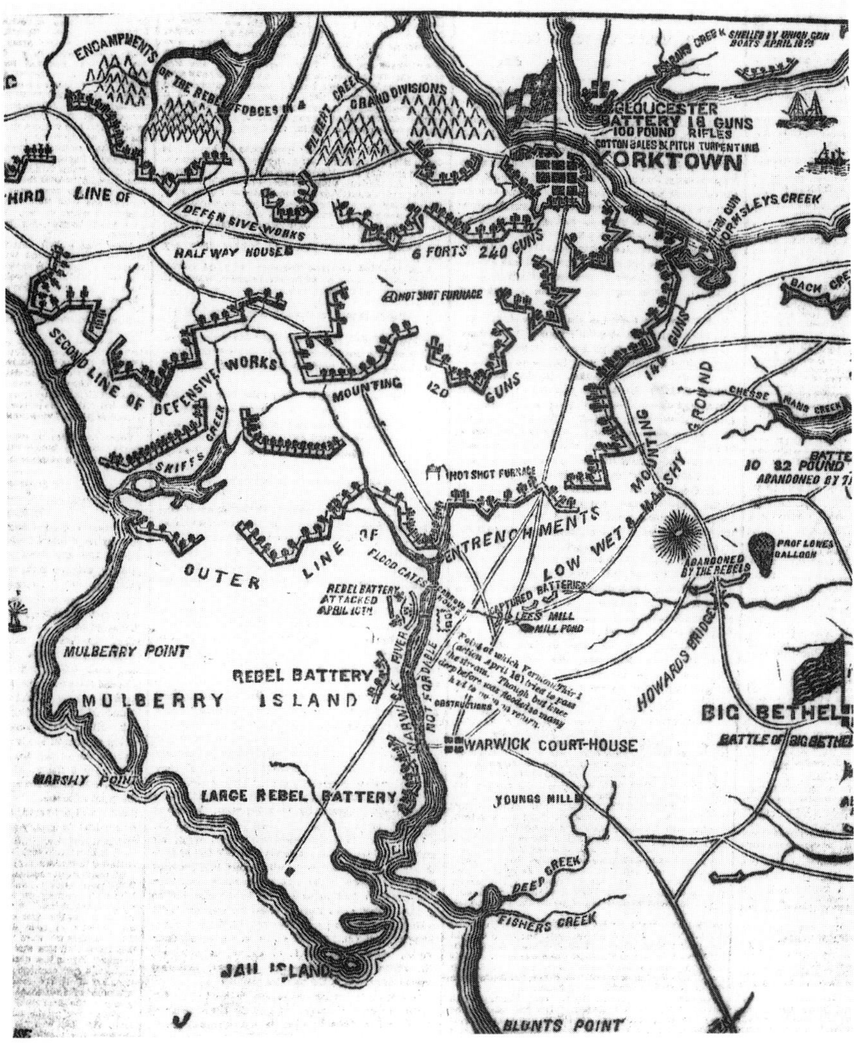

Figure 8. Detail of the *New York Herald*'s map of the siege of Yorktown showing Confederate positions.

all. I told Mr. Hudson that the map he printed was nonsense and that the stream put down there was made to run into its spring instead of its mouth."[53] The severity of Townsend's complaint does not seem entirely justified, for the map provides an adequate depiction of the battle, despite the confusion over certain streams (see map 20).

Unfortunately, like so many other correspondents' maps, Townsend's original did not survive, or we might compare it with the *Herald*'s map. Virtually all maps sent from the field fell victim to the process of cartographic production. It is possible that sketches for small maps were simply attached to the engraving block and the engraver cut right through the paper into the wood. In other cases, after being redrawn onto the block, the original maps were seemingly discarded. Since no good description of newspaper map engraving exists, the exact fate of correspondents' sketches is unknown.

Figure 9. A ten cylinder type-revolving press manufactured by Robert Hoe & Company. The impression cylinders can be seen positioned around the central printing cylinder on which type or stereotypes were mounted. (J. Luther Ringwalt, *American Encyclopedia of Printing*, 1871.)

Figure 10. Beating a papier-mâché matrix to take an impression for stereotyping. (J. Luther Ringwalt, *American Encyclopedia of Printing*, 1871.)

The Production of Newspaper Maps

THAT DAILY NEWSPAPERS BECAME A PRINCIPAL SOURCE OF INEXPENSIVE CARTOGRAPHY was largely due to developments in the printing trades. Steam-powered rotary printing presses alone altered production practices, by dramatically increasing productivity. These presses consisted of a large horizontal printing cylinder, ink rollers, and from two to ten impression cylinders (see Fig. 9). After curved forms bearing the handset type were locked onto the bed of the printing cylinder, paper was fed onto the rotating impression cylinders, printing up to ten pages simultaneously. As early as 1861, Robert Hoe & Company of New York manufactured presses capable of twenty thousand impressions per hour.[54] Even this rate of production barely kept pace with the wartime demand for news.

The cost of metal type figured as another important component in mass publishing. In the 1850s daily newspapers with large circulations replaced worn type every three months or so to assure legibility.[55] To circumvent this expense, papier-mâché or wet-mat stereotyping developed as an alternative method of printing newspapers. Wet-mat stereotypes were made by laying four or five sheets of papier-mâché on the oil coated surface of a page of type set in a frame, or chase. To take an exact impression of the type required beating the papier-mâché (matrix) with a special brush (see Fig. 10). After drying in a steam press, the matrix and the type were separated. Next the matrix was molded in a casting box to conform to the curved surface of the printing cylinder. Finally, molten type metal was poured into the indented matrix, which when cooled and trimmed formed a durable printing plate.[56]

The credit for adapting the wet-mat process to newspaper production goes to Charles Craske. Craske first cast experimental plates in 1854, and with the support of the *New York Tribune* continued to refine the process.[57] On April 10, 1861, the *Tribune* became the first American newspaper to be printed from wet-mat stereotype plates. The *Tribune* proclaimed that stereotypes not only saved wear on type but also provided greater legibility and reduced printing time.[58] By quickly and inexpensively duplicating entire pages of a newspaper, stereotyping eliminated the need for a large type stock and reduced the considerable labor of handsetting type. These advantages appealed to other New York dailies, and soon the *Sun*, the *Herald*, and the *Times* began printing from stereotype plates cast in as little as seventeen minutes.[59]

Stereotypes also played an important role in the reproduction of newspaper maps and drawings. At the time of the Civil War, wood engravings were the chief means of illustrating newspapers and periodicals. Contrary to what the name implies, wood engraving was a relief process closely related to the woodcut. Like that of the woodcut, the raised surface of a wood engraving made it ideal for printing simultaneously with letterpress text. However, wood blocks often split after repeated printing, and they proved incompatible with rotary presses. Experiments conducted in 1856 by the *Illustrated London News* demonstrated the futility of engraving curved wood blocks for use on printing cylinders.[60] The refinement of wet-mat stereotyping provided the solution by offering an economical and practical means of printing illustrations on rotary presses.[61] Even newspapers that printed their text directly from type rather than from stereotypes could mount stereotyped illustration plates on curved wood blocks such as those sold by press manufacturer Robert Hoe.[62]

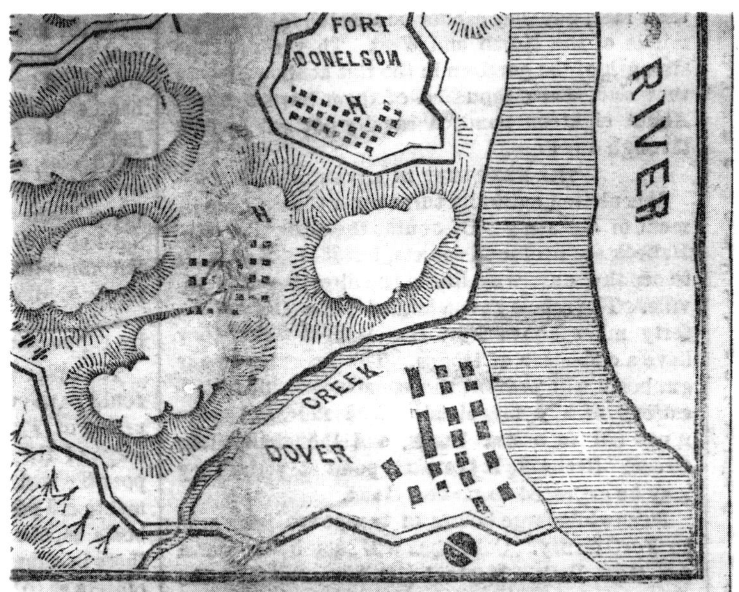

Figure 11. Detail of a map of Fort Donelson, on which appears (*near bottom edge*) the print of a screw used to mount the map stereotype on a supporting wood block during printing. From the *World*, February 22, 1862.

Wood engravings differed from woodcuts in being cut on the end grain rather than the side or plank, with engraving tools such as a burin rather than a blade. In the nineteenth century, wood engravers practiced two contrasting styles, although in each case the nonprinting surface was removed. White-line engraving, which, like wood engraving generally, had long been in decline, was revived at the end of the eighteenth century by the English engraver Thomas Bewick. White-line engraving resulted in an image of white lines on a black (printed) background (see Fig. 12). Conversely, black-line engraving imitated line drawing by printing the image on a white (nonprinted) background. Black-line maps far outnumber any other style printed in Civil War era newspapers.[63]

Although the white-line technique offered considerable savings in time since only the design needed engraving, newspapers used it sparingly. Difficulties in inking and printing the relatively unbroken relief surface of white-line maps may account for their scarcity in the daily press. Adherence to the labor-intensive black-line technique may also reflect the dominance of lithographed maps and maps engraved on copper, steel, or wax. Editors may have favored black-line maps on the basis of their resemblance to those familiar cartographic formats.

The majority of newspaper maps were printed from blocks composed of several sections of wood joined by screws or bolts (see Fig. 13). Frank Leslie, an enterprising

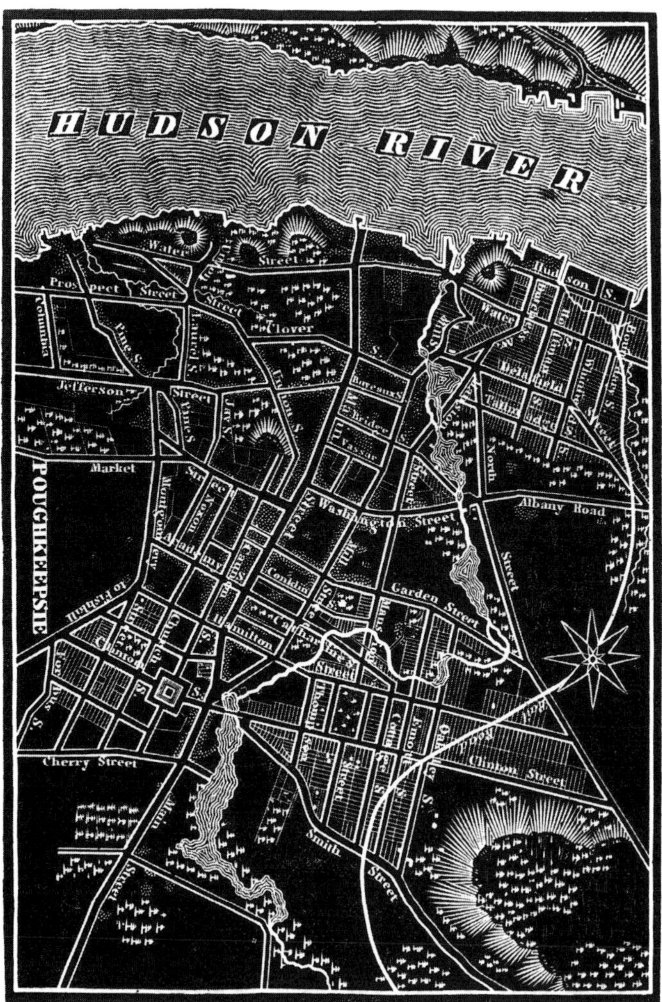

Figure 12. An example of white-line wood engraving. Map of Poughkeepsie, New York, in Thomas Gordon's *Gazetteer of the State of New York* (Philadelphia, 1836).

British engraver turned publisher, possibly brought the technique with him when he immigrated to the United States in 1849.[64] The sectioned block offered two immediate benefits: it created a large printing surface, and when disassembled it allowed simultaneous engraving of multiple parts of the same map or illustration. Due to the time limitations confronting the daily press, the only feasible means of engraving large maps, some of which measured as much as 50 × 40 cm., required a sectioned block. In this way a map that would take a single engraver several days to complete could be cut by several engravers in just a few hours.[65]

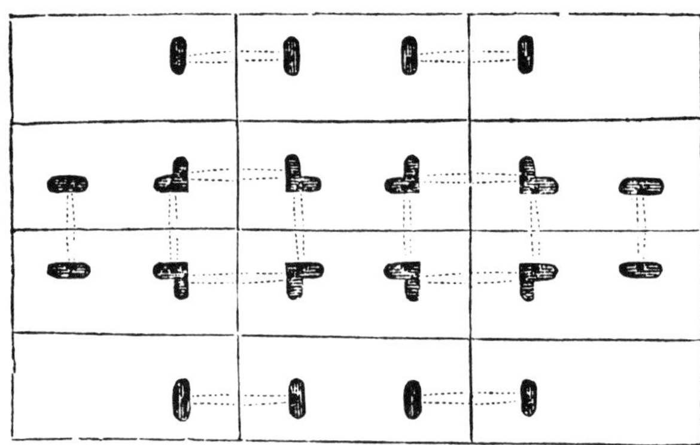

Figure 13. Illustration showing the manner of joining a multisectioned wood block. From *Frank Leslie's Illustrated Newspaper*, August 2, 1856.

Daily newspapers did not have in-house art departments in the mid-nineteenth century but relied instead on outside engraving firms.[66] Wood-engraving workshops may have assigned sections of the map to engravers on the basis of their experience or talent. Illustrated weeklies, following this practice, hired engravers who specialized in human figures, buildings, or trees, working only on those portions of the design.[67] Map work consisted of "lettering and plain work," according to one contemporary characterization of wood engraving, but in the interests of expedience engravers of maps for the daily press probably cut everything on the section of the block assigned to them.[68]

Engravers preferred working with close-grained hardwoods such as boxwood, mahogany, or fruit woods. Blocks of the end grain, often measuring no more than six square centimeters so as to prevent warping, were cut, planed, sorted by size, and stored. An application of chalk or white enamel prepared the surface of the block to receive the design.[69] The map could be drawn directly on the block in reverse or transferred to the block by placing a map drawn in soft lead pencil face down on the block and tracing it.[70] A master engraver then cut the lines of the map where they crossed sections of the block, to assure some harmony to the whole.[71] The block was next divided and the sections

Figure 14. View of a wood-engraving workshop. From *Frank Leslie's Illustrated Newspaper*, August 2, 1856.

Figure 15. Wood blocks being planed and surfaced in preparation for engraving. From *Frank Leslie's Illustrated Newspaper*, August 2, 1856.

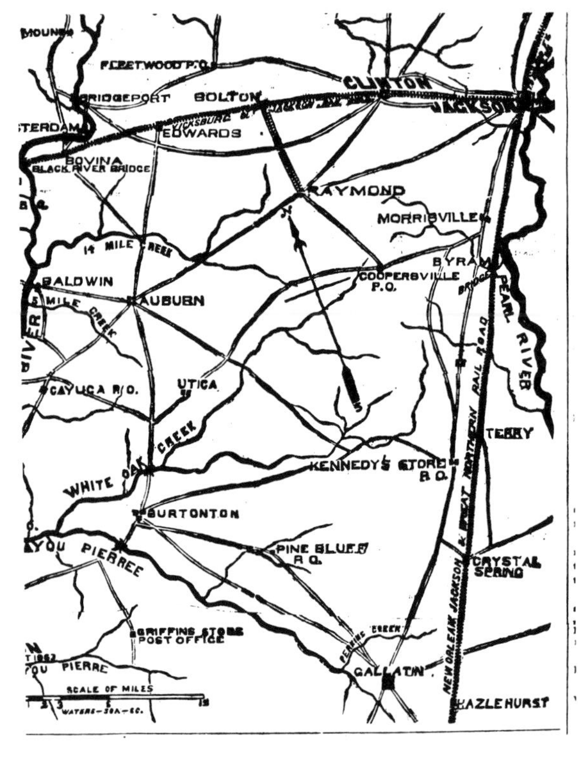

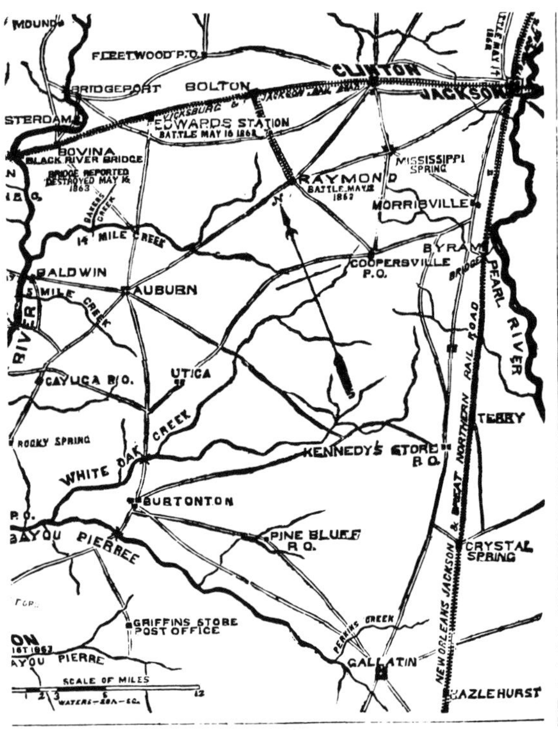

Figures 16a and 16b. *Top*, section of a map of the Vicksburg campaign printed in the *New York Herald* on May 17, 1863. *Bottom*, the same section as it appeared in a map printed in the *Herald* May 23, 1863. Numerous changes can be seen west of Jackson.

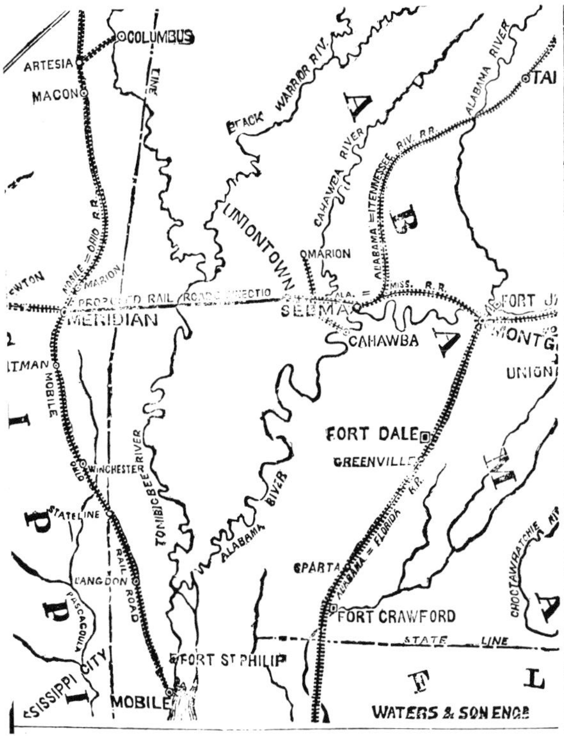

Figure 17. On this detail of a map of central Mississippi and Alabama, printed in the *New York Herald*, May 31, 1862, incomplete names for Talladega, Fort Jackson, Montgomery, and Union Springs along right edge show that it was originally part of a larger map.

distributed. When the sections were engraved and reassembled, the master engraver corrected any discrepancies.

Dividing wood blocks not only reduced engraving time but also made it far easier to revise maps. Changing a woodcut map, for which the design formed the raised printing surface, meant painstakingly cutting out the required area and inserting a precisely measured wood plug for recutting to preserve the integrity of the block.[72] Amending maps printed from multisectional blocks simply required disassembling the block and substituting corrected sections (see Figs. 16a and 16b).

Multisectional wood blocks also presented the possibility of generating several maps from a single block. Formed of as many as twenty-four sections, the engraved block essentially consisted of a variety of smaller maps. Disassembling the engraved block and reconfiguring sections allowed editors to create maps as needed. To increase a map's geographic coverage, engraved sections need only be joined to the original wood block. Since titles rarely appeared on the map itself, typesetting a title to reflect the purpose of the new map presented little difficulty.

Stereotyping engraved blocks before printing assured the block's preservation and made it possible to reprint a map or a portion of it over a lengthy period, sometimes as

Figure 18. Proof copy of a map drawn by Edward S. Hall and engraved by Waters & Son, first printed in the *New York Herald* on September 8, 1861. The original bears blue penciled editorial changes. The entire map was printed on three different occasions; sections, indicated by the vertical and horizontal editorial lines, were printed on four occasions.

much as two years. Numerous maps saw repeated use, and toward the end of the war some newspapers ran previously printed maps nearly as often as new ones. This scheme obviously benefited newspapers if they, rather than the engraver, retained ownership of the blocks. In November 1861, the *World*, the *Philadelphia Inquirer*, and the *New York Tribune* printed identical maps of the vicinity of Beaufort, South Carolina, engraved by the firm of G. W. Colton. Multiple use suggests that Colton owned the wood block or printing plate, but maps reprinted in the *Rebellion Record*, an 1861 compilation of war documents, raise doubts over the question of ownership.[73] Two Colton maps in the *Record* credit the proprietors of the newspapers that originally printed them, which would indicate that the plates did not belong to the engraver.

The assembly-line approach to preparing and engraving wood blocks made rapid map production possible and enabled daily newspapers to provide timely cartographic coverage of military news. The firm of Waters & Son regularly prepared maps for the *New York Herald* in less than twenty-four hours. On one occasion Frederic Hudson, managing editor of the *Herald*, noted that a twenty-block map of a major battle appeared in the morning's paper after a night of frantic engraving.[74] The cartographic efficiency of the daily press easily surpassed that of any other form of contemporary mapmaking.

That so many daily newspapers printed maps during the Civil War is indicative of the rapid growth of wood engraving in America. In 1840, fewer than twenty professional engravers operated in the entire country, but by 1860, 147 workers were employed by twenty-nine wood-engraving establishments in New York City alone.[75] Two New York engravers—Waters & Son (*New York Herald*, *Times*, and *Tribune*, and *Philadelphia Inquirer*) and G. W. Colton (*New York Times*, *Tribune*, *Sun*, and *World*, and *Philadelphia Inquirer*)—accounted for the majority of all newspaper maps printed during the war.[76] Other wood engravers who signed maps included William D. Baker (*Chicago Post*, *Chicago Times*), Jessie Haney (*New York Tribune*), William Mackwits (*Daily Missouri Republican*), Henry L. Penfield Company (*New York Times*), David Scattergood (*Philadelphia Inquirer*), Schonberg & Company (*Sun*), Charles Sears (*New York Tribune*), Richard Shugg (*World*), and George K. Stillman (*Cincinnati Daily Commercial*).

These engravers employed essentially the same methods and materials and faced similar obstacles in their labors for the daily press. Even engravers who used divided wood blocks worked under severe time constraints. In order to maintain circulation in an era of intense competition between papers, news had to be published promptly. New York and Philadelphia papers regularly featured maps of battles in the Virginia theater of war within five days of their occurrence, and getting information from the field to the newspaper office accounted for most of that interval. Under these circumstances, engravers were denied the luxury of circumspection.

Of course, expedience carried a price. The managing editor of the *New York Herald* estimated that his paper alone spent over $500,000 covering the war.[77] Wages and materials for map engraving must have amounted to a small portion of those costs, but they undoubtedly exceeded any previous expenditures on wood-engraved maps. Using a conservative estimate of twenty-five thousand impressions (the number of issues printed) per map, the daily Northern press printed over fifty million copies of war-related maps between 1861 and 1865. When taking into account the additional maps in weekly papers, periodicals, and books, the Civil War must be considered the preeminent period of wood-engraved cartography in America.

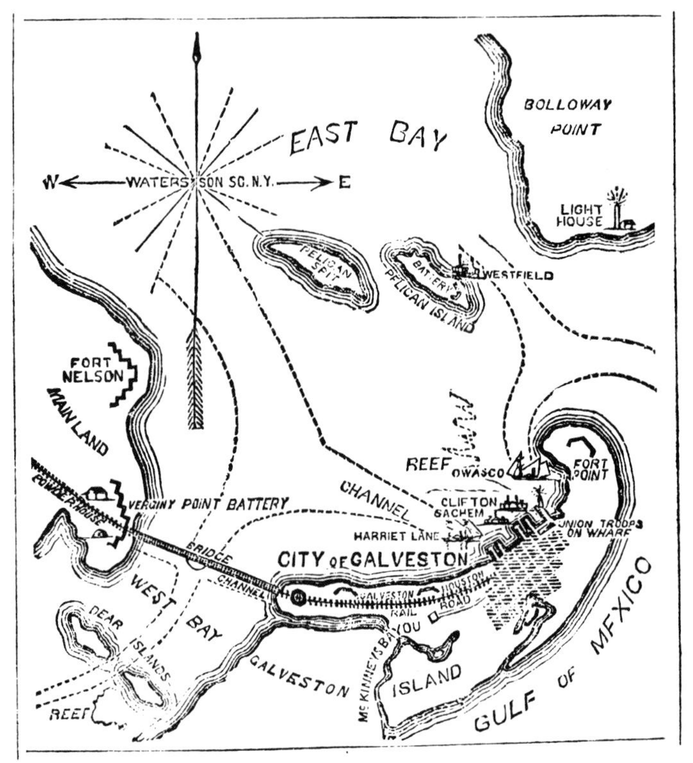

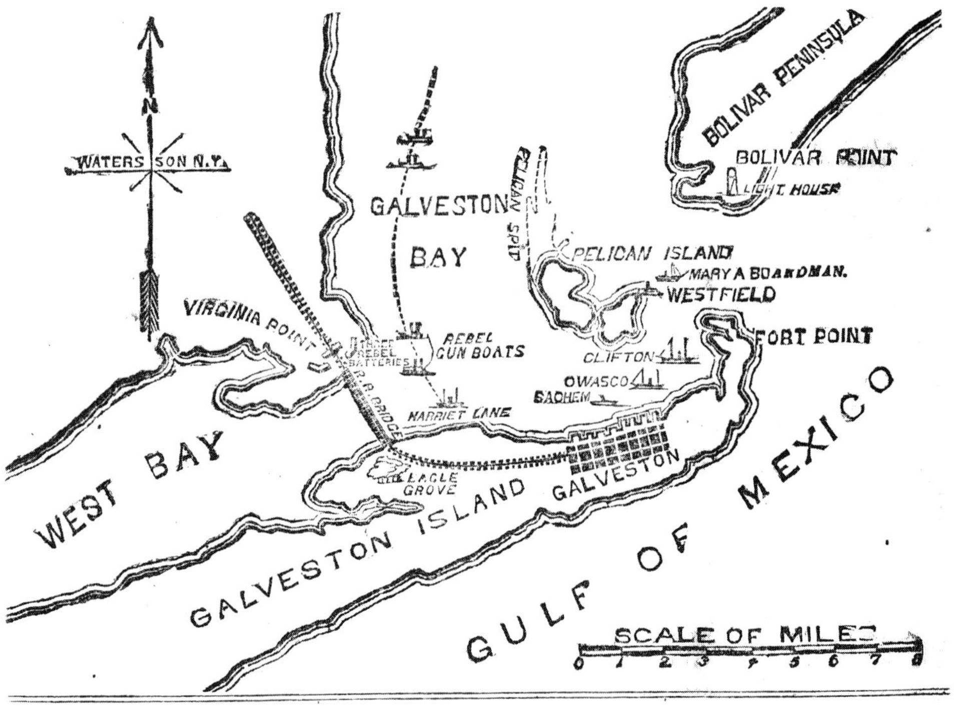

Figures 19a and 19b. Two maps of Galveston, Texas, both engraved by Waters & Son and printed on the same day, January 19, 1863, one in the *New York Herald* (*top*) and the other in the *New York Tribune*. The maps differ considerably.

The Design and Appearance of Newspaper Maps

THE VISUAL CHARACTERISTICS OF DAILY NEWSPAPER MAPS REFLECTED A VARIETY OF influences. The medium of reproduction, the time constraints, and the requirements of information transfer together shaped the appearance of these maps. Wood engraving, the first of these factors, presented certain limitations which, in turn, restricted design options. The black-line style of engraving favored the use of line work and point symbols even though more of the surface of the block had to be cut away. Engravers for the daily press were capable of fashioning area symbols to represent features like hills and vegetation, but with the exception of Waters & Son, few did so with any frequency. By and large, maps printed in daily newspapers selectively employed nonlinear techniques for battle maps, to reduce engraving time.[78] The emphasis on lines and lettering, which tended to be bold and simple, often gave newspaper maps a stark quality.

A minimalist approach to engraving complemented journalistic cartography's requirement of visual simplicity; the design of newspaper maps had to remain elementary to be readily understood by a broad audience.[79] Civil War newspaper maps achieved clarity through an economy of line and lettering. In addition, pertinent map data, such as troop positions or particular topographical features, were emphasized while details not germane to the map's message were suppressed. Selectivity served to direct the viewer's attention and also aided in the transfer of cartographic information.

The extent to which conscious design decisions contributed to the effectiveness of journalistic maps is, however, questionable. As we have seen, neither correspondents nor editors possessed much in the way of cartographic knowledge. Most of the wood engravers employed by the daily press also had little experience with maps, for at this time maps tended to be reproduced by lithography or steel engraving rather than wood engraving.[80] Commercial wood engravers may have regarded maps as simply a printing job consisting of lines and lettering, an attitude that prevailed among some noncartographic wax-engraving firms into the twentieth century.[81] A comparison of two maps of Galveston, Texas, engraved by the firm of Waters & Son lends weight to this contention. Printed in the January 19, 1863, issues of the *New York Herald* and the *New York Tribune*, the maps contain numerous discrepancies in topography and place names that the engravers took no pains to reconcile (see Figs. 19a and 19b).

The production of Civil War newspaper maps may have paralleled the procedures weekly newspapers followed for preparing illustrations. When a drawing reached the

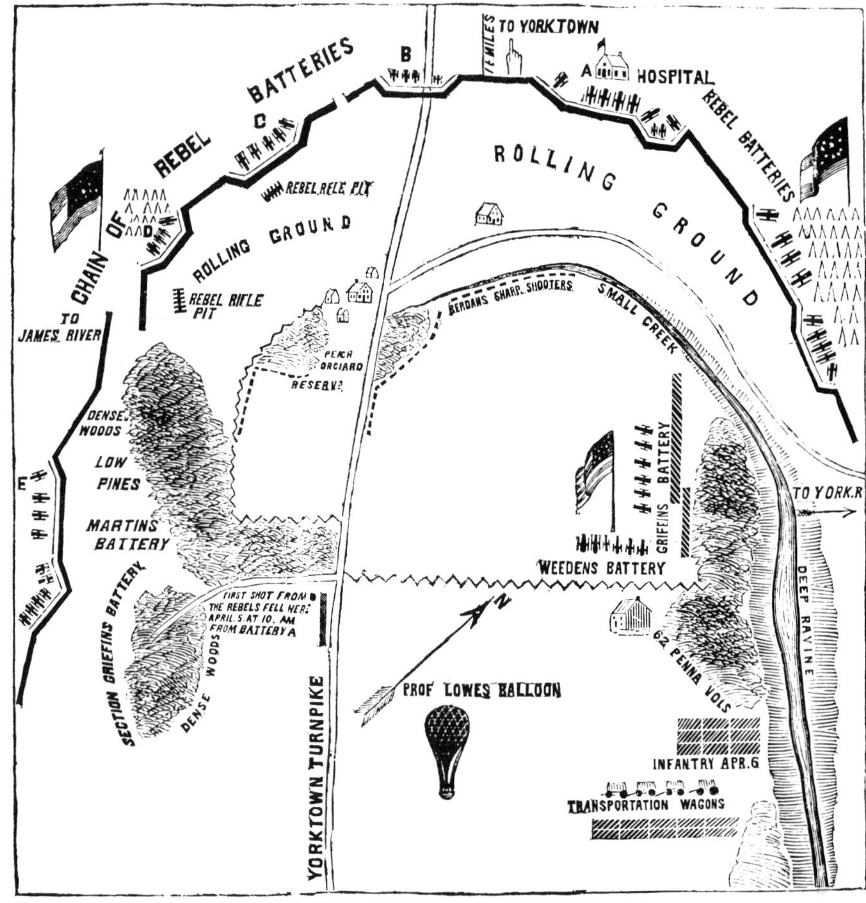

Figure 20. Detail of a map of the siege of Yorktown, Virginia, on which can be seen numerous pictorial symbols. Printed in the *Philadelphia Inquirer*, April 19, 1862.

offices of an illustrated paper, a draftsman redrew the map on a wood block, then turned it over to an engraver.[82] Correspondents for dailies sometimes delivered their maps in person and may have drawn them directly on the wood blocks. Draftsmen compiled theater-of-war and small-scale maps at the newspaper office, perhaps superintended by an editor. Engravers apparently played a small role in devising maps. In the early part of the century, wood engravers both designed and cut their blocks, but the practice of book and periodical illustration suggests that by 1860 a distinction existed between design and engraving in the United States.[83]

Newspapers faced the same shortage of detailed maps of the interior South that initially hindered the military. At the beginning of the war the daily press made particular use of small-scale commercial cartography, and perhaps for this reason had greater need of draftsmen to copy maps. In the case of the *New York Herald*, twenty-one maps printed in 1861 named the draftsman (indicated by "del.," an abbreviation of *delineavit*). By 1862, when the number of maps printed in the *Herald* had more than doubled, only thirteen maps named the individuals who had drawn them. This decrease reflected the overall anonymity of journalistic cartographers, but it also may have denoted a diminishing reliance on commercial artists. Apparently none of the *Herald*'s draftsmen had the benefit of cartographic training. Edward S. Hall, who signed more than a dozen maps printed in the *Herald*, was perhaps typical. Hall, a young New York book illustrator, turned to cartographic drafting when the war began and prepared "Lloyd's New Military Map of the Border and Southern States."[84] He later served as an artist for *Frank Leslie's Illustrated Newspaper*, after his name ceased to appear in the *Herald*.

Like written reports, whose language became less sensational and more judicious during the course of the war, the cartographic vocabulary of journalistic maps changed subtly.[85] The design of small-scale newspaper maps, which most resembled other commercial maps, remained relatively constant. In the case of large-scale battle plans, the choice of symbols for geographical, cultural, or military features gradually changed. During the first year of the war, maps frequently employed pictorial or iconic symbols for artillery, buildings, trees, and vessels. These appeared in perspective or profile, usually combined with representations in plan (vertical view) for roads, bridges, rivers, and troop locations. Newspaper mapmakers never completely abandoned pictorial symbols, but their use declined on later maps. A change in the nature of newspaper map symbols may indicate the influence of commercial maps, which generally shunned iconic symbols.

Figure 21. Detail of a map of eastern Virginia printed in the *Philadelphia Inquirer*, April 23, 1862. Place names in the upper and lower halves are engraved in noticeably different styles.

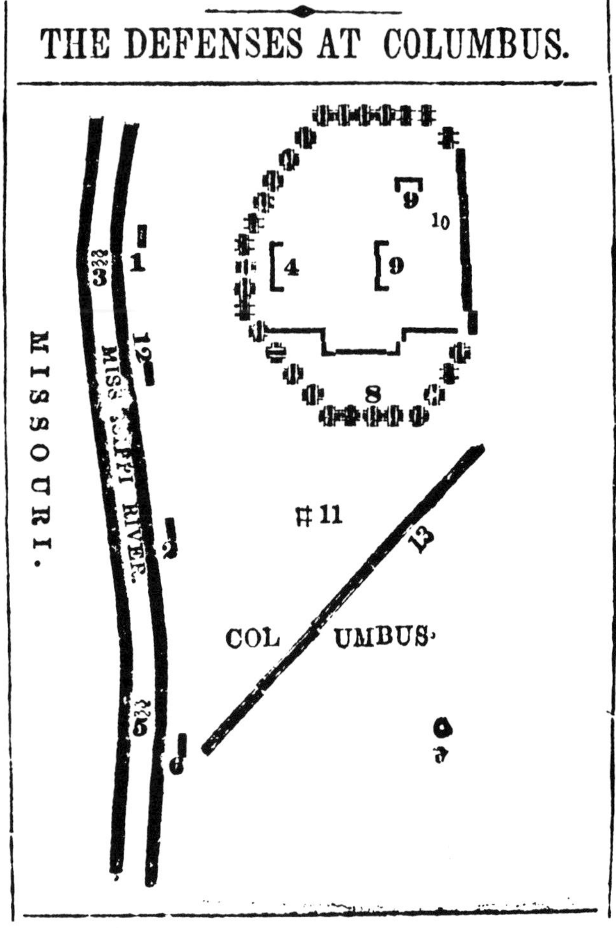

Figure 22. Map printed in the January 27, 1862, *New York Tribune*, composed entirely of printer's type.

Lettering formed one of the most conspicuous and onerous design elements of newspaper maps. Although freer and less angular than that of early woodcut maps, wood-engraved lettering showed noticeable inconsistencies in size, spacing, and style. Nearly all newspaper map lettering was handcut in relief, a laborious and tedious undertaking. Unintentional variations in lettering on the same map provide further evidence that individual engravers cut everything on their section of the wood block, whether they were particularly skilled at all those elements or not (see Fig. 21). With few exceptions newspaper map lettering consisted solely of plain large and small roman capitals. Although not commonly used, italics differentiated classes of data, such as rivers, on some maps.

Place names on newspaper maps could also be printed from type inserted through slots cut in the block or attached to the block as individual stereotypes. This allowed newspapers to print maps composed entirely of type (see Fig. 22), but few took advantage of this seemingly quick approach to mapping. Typeset lettering tended to be

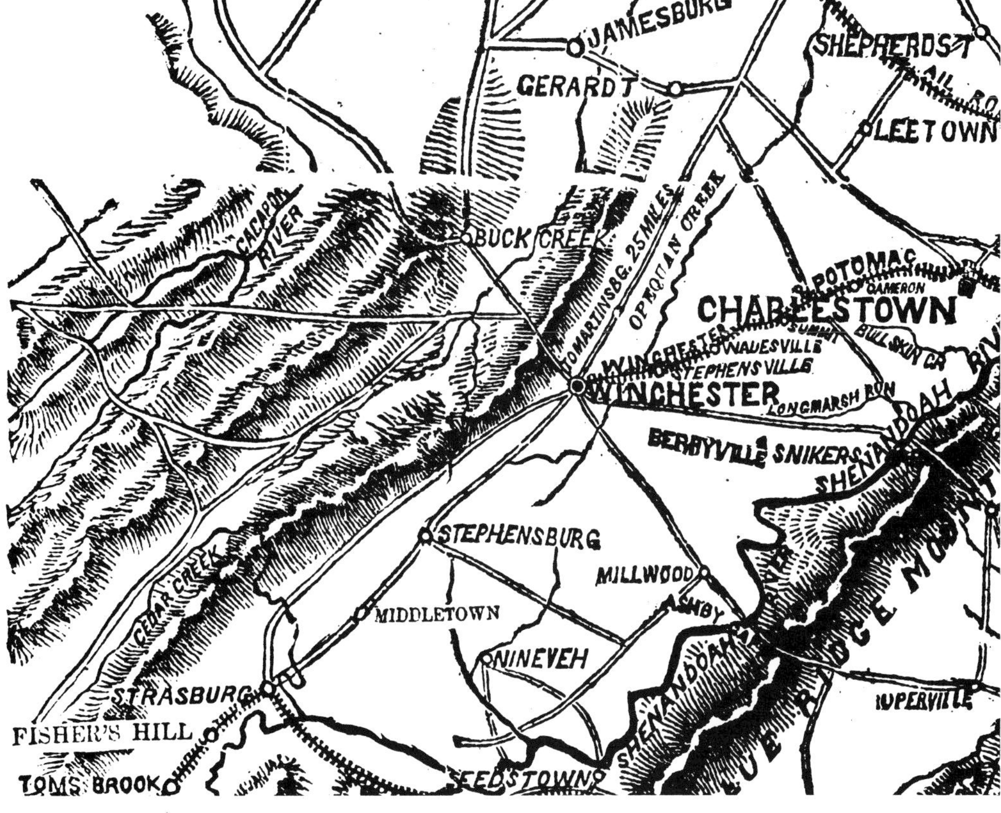

Figure 23. Detail of a map of the Shenandoah Valley with both typeset (Middletown, Fisher's Hill, Opequan Creek) and engraved lettering. A further indication that engravers cut everything on their section of the wood block is the variant styles of depicting hills, seen at the top of the illustration. Printed in the *New York Herald*, September 24, 1864.

confined to a few place names on otherwise entirely engraved maps, indicating that its chief use was for revising maps or making late additions (see Fig. 23). The physical separation of engraving workshops from composing rooms made cooperative map design less likely and contributed to the dearth of typeset lettering on maps.

Titles, which generally consisted of typeset banner headlines above the map, were not strictly part of the cartographic design process but often had a significant presence. Because titles functioned as an indication of a map's intent, giving an existing general map a new title allowed an editor to press it into service for a specific use, even if that purpose was not reflected in the map's content (see Fig. 24). Some map titles, such as the following from the April 10, 1862, issue of the *Philadelphia Inquirer*, consisted of long and tedious editorial commentaries: "Seat of military operations in the south-west. New Madrid and Island No. 10, scene of the glorious victory of General Pope and Commodore Foote over the Rebel forces; Memphis, Decatur, Corinth, Florence, Savannah, and Pittsburg Landing, and surroundings, showing the locality of the terrible conflict be-

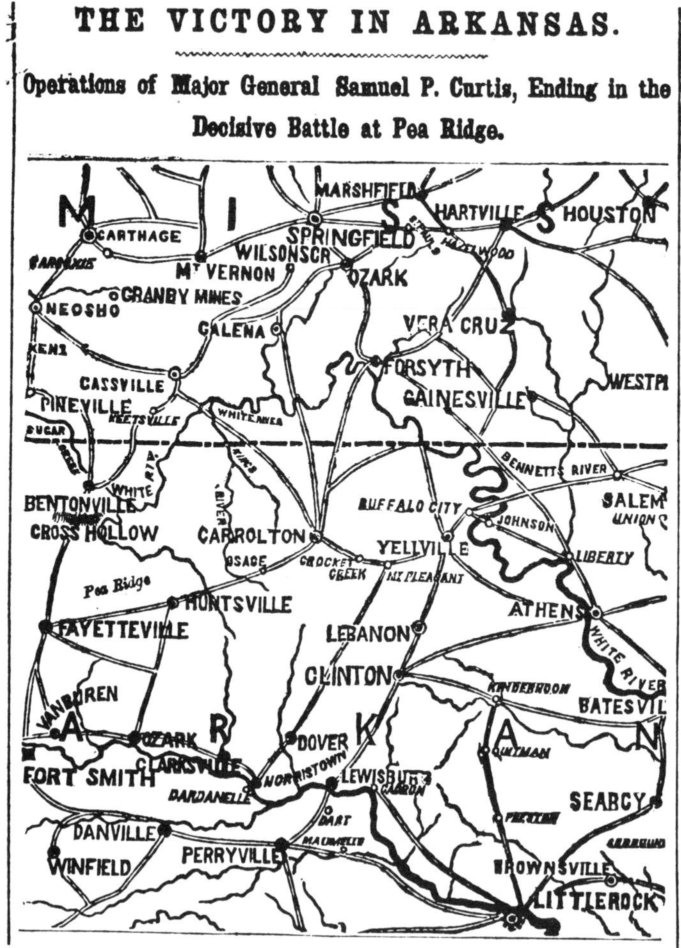

Figure 24. A general map of part of western Missouri and Arkansas with a title suggestive of greater detail. Printed in the *New York Herald*, March 12, 1862. The typeset words *Pea Ridge* (*middle left*) have been squeezed into an existing map to indicate the location of the battlefield.

tween the Union armies, under command of major generals Halleck, Grant, and Buell, and the Rebel hordes under Beauregard and Johnston." A good example of the colloquialism that crept into titles accompanied a map of Charleston, South Carolina, printed in the *Cincinnati Daily Times* on August 26, 1863: "Charleston and its defenses. The surrender of Fort Sumter. The 'Yankee vandals' too much for the Southern chivalry."

Editorial ridicule of military policy frequently found expression in map titles. As John Pope's Army of the Potomac retired northward in the face of Confederate maneuvers, the *Cincinnati Daily Times* printed a map of northern Virginia with a title that sneered at the Union course of action: "Pope's 'change of base'—another stroke of strategy—the army across the Rappahannock."[86] One suspects that titles may have been the sole aspect of cartographic journalism that editors, who had little experience with the genre, controlled completely.

Contemporary Criticism

POLITICAL CARTOONS AND CARICATURES ABOUNDED DURING THE CIVIL WAR, AND just as politicians and military leaders found themselves the subjects of ridicule, so too did newspaper maps and their makers. *Vanity Fair*, a humorous weekly paper that began publication in New York just before the war, sarcastically warned against the deleterious effects of newspaper maps. The November 30, 1861, issue included a drawing of a demented map user confined to a cell and shrouded in a haze of cartographic symbols. The caption explained, "Lamentable condition of an intelligent gentleman who lately devoted himself to the study of the *N.Y. Herald*'s maps" (Fig. 25).

The *Herald*'s maps were again singled out for abuse in the May 3, 1862, issue of *Vanity Fair*. A deliberately perplexing map, allegedly of the siege of Yorktown, accompanied a letter from one McArone, *Vanity Fair*'s fictitious war correspondent. "The subjoined diagram," he wrote, "shows my plan of investment; it will be understood at a glance. This was designed by the gentleman who does all the *Herald* war-maps" (Fig. 26).

In a spurious letter published in the May 24, 1862, issue of *Vanity Fair*, a "bothered contributor" railed against the ambiguity of newspaper maps. The writer, who stated that he subscribed to all the daily and weekly "illustrated papers," characterized the typical newspaper map as being "spotted all over with letters as if it had measles. Dotted lines running in every direction. Big blots to represent forts. Little blots to represent camps. Spider trenches—intoxicated spiders, too, to represent roads. Smooches to represent water. Cyphers to represent where Burnside was last week. More cyphers to represent where he will be next week. It's all a muddle." This echoes the remonstrance of a Cincinnati newspaper correspondent who charged that the "small pox maps of the Herald are a standing jest in the army."[87] Continuing in a similar vein, a journalist in Louisville, Kentucky, derisively compared maps "improvised by sensation papers" to "striking and lifelike pictures of a drunkard's stomach."[88]

Robert H. Newell, a correspondent for the *New York Herald* who signed himself Orpheus C. Kerr, deprecated newspaper maps and perhaps himself in the bargain. Newell related the imaginary interrogation of a correspondent arrested for suspicious behavior:

> "Well Samyule," says the general to one of the pickets, "what is your charge against the prisoner?"
>
> "He is a young man which is a spy," replied Samyule holding up the sheet of

paper; "and I take this here picture of his to be the Great Seal of the Southern Confederacy."

"Why thinkest thou so . . . and what does the work of art represent?" inquired the general.

"The drawing is not of the best," responded Samyule, closing one eye and viewing the picture critically; "but I should say it represented a ham, with a fiddle laid across it, with beefsteaks in the corners."

"Miserable vandal!" shouted the longhaired chap excitedly, "you know not what you say. I am a Federal artist; and that picture is a map of the coast of North Carolina, for a New York daily newspaper."[89]

As amusing as they may be, satirical portrayals of confused map users hardly amount to a reliable measure of public opinion. Daily newspapers reached a vast audience whose cartographic sophistication varied widely, so gauging the perceived value of newspaper maps presents obvious difficulties. In addition, it is doubtful whether many readers were capable of distinguishing good newspaper battle maps from bad on the basis of the information they contained. Except for occasional jabs from humorists and rival correspondents, little commentary on the quality of newspaper maps exists. Nor do we learn much on this subject from military memoirs and accounts of the war.

Soldiers, officers in particular, often found themselves in a position to judge the success or failure of newspaper maps, but few who took notice of them left a record of

LAMENTABLE CONDITION OF AN INTELLIGENT GENTLEMAN WHO LATELY DEVOTED HIMSELF TO THE STUDY OF THE *N. Y. Herald* MAPS.

Figure 25. Cartoon in *Vanity Fair*, November 30, 1861, lampooning newspaper maps.

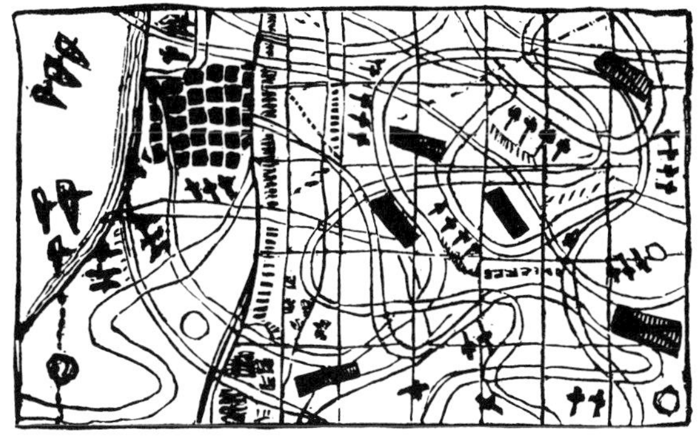

THE SIEGE OF YORKTOWN.

Figure 26. A spoof on *New York Herald* maps, in *Vanity Fair*, May 3, 1862.

their comments. One officer who did was Henry Hitchcock, an adjutant on William T. Sherman's staff. Hitchcock chided the *Herald* for publishing a map incorrectly depicting the Union army's location after leaving Atlanta: "One number of the New York *Herald* had a big map of 'Sherman's field of operations' with a very black line marked 'Route of Slocum's column,' which carefully avoided the actual line the column took, in a manner lovely to see."[90] Similarly, Gen. Alpheus S. Williams, commander of the First Division of the Army of the Potomac's Twelfth Corps, lamented the published accounts of the Battle of Chancellorsville. In a letter dated May 18, 1863, he stated, "I have seen in the illustrated newspapers and in the *Herald*, diagrams and drawings of furious onslaughts made by troops which never fired a gun."[91]

Not all opinions criticized the efforts of the press. Following the Battle of Antietam, Stephen Weld, a lieutenant on Gen. Fitz-John Porter's staff, enclosed a map from the *Philadelphia Inquirer* in a letter to his sister. Weld provided his version of the action by making reference to the map that he thought did justice to the battlefield.[92] A newspaper map of the siege of Petersburg pleased a Union soldier who had just received a different map from home: "The map I like; I am sorry it does not include Petersburg and surroundings of our present scene of operations. Ask father if he cannot procure the *New York Herald* with such a map on the front page. I believe I saw it today, and it is cheap and good; I would like it."[93]

These personal reactions to individual maps offer a narrow perspective on the issue. From our vantage point more than a century later it seems clear that newspaper maps furnished economical and timely information. They located the scene of events, established spatial relationships, and depicted military operations with surprising accuracy. Battle plans were especially noteworthy for providing the public with the earliest, and occasionally the only, cartographic intelligence of operations. The nearly immediate publication of maps that would otherwise be unavailable to the public until long after the fact, if ever, stands as one of the greatest achievements of Civil War journalism.

The Published Record

BETWEEN APRIL 1, 1861, AND APRIL 30, 1865, THE DAILY NORTHERN PRESS PRINTED 2,045 maps relating to the war.[94] These ranged from plans of fortifications and battles to campaign and theater-of-war maps. The New York and Philadelphia presses published by far the greatest number of maps, the majority of which represented the eastern theater of war. Two main factors accounted for the geographical distribution of newspaper map coverage. First, the effort to capture Richmond and the need to protect Washington made Virginia the major theater of war and focused the attention of the Northern press there. Second, readers of daily newspapers such as the *New York Herald* and *Philadelphia Inquirer* were especially interested in their local and state troops operating in the East. That maps of Virginia accounted for about half of all maps printed by the daily press confirms the importance attached to eastern campaigns.

While the vast majority of Civil War journalistic maps represent original cartography, newspapers also reprinted previously published maps, with or without modification, and even appropriated maps from other papers. Cartographic piracy was confined to maps of battles rather than small-scale maps locating places or campaigns. Some western papers often relied on maps in the *New York Herald* or *Philadelphia Inquirer*, while eastern papers copied maps of western battles from Chicago, Cincinnati, or St. Louis papers, especially early in the war. Usually the source of the pirated map went unacknowledged, leaving readers none the wiser.

Editors turned to maps printed in other newspapers when their own coverage lagged behind. Often the blame for this rested on the paper's correspondent. Thomas Gunn's dilatory reporting of the Battle of Lee's Mills, Virginia, for the *New York Tribune* evoked the ire of Sydney Howard Gay, his managing editor:

> Your sketch of ye battle-ground of the 16th came just eight days after ye battle. Of course it was useless. The corr. of ye Philadelphia Inquirer had sent one to that paper, which it had engraved and published, which I had also had engraved & published, three days before yours reached me. I pray you remember ye Tribune is a daily newspaper—or meant to be—& not a historical record of past events.[95]

Rarely did newspapers alter or correct plagiarized maps, a fact noted by George Smalley of the *Tribune* in a letter to his editor. Smalley commented on a map of the Battle of Antietam, saying, "I see your map copied in the Philadelphia Inquirer without credit which need not be much regretted—as I think it unsatisfactory."[96] The slavish copying of maps implies that a lack of knowledge and resources, as well as time, affected editorial decisions regarding journalistic cartography.

It is quite conceivable that newspaper maps, being readily available and affordable, helped create an interest in maps as collectible war relics. A. Homer Byington, a correspondent of the *New York Tribune*, offered his opinion on the demand for a map of Gettysburg. Writing from Hanover, Pennsylvania, on the second day of the battle, he told his editor: "I send you a map of Adams County [Pennsylvania]. . . . It will aid you in getting a complete map of the greatest battle-ground. I think it will pay you to have it cover an entire page. Could sell 10,000 or more Tribunes in the army with it I have no doubt."[97] Byington's estimate seems entirely reasonable, for after an important engagement the sales of a major daily newspaper might exceed its normal circulation by as much as five times.[98] Given the public's abiding interest in the outcome of battles, many civilian readers as well as soldiers in the Army of the Potomac purchased newspapers for the maps they contained.

Commercial publishers such as Louis Prang, James T. Lloyd, Charles Magnus, and W. H. Forbes celebrated Union operations cartographically with the knowledge that eager buyers awaited.[99] Despite having the means for prolific production, commercial publishers could not issue maps at the rate newspapers did, and they occasionally followed the lead of cartographic journalism by copying information. One instance of commercial imitation involved a map of Port Hudson, Louisiana, published in the *New York Herald* on June 12, 1863. Based on information furnished by one John Harris, a captured Confederate soldier, the *Herald*'s large-scale map (ca. 1:50,000) showed considerable detail not commonly available (see Fig. 27). Within a matter of weeks George W. Tomlinson of Boston published a nearly identical map at a similar scale (ca. 1:65,000).[100] Tomlinson's map commemorated the campaign of Gen. Nathaniel P. Banks, former governor of Massachusetts, noting that Banks accepted the surrender of Port Hudson on July 9. The Tomlinson map extended farther west and south but clearly relied on the *Herald*'s depiction of the town and its defenses (see Fig. 28).

Several newspapers tried to market maps in a different format early in the war, leading at least one commercial publisher to follow suit. In 1861, the *Chicago Post*, the *New York Tribune*, and the *New York Herald* published cartographic supplements as large broadsides or smaller folded pages.[101] These contained ten, seventeen, and thirty-four maps respectively, all of which had previously run in the papers. New York map publisher J. H. Colton adopted a similar format the following year, publishing a lithographed sheet of twenty-three maps depicting harbors and coastal defenses.[102]

While other forms of commercial cartography flourished throughout the war, newspaper map publication abated as expenditures for wages, materials, and reporting grew.

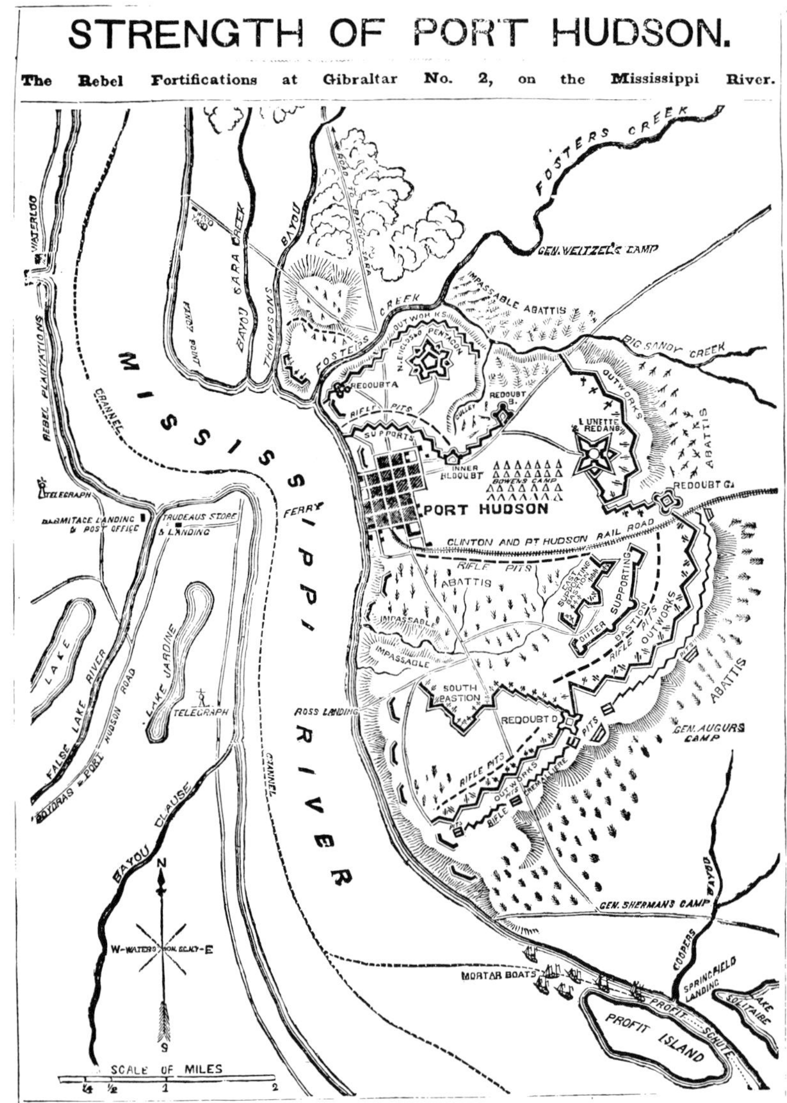

Figure 27. Map of the defenses of Port Hudson, Louisiana, based on information supplied by a captured Confederate soldier. Printed in the *New York Herald*, June 12, 1863.

As early as 1862, the *Scientific American* announced an unprecedented crisis in newspaper publishing, brought about by a sudden increase in paper costs.[103] Other costs mounted as well. Most newspapers raised the price of an issue, in some cases as much as doubling it, only to see circulation falter.[104] Declining sales in turn forced several newspapers to discontinue Sunday issues and reduce the number of maps they printed.

Newspapers across the country felt the financial strain. The August 21, 1864, issue of the *Chicago Daily Tribune* complained that printing paper had increased from nine to twenty cents per pound while typesetting costs had nearly doubled. That year the *Tribune* printed one-third the number of maps it had in 1863. The *New York Times* spent twenty-five thousand dollars more on maintaining correspondents during the second

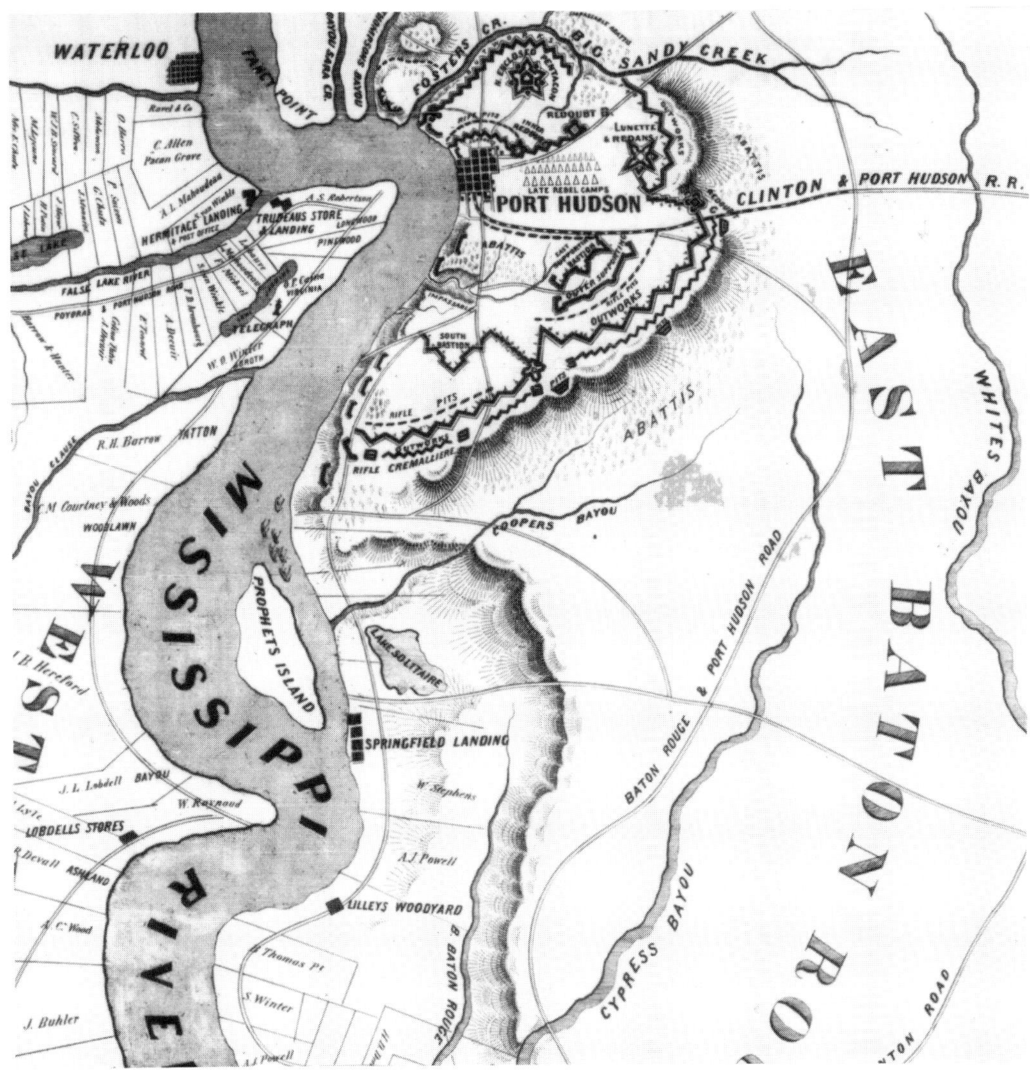

Figure 28. Detail of G. W. Tomlinson's map of Port Hudson, published in Boston to mark Port Hudson's surrender to Gen. Nathaniel P. Banks. Not drawn from first-hand information, the map owed much to the *New York Herald* map shown in Figure 27.

year of the war than it had in 1861.[105] In 1861 and 1862 the *Times* published a total of 116 maps, but managed only nine more during the entire remainder of the war. Even the prolific *New York Herald* suffered. This giant among illustrated dailies printed 104 war maps in 1864, just over half of its production for 1863 and far fewer than the 257 maps it had printed in 1862.

Over the course of the war newspaper maps appeared less frequently, but virtually every military campaign received coverage. After major battles like Shiloh (Pittsburg Landing) and Gettysburg, daily newspapers printed as many as a dozen different maps. Even obscure skirmishes were mapped, thanks to the largely unacknowledged efforts of correspondents. In fact, newspapers supplied the only contemporary printed maps for several of the war's engagements. These included Blackwater Creek or Shawnee Mound, Missouri (*New York Times* and *World*, December 27, 1861), Tranter's Creek, North Carolina (*New York Herald*, June 13, 1862), and Milton, or Vaught's Mill, Tennessee (*Chicago Times*, March 28, 1863).

With the dispatch achieved by the telegraph and railroad and the development of a corps of correspondents, the daily press provided detailed coverage of the war from strange, distant locales that later became household names. Journalistic maps played a prominent role in the diffusion of military and geographical information in a manner that facilitated the public's comprehension of the war's spatial dimension. It was not without justification that the *New York Herald* proudly pointed to its cartographic accomplishment:

> Military maps and plans of battles have no doubt been made [in the past], but they have usually been locked up in government archives and kept carefully from the public eye. Here, on the contrary, they have been promptly and minutely prepared for our columns, at our own expense, and our readers scarcely hear of a battle before it is made intelligible to them by carefully executed maps, prepared by or for our correspondents on the spot, and at once engraved and published in our columns. Our readers, if they have chosen to preserve them, have now the best atlas extant of those sections of the country which have been the scene of hostile encounters or curious strategy.[106]

The *Herald*'s statement correctly noted that the reading public had been given unprecedented access to military intelligence. Critics of the Northern press denounced the free publication of war news as ill advised and dangerous, claiming that it also benefited the enemy.[107] Viewing the conflict as a "people's war," editors felt justified in printing virtually anything on military matters—especially if they did so before their rivals.

Early in the war the *New York Tribune* expressed its position on the matter of national security rather dramatically:

> Millions of men and women, fathers, mothers, children, wives, sweethearts, who have sent those dearer than life to these wars, look every day at this journal, and at other journals, with eyes brimful of anxious tears, and turn these pages with hands made unsteady by emotion. It is quite as important that this love should be respected, that these apprehensions should be allayed, that these tortures of suspense should be averted, as that Gen. Benjamin F. Butler should keep secret any expedition which he is likely to undertake.[108]

A sense of moral indignation incited the press to spar with politicians and military authorities over freedom of information, including maps. Both sides achieved victories, but correspondents and editors persevered in their efforts to inform the public, and by doing so they created an enormous body of cartographic documentation.

The Accuracy of Newspaper Maps

When the reliability of old maps used as historical evidence comes into question, few simple answers can be found. Determining a map's accuracy requires a careful review of internal cartographic content and external factors such as the mapmaker's sources and the map's intended purpose and audience. Because the various representations on a map (of roads, vegetation, terrain, etc.) coincide to greater or lesser extents with reality, different levels of accuracy exist within a single map.[109] To further complicate matters, the informational requirements of the local historian, the military historian, and the historical geographer vary, and so will their opinion of any given map's utility.

Central to an assessment of Civil War journalistic cartography should be an awareness of its unique place in the publication of military intelligence. Almost without exception, the first published battle maps came from the pens of correspondents. In order to achieve this priority newspapers executed maps as quickly as possible from available information. Obviously such circumstances placed restrictions on a map's contents. Comparing correspondents' maps to their modern equivalents will confirm that news maps lacked the planimetric precision of later surveys and that their makers did not possess all relevant facts. A more telling exercise is to judge these maps in relation to other contemporary cartography originating in the field.

The many maps depicting the Battle of Gettysburg (July 1–3, 1863) signal its military and political importance.[110] On July 4, the *Philadelphia Inquirer* printed the first map of the battle, showing the first day's fighting. Other newspapers followed, providing the North with the earliest maps of the Union victory. On July 6, 1863, the *New York Herald* printed the most detailed newspaper map of the fighting of July 2 (see Fig. 29), encompassing incidents occurring throughout the day. Eight correspondents covered the battle for the *Herald*, and each of them may have contributed notes and sketches for the map. Certain of the map's notations, for example the presence of sharpshooters on buildings in the town, are traceable to a particular correspondent, but the map's author remains unknown.[111]

Portraying dynamic events through a static medium presented one of the greatest challenges to the newspaper mapmaker. Employing a combination of symbols, directional signs, and text, newspaper maps illustrated evolving battles with varying degrees of success. On the *Herald*'s July 6 map, for instance, the relative positions of Union

Scene of the Second Day's Battle, Thursday, July 2—The Repulse of the Rebels.

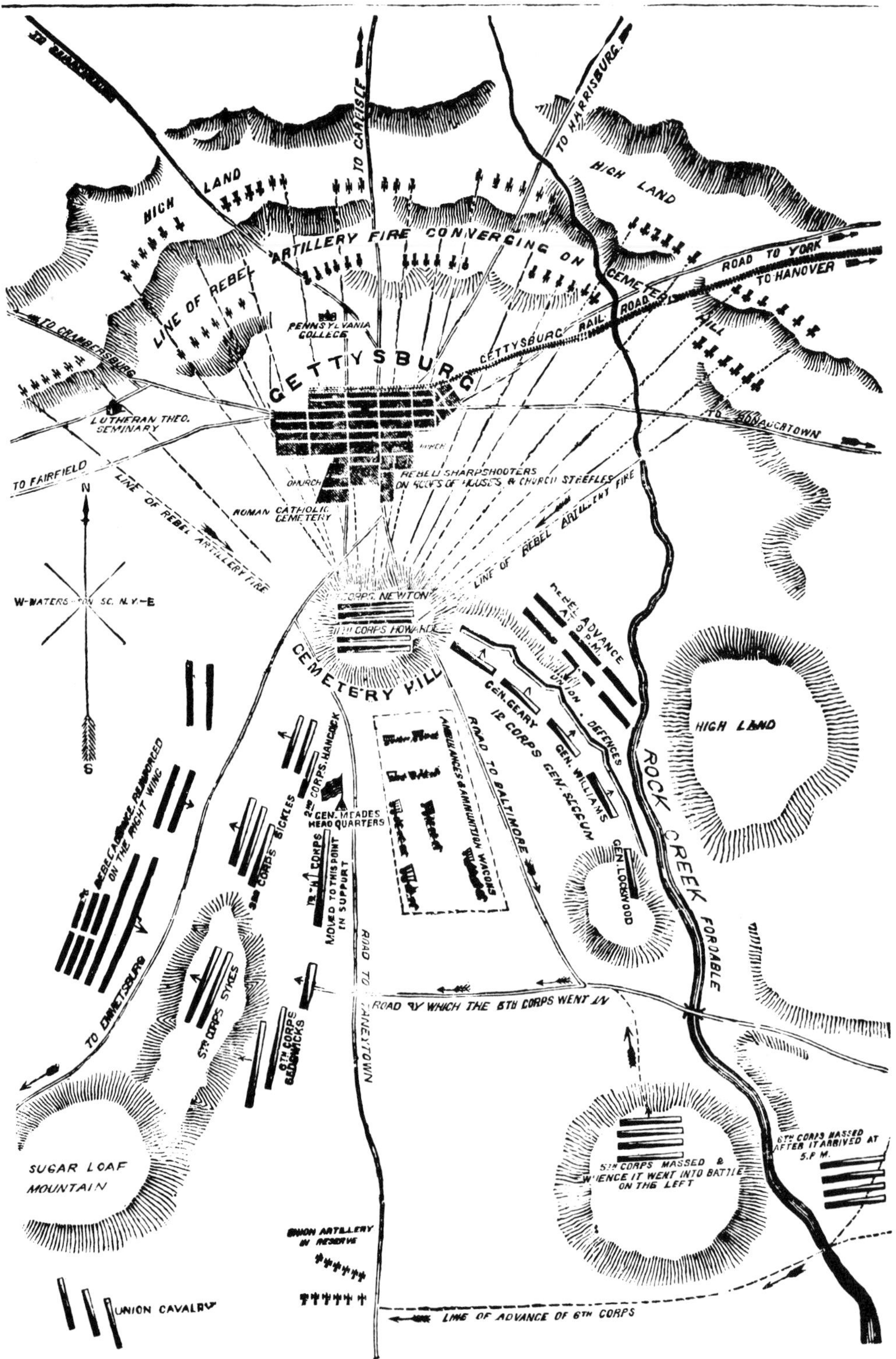

Figure 29. The *New York Herald*'s second map of Gettysburg, printed July 6, 1863.

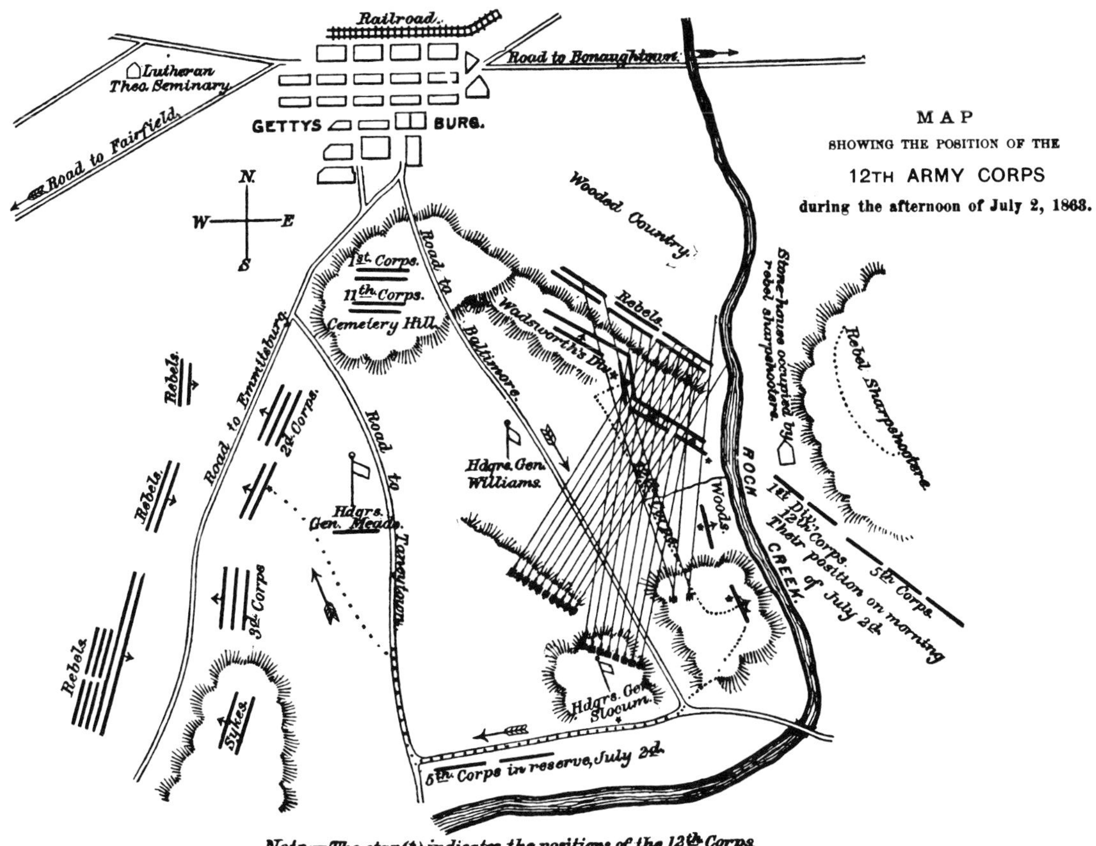

Figure 30. Map accompanying Gen. Henry Slocum's report in series 1, volume 27, part 1 of the *War of the Rebellion*.

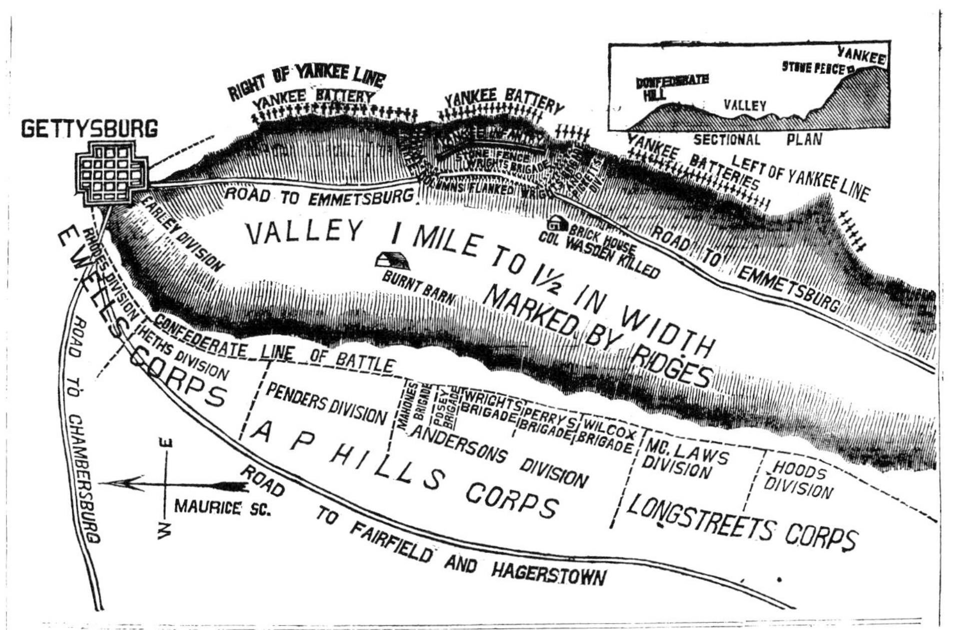

Figure 31. The battle of Gettysburg as portrayed in the *Augusta Constitutionalist*. The map is rather unusual in that it includes a profile of the terrain.

units and their commanders are generally correct as marked, but the map fails to provide details of certain phases of the battle. Arrows seem to indicate a general Union advance when only the Third Corps moved ahead to the Emmitsburg Road. The corps's subsequent retreat following the Confederate attack does not appear, nor does the movement of the First Corps to reinforce the threatened portion of the Union line. The arrival of the Fifth and Sixth Corps and their deployment in the afternoon are noted, however.

Most of the Twelfth Corps shifted from the Union right to a position backing the Third Corps, depicted by a symbol and the words "moved to this point in support." Below the map a note reads, "though the Twelfth held the position on our right all day, it was moved over to the left when we were hard pressed there towards night—all except Greene's brigade of Geary's division which was left on the right—and thus sustained alone the fierce night battle." This synopsis agrees with the report later filed by Gen. Henry Slocum, commander of the Twelfth Corps.[112] Slocum also submitted a map of the second day's battle, focusing on the activity of his corps. It can safely be assumed that a staff officer compiled the map from the reports and sketches of Slocum and his subordinates. Interestingly, this "authorized" version differs little from the map in the *Herald* and surpasses it only in representing the troop movements over time. Despite its military precision, the Twelfth Corps map nevertheless erred in its plotting of the course of Rock Creek.

Newspaper battle maps usually accompanied written reports, and one normally helped interpret the other. In the case of the *Herald*'s map of Gettysburg (Fig. 29), the text does not enhance the accuracy of the map. Early on July 2, John Buford's cavalry (*bottom of map*) occupied the position shown, but they soon moved farther southeast, to cover the Union rear during the day's action.[113] It is impossible to learn from text or map whether the *Herald* believed that cavalry operated on the Union flank all day or whether the paper simply neglected to indicate the change in Buford's position.

The *Herald*'s map also illustrates the relatively common failing of newspaper maps to identify the enemy—invariably referred to in Northern papers as rebels—by commands. Ambiguity regarding the composition of Confederate forces resulted from inadequate information and, to a lesser extent, the bias of those responsible for the map.[114] Similarly, the only known Southern newspaper map of Gettysburg, printed in the Augusta *Constitutionalist* of July 23, indicated a mass of "Yankee" forces without differentiation (Fig. 31).

Commercial publishers quickly exploited the Gettysburg victory with a rash of maps, a number of which were drawn by officers. Capt. William H. Willcox, an aide on the staff of Gen. John Reynolds of the First Corps, depicted the second day's battle in a map published shortly thereafter in Philadelphia. Willcox served throughout the battle, but his map cannot be considered official cartography (see Fig. 32). As an officer, Willcox would have had access to military maps, which could account for the topographical

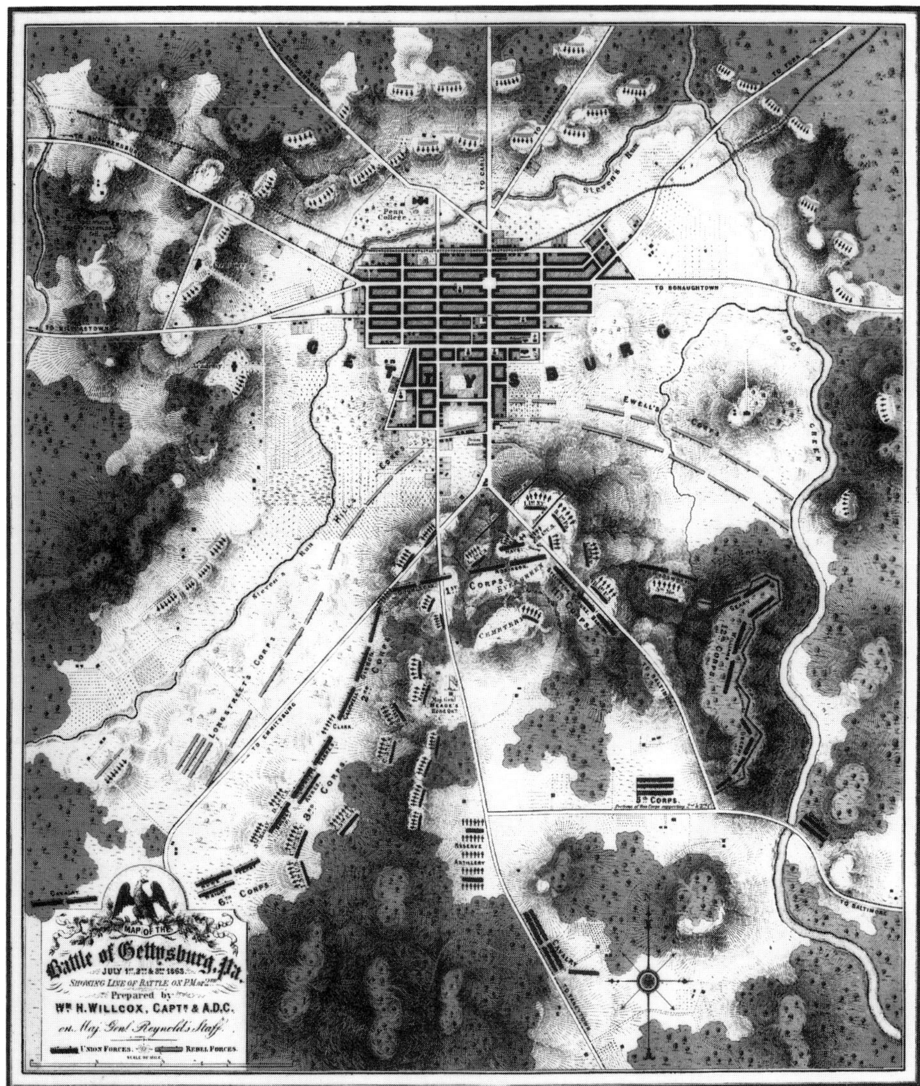

Figure 32. Capt. William H. Willcox's map of Gettysburg, published shortly after the battle.

accuracy of his own product. The map, however, contains errors. Steven's Run (*top of map*) originates too far to the south, and the Sixth Corps is mistakenly placed to the west of Round Top, which is not labeled. Like the map published in the *Herald*, Willcox's shows cavalry operating on the far left flank. Willcox also transposed the Confederate corps of A. P. Hill and James Longstreet.

In the context of all Civil War cartography, newspaper maps exhibited a degree of accuracy comparable to or surpassing that of many of their contemporaries. Given the constraints suffered by correspondents, editors, and engravers, the maps they created interpreted complex events remarkably well. They were not, of course, faultless in their representation of either topographical or military data, and on occasion they faltered badly (see Map 28). Yet those relatively few instances do not negate the overall informational value of newspaper maps.

A final question to be posed when considering the accuracy of newspaper maps concerns objectivity. Did maps, either subtly or overtly, attempt to influence the newspaper reader's opinion of the nature of battles and their outcome? If the written accounts prematurely proclaimed a great Union victory, might maps have contained a similar message? Here little parallel existed between maps and reports.

A map's title might indicate potential bias, but those of newspaper battle maps remained essentially neutral by being descriptive rather than dogmatic. Evidence of cartographic subjectivity did surface in the content of some battle maps, in both inclusions and omissions. As we have seen, the Northern press often neglected to identify Confederate units, but Union officers and military units also experienced selective recognition on maps. A number of reasons accounted for this. Presumably the importance of a given unit's actions in the outcome of a battle had the greatest influence on its prominence on the map, but favoritism, bias, and incomplete information also played a role in deciding who received credit. If an officer fell out of favor with the press, as happened to Gen. George Meade in 1864, correspondents might go so far as to suppress all mention of him.[115] When assessing the military data on any map, it is difficult, if not impossible, to determine the motives or knowledge of the correspondents and editors who generated it.

Bias and misinformation had a greater influence on the depiction of Confederate forces. Maps occasionally misrepresented armies by employing a large number of symbols or symbols of exaggerated size. The *New York Times*'s map of the Battle of Seven Pines, Virginia, published June 13, 1862, provides an example of cartographic distortion (see Map 17). At the top of the map (east), large rectangles representing Joseph E. Johnston's army give an impression of overwhelming strength, while in reality Confederate forces were outnumbered.[116] Interestingly, it was an officer on the staff of Gen. Silas Casey, whose division retired in the face of the initial Confederate attack, who prepared the map. Other maps overstating Confederate forces include those of Wilson's Creek (Map 3) and Chancellorsville (Map 27a).

Evaluating the newspaper maps contained in the following atlas necessitated comparing numerous contemporary and modern maps and texts. In doing so a number of discrepancies emerged, reinforcing the need to examine a wide range of documents when reconstructing battles. The maps that follow were chosen primarily to illustrate the manner in which newspapers informed the Northern public, but they also provide details not found on any other maps of the war. It is hoped that these maps will prompt researchers to make fuller use of this overlooked primary source.

Notes to the Introduction

1. Although exact figures for the various forms of maps are not available, Union officers alone were issued over forty-five thousand printed sheet maps between 1864 and 1865. "Report of the Chief of Engineers," in U.S. War Department, *Report of the Secretary of War, 1864*, vol. 2 (Washington, D.C.: Government Printing Office, 1865), 927; "Report of the Chief of Engineers," in *Report of the Secretary of War, 1865*, vol. 2 (Washington, D.C.: Government Printing Office, 1866), 919.
2. Henry W. Halleck to Don Carlos Buell, February 13, 1862, in U.S. War Department, *The War of the Rebellion: A Compilation of the Official Records of the Union and Confederate Armies*, ser. 1, vol. 7 (Washington, D.C.: Government Printing Office, 1882), 609. Cited in T. Harry Williams, *Lincoln and His Generals* (New York: Grosset & Dunlap, 1952), 5. For information on how a lack of maps affected the Peninsular campaign see George B. McClellan, *McClellan's Own Story, the War for the Union* (New York: Charles Webster, 1887), 253.
3. Richard W. Stephenson, *Civil War Maps: An Annotated List of Maps and Atlases in the Library of Congress* (Washington, D.C.: Library of Congress, 1989), 9.
4. The first map printed in any newspaper within the limits of what would become the United States dates from 1732 (James C. Wheat and Christian Brun, *Maps and Charts Published in America before 1800* [New Haven: Yale University Press, 1969], 58). American wars generated only a handful of newspaper maps prior to the Civil War. Maps of European wars, such as that in northern Italy in 1859, can also be found in certain newspapers.
5. Budd L. Gambee, "American Book and Magazine Illustration of the Later Nineteenth Century," in Frances Brewer, ed., *Book Illustration: Papers Presented at the Third Rare Book Conference of the American Library Association* (Berlin: Gebr. Mann Verlag, 1963), 45.
6. "To the Reader," *Illustrated News*, January 1, 1853, 6.
7. Budd L. Gambee, *Frank Leslie and His Illustrated Newspaper* (Ann Arbor: University of Michigan, Department of Library Science, 1964), 69–72.
8. "How Illustrated Newspapers Are Made," *Frank Leslie's Illustrated Newspaper*, August 2, 1856, 124.
9. This view found expression in the first issue of *Frank Leslie's Illustrated Newspaper* (December 15, 1855). The writer, presumably Leslie himself, also blamed a want of suitable engraving wood and inferior presswork for the demise of predecessors such as the *American Illustrated News* and the *Illustrated News*, both of New York.
10. *Southern Illustrated News*, July 18, 1863; J. Cutler Andrews, *The South Reports the Civil War* (Princeton: Princeton University Press, 1970), 42–43.
11. Newspaper presses such as the *Richmond Enquirer*, the *Mobile Advertiser*, and the *Galveston News* printed an occasional broadside map, but these fall into the category of job printing rather than journalistic cartography.
12. Daniel J. Kenny, *American Newspaper Directory and Record of the Press* (New York: Watson, 1861).
13. A discussion of the changing role of the press during the Civil War can be found in Edwin Emery and Michael Emery, *The Press and America: An Interpretive History of the Mass Media* (Englewood Cliffs, N.J.: Prentice-Hall, 1978); James M. Lee, *History of American Journalism* (Boston: Houghton Mifflin, 1923); and Frank Luther Mott, *American Journalism: A History of Newspapers in the United States through 260 Years* (New York: Macmillan, 1953).

14. From a description of the skirmish at Chicamacomico, North Carolina, published in the *New York Herald*, October 13, 1861.
15. Although modest in terms of reporting, a few correspondents, mostly representing New Orleans newspapers, covered the Mexican War (1846–48). Their efforts have generally been overlooked by historians of the press.
16. J. Cutler Andrews, *The North Reports the Civil War* (Pittsburgh: University of Pittsburgh Press, 1955). A list of Northern reporters appears on pages 751–59.
17. From the *Herald*'s confidential circular to correspondents. Albert D. Richardson enclosed a hand-written transcript in a letter dated April 14, 1863, to Sydney Howard Gay. Sydney Howard Gay Papers, Rare Book and Manuscript Library, Columbia University.
18. Albert D. Richardson to Sydney Howard Gay, May 24, 1862. Gay Papers.
19. Andrews, *The North Reports the Civil War*, 359.
20. War Department, *The War of the Rebellion*, ser. 1, vol. 27, pt. 3 (1889), 192.
21. William E. Griffis, *Charles Carleton Coffin, War Correspondent, Traveller, Author and Statesman* (Boston: Estes & Lauriat, 1898), 87.
22. It should be noted that not all maps of battles printed in newspapers were drawn by correspondents.
23. *New York Tribune*, January 27, 1862.
24. *New York Herald*, June 12, 1861.
25. *New York Herald*, August 13, 1862.
26. Townsend provided a slightly different version in his *Campaigns of a Non-Combatant* (New York: Blelock, 1866). When assured that the sketch would become a "newspaper engraving," Stuart replied, "Umph!" During the truce following the battle Stuart met with Union generals Samuel Crawford and George Bayard, whom he had known at West Point. According to Charles M. Blackford, a Confederate officer present, Stuart bet his hat that Northern newspapers would declare Cedar Mountain a Union victory. Crawford accepted, remarking that even the *New York Herald* would not go so far as that. Susan L. Blackford, comp., *Letters from Lee's Army, or Memoirs of Life In and Out of the Army in Virginia During the War Between the States* (New York: Charles Scribner's Sons, 1947), 111.
27. Henry Villard, "Army Correspondence," *Nation* 1 (1865), 145.
28. A manuscript map of the battle of Gettysburg in the George Hay Stuart Papers, Library of Congress, Manuscript Division, bears the annotation, "drawn by reporter of Pittsburg [*sic*] Gazette." However, the *Daily Pittsburgh Gazette* printed no Gettysburg maps, and no documentation regarding the manuscript map exists.
29. Thomas Knox to James Gordon Bennett, June 28, 1862. James Gordon Bennett Papers, Library of Congress.
30. White sent the map to Sydney Gay via "Captain Holmes." White to Sydney Howard Gay, April 6, 1863. Gay Papers.
31. Numerous examples of this are discussed in Andrews, *The North Reports the Civil War*; Emmet Crozier, *Yankee Reporters, 1861–65* (New York: Oxford University Press, 1956); Louis M. Starr, *Bohemian Brigade: Civil War Newsmen in Action* (New York: Alfred Knopf, 1954); and Bernard Weisberger, *Reporters for the Union* (Boston: Little, Brown, 1953).
32. Frederick Reeder's map of Wilson's Creek reputedly accompanied Samuel Sturgis's report of the battle, but no such report is found in *The War of the Rebellion*.
33. McDowell's report dated from August 4, 1861. The map appears as pl. 3, no. 2, in U.S. War Department, *Atlas to Accompany the Official Records of the Union and Confederate Armies* (Washington, D.C.: Government Printing Office, 1891–95).
34. Outside of New York, papers such as the *Herald* and *Tribune* could sell for as much as twenty-five cents an issue, especially when they contained news of a major battle (Margaret Leech, *Reveille in Washington 1860–1865* [New York: Harper & Bros., 1941], 76).
35. Villard, "Army Correspondence," 116.
36. William F. G. Shanks, "How We Get Our News," *Harper's New Monthly Magazine* 34 (1867), 519.

37. George Alfred Townsend Scrapbooks. Quoted in Andrews, *The North Reports the Civil War*, 192. Townsend's papers are now housed in the Hall of Records, Maryland State Archives, but the scrapbooks Andrews examined nearly forty years ago in New York City remain unlocated.
38. As an example, in a letter written to Sydney H. Gay, Henry Villard contended that the correspondent of the *New York Herald* wrote his account of the battle of Stones River, Tennessee, from a hotel room in Louisville, Kentucky. Villard to Gay, September 26, 1863. Gay Papers.
39. Franc Wilkie, *Pen and Powder* (Boston: Ticknor, 1888), 124–29. In his published memoirs, Knox, for reasons unknown, only recounted the battle, making no mention of Browne's actions.
40. Albert D. Richardson, *The Secret Service, the Field, the Dungeon, and the Escape* (Hartford: American Publishing, 1865), 270–71.
41. See Henry Villard's discussion of the official reports of the Battle of Shiloh in *Memoirs of Henry Villard, Journalist and Financier, 1835–1900*, vol. 1 (Boston: Houghton Mifflin, 1904), 253–55.
42. Boynton's comments, written in 1881, are quoted by Royal Cortissoz, *The Life of Whitelaw Reid*, vol. 1 (New York: Charles Scribner's Sons, 1921), 98.
43. George Alfred Townsend, "Campaigning with General Pope," *Cornhill Magazine* 6 (1862), 767.
44. Thomas Knox, *Camp-Fire and Cotton-Field: Southern Adventure in Time of War* (Cincinnati: Jones Brothers, 1865), 73.
45. *New York Tribune*, February 3, 1862.
46. Censorship of the press during the Civil War is discussed in James G. Randall, "The Newspaper Problem and Its Bearing upon Military Secrecy during the Civil War," *American Historical Review* 23 (1918), 303–23; Quintus C. Wilson, "Voluntary Press Censorship during the Civil War," *Journalism Quarterly* 19 (1942), 251–61; John Marszalek, *Sherman's Other War: The General and the Civil War Press* (Memphis: Memphis State University Press, 1981); and is touched upon in several general histories of the war and Civil War journalism.
47. Simon Cameron to Henry Raymond, December 11, 1861, and Raymond to Cameron, December 13, 1861. Henry J. Raymond Papers, New York Public Library.
48. Knox, *Camp-Fire and Cotton-Field*, 254–58; Richardson, *The Secret Service*, 317–19.
49. *New York Herald*, January 18, 1863.
50. Andrews, *The North Reports the Civil War*, 552.
51. "Regulations for Correspondents of the Press with the Army of the Potomac," *Philadelphia Inquirer*, April 19, 1862.
52. *Cincinnati Daily Commercial*, April 30, 1862.
53. George Alfred Townsend Scrapbooks. Quoted in Andrews, *The North Reports the Civil War*, 265.
54. Frank Comparto, *Chronicles of Genius and Folly: R. Hoe & Company and the Printing Press as a Service to Democracy* (Culver City, Calif.: Labyrinthos, 1979), 284.
55. George A. Kubler, *A New History of Stereotyping* (New York: privately printed, 1941), 173–74.
56. The wet-mat process is described in detail in Kubler, *A New History of Stereotyping*, 249–63; J. Luther Ringwalt, *American Encyclopedia of Printing* (Philadelphia: Menamin & Ringwalt, 1871), 443–47; Michael Winship, "Printing with Plates in the Nineteenth-Century United States," *Printing History* 5 (1983), 15–20.
57. Kubler, *A New History of Stereotyping*, 174.
58. *New York Tribune*, April 10, 1861.
59. Frank O'Brien, *The Story of "The Sun"* (New York: George H. Doran, 1918), 193. The *Herald* considered the use of stereotypes while the process was being perfected. A letter from Richard Hoe to James Gordon Bennett, dated April 9, 1861, outlined the costs of fabricating the forms necessary to stereotype the *Herald*. James Gordon Bennett Papers, New York Public Library.
60. Letter from Herbert Ingram to Robert Hoe, June 1856. Quoted in Comparto, *Chronicles of Genius and Folly*, 425.
61. Electrotype plates, usually reserved for book illustration or fine drawings in periodicals, could also be used to print newspaper graphics. Only one example of an electrotyped map, identified as such, has been

found in a daily newspaper. See Winship, "Printing with Plates," 20–21, for information on electrotyping.

62. George Everett, "Printing Technology as a Barrier to Multi-Column Headlines, 1850–1895," *Journalism Quarterly* 53 (1976), 530.
63. Wood engravings did not account for all Civil War newspaper maps. The *Sun* (New York) printed some of their maps from graphotypes, a newly invented process that created a relief plate directly from a drawing. A map was drawn on a chalk-covered plate, using a special chemical ink that caused the chalk beneath the lines to harden. After removing the remaining chalk from the plate, a drawing stood in relief, ready for stereotyping.
64. Gambee, *Frank Leslie and His Illustrated Newspaper*, 47–48.
65. Prior to 1884, a double-page wood engraving in the *Illustrated London News* could be completed by twenty-four engravers in approximately twelve hours (Clement K. Shorter, "Illustrated Journalism: Its Past and Future," *The Contemporary Review* 75 [1899], 491).
66. For example, the *Chicago Daily Tribune*, which published over two hundred maps during the war, did not establish its own engraving shop until 1887 (Lloyd Wendt, *Chicago Tribune: The Rise of a Great American Newspaper* [Chicago: Rand McNally, 1979], 292). Surprisingly, not all weekly illustrated newspapers had art departments either. *Harper's Weekly* established an in-house art department in April 1863, six years after it began publication (Joseph Henry Harper, *The House of Harper* [New York: Harper & Bros., 1912], 204–5).
67. Mason Jackson, *The Pictorial Press, Its Origin and Progress* (London: Hurst & Blackett, 1885), 322–24; Sue Rainey, "Wood Engraving in America," in Mildred Abraham, ed., *Embellished with Numerous Engravings: The Works of American Illustrators and Wood Engravers, 1670–1880* (Charlottesville: University of Virginia Library, 1986), 24; Shorter, "Illustrated Journalism," 491; David Woodward, "The Decline of Commercial Wood-Engraving in Nineteenth-Century America," *Journal of the Printing Historical Society* 10 (1974), 58.
68. Virginia Penny, *The Employments of Women: A Cyclopedia of Woman's Work* (Boston: Walker, Wise, 1863), 98.
69. Ringwalt, *American Encyclopedia of Printing*, 497; Thomas Gilks, *The Art of Wood Engraving* (London: Winsor & Newton, 1867), 25; William A. Emerson, *Practical Instruction in the Art of Wood Engraving* (East Douglas, Mass.: Charles Batcheller, 1876), 16.
70. Samuel E. Fuller, *A Manual of Instruction in the Art of Wood Engraving* (Boston: J. Watson, 1867), 11–14.
71. Jackson, *The Pictorial Press*, 321.
72. Details of this process are discussed in David Woodward, "*The Woodcut Technique*," in Woodward, ed., *Five Centuries of Map Printing* (Chicago: University of Chicago Press, 1975), 48–49.
73. The maps were published in the *New York Tribune* (April 23) and the *New York Times* (May 26) and reprinted on page 31 and after page 52 of the *Rebellion Record: A Diary of American Events*, vol. 1 (New York: G. P. Putnam, 1861).
74. Frederic Hudson, *Journalism in the United States from 1690 to 1872* (New York: Harper & Bros., 1873), 705.
75. Benson Lossing, *A Memorial of Alexander Anderson, M.D., the First Engraver on Wood in America* (New York: privately printed, 1872), 80; *Manufacturing Schedule, New York County. Census of the State of New York*, 1865.
76. Colton also engraved maps for *Frank Leslie's Illustrated Newspaper* and *Harper's Weekly*.
77. Hudson, *Journalism in the United States*, 717.
78. A "linear mode of expression" permeated wood-engraved illustrations as well (Philip Beam, *Winslow Homer's Magazine Engravings* [New York: Harper & Row, 1979], 39).
79. The same can be said of modern newspaper maps. See Patricia Gilmartin, "The Design of Journalistic Maps: Purposes, Parameters, and Prospects," *Cartographica* 22 (1985), 6–8; Mark Monmonier, *Maps*

with the News: The Development of American Journalistic Cartography (Chicago: University of Chicago Press, 1989), 14–15.

80. The only firms with cartographic experience were G. W. Colton, publisher primarily of steel engraved and lithographed maps, and Schonberg & Company, a minor New York City cartographic publishing firm which appears to have specialized in wood-engraved maps.
81. David Woodward, *The All American Map: Wax Engraving and Its Influence on Cartography* (Chicago: University of Chicago Press, 1977), 87.
82. Beam, *Winslow Homer's Magazine Engravings*, 30; Gambee, *Frank Leslie and His Illustrated Newspaper*, 46–47; Jackson, *The Pictorial Press*, 317–21; Imre Reiner, *Woodcut/Wood Engraving: A Contribution to the History of the Art* (London: Publix Publishing, 1947), 15.
83. The separation of designers and engravers is discussed in Gillett Griffin, "The Development of Woodcut Printing in America," *Princeton University Library Chronicle* 20 (1958), 15–17; Beam, *Winslow Homer's Magazine Engravings*, 33–34; "How Our Pictures Are Made," *The Child At Home*, vol. 2 (1860), 19; and "Desultory Thoughts on Wood-Engraving and Wood-Cut Printing," *The Knickerbocker or New York Monthly Magazine* 41 (1853), 53.
84. "Lloyd's New Military Map of the Border and Southern States" (New York: H. H. Lloyd, 1862; reissued thereafter to 1865). Sinclair Hamilton, *Early American Book Illustrators and Wood Engravers, 1670–1870* (Princeton: Princeton University Library, 1958), 135.
85. For a discussion of the changing quality of journalistic prose, see Starr, *Bohemian Brigade*, 255–71.
86. *Cincinnati Daily Times*, August 23, 1862.
87. *Cincinnati Daily Commercial*, April 30, 1862. Cited in Andrews, *The North Reports the Civil War*, 643.
88. *Daily Missouri Democrat*, April 1, 1863. Cited in Andrews, *The North Reports the Civil War*, 643.
89. Robert H. Newell, *The Orpheus C. Kerr Papers*, vol. 1 (New York: Blakeman & Mason, 1862), 193.
90. Letter from Henry Hitchcock to his wife, December 16, 1864, quoted in M. A. DeWolfe Howe, ed., *Marching with Sherman: Passages from the Letters and Campaign Diaries of Henry Hitchcock* (New Haven: Yale University Press, 1927), 192. The map appeared in the November 28 issue. Sherman imposed a fairly effective news blackout, which left the public wondering about his movements. For a discussion of Sherman's opposition to the press, see Marszalek, *Sherman's Other War*.
91. Milo Quaife, ed., *From the Cannon's Mouth: The Civil War Letters of General Alpheus S. Williams* (Detroit: Wayne State University Press, 1959), 179.
92. *War Diary and Letters of Stephen Minot Weld, 1861–1865* (Boston: Massachusetts Historical Society, 1979), 140. The map of Antietam was published on September 22, 1862.
93. Letter dated June 21, 1864. Robert G. Carter, *Four Brothers in Blue or Sunshine and Shadows of the War of the Rebellion* (Austin: University of Texas Press, 1978), 444–45. It is impossible to tell who the author of the letter was, since no names are given. Both Walter Carter and Robert G. Carter served at Petersburg.
94. David Bosse, *Civil War Newspaper Maps of the Northern Daily Press: A Cartobibliography* (Westport, Conn.: Greenwood Press, 1993). See appendix for additional information on the frequency of map publication and the newspapers that printed them.
95. Letter from Sydney H. Gay to Thomas Gunn, which the *New York Herald* published in its May 16, 1862, issue. Presumably the letter came into the possession of the *Herald* by nefarious means. The *Tribune* published the map of Lee's Mills in its April 22, 1862, issue, with credit given to the *Philadelphia Inquirer*.
96. George Smalley to Sydney H. Gay, September 23, 1862. Gay Papers.
97. A. Homer Byington to Sydney H. Gay, undated letter. Gay Papers.
98. Andrews, *The North Reports the Civil War*, 32–33.
99. Stephenson, *Civil War Maps*, 11.
100. The copyright deposit date on the copy of the map in the Library of Congress is July 23, 1863.
101. Stephenson, *Civil War Maps*, numbers 6.2 and 14.65, 14.7, 14.75, 14.8.

102. Ibid., number 26.

103. *Scientific American* 7 (1862), 1. Other print media also suffered, and retail book prices increased by as much as 30 percent during the war (John Tebbel, *A History of Book Publishing in the United States* [New York: R. R. Bowker, 1972], 281).

104. Theodore DeVinne, "Trade Unions," *The Printer* 5 (1864), 1.

105. Francis Brown, *Raymond of the "Times"* (New York: W. W. Norton, 1951), 226.

106. *New York Herald*, November 9, 1864.

107. This point is debated in the previously cited works on Civil War censorship. An unequivocal statement of the situation is found in a circular from Leroy P. Walker, Confederate secretary of war, "To Newspaper Correspondents," dated July 1, 1861. Walker pleads for discretion on the part of members of the press, adding, "You are aware of the great amount of valuable information obtained by us through the medium of the enterprising journals of the North." Original in the manuscript collection, Chicago Historical Society.

108. *New York Tribune*, July 13, 1861. Quoted in Weisberger, *Reporters for the Union*, 84.

109. M. J. Blakemore and J. Brian Harley, "Concepts in the History of Cartography, A Review and Perspective," *Cartographica* 17 (1980), 54–55. The authors identify chronometric, planimetric, and topographical accuracy as interdependent aspects of cartographic evidence.

110. A survey of the maps in the Library of Congress shows Gettysburg to be the most mapped battle of the war. Stephenson, *Civil War Maps*.

111. George Hosmer reported that he was standing on Cemetery Hill with Gen. George Meade when they were fired on from a church steeple. Andrews, *The North Reports the Civil War*, 421–22.

112. *The War of the Rebellion*, ser. 1, vol. 27, pt. 1, 758–63.

113. Report of Gen. John Buford, First Cavalry Div., in *The War of the Rebellion*, ser. 1, vol. 27, pt. 1, 927–28.

114. By interviewing prisoners and observing battle flags, Northern correspondents usually could identify Confederate troops. A number of newspaper maps note the locations and names of Confederate units, but never with the precision accorded Union troops.

115. Andrews, *The North Reports the Civil War*, 548.

116. According to official returns, 11,853 Union troops were engaged on May 31 at Seven Pines compared to 9,520 Confederates ("Opposing Forces at Seven Pines, May 31–June 1, 1862," in Robert U. Johnson and Clarence Buell, eds., *Battles and Leaders of the Civil War*, vol. 2 [New York: Century, 1887], 218–19).

ATLAS

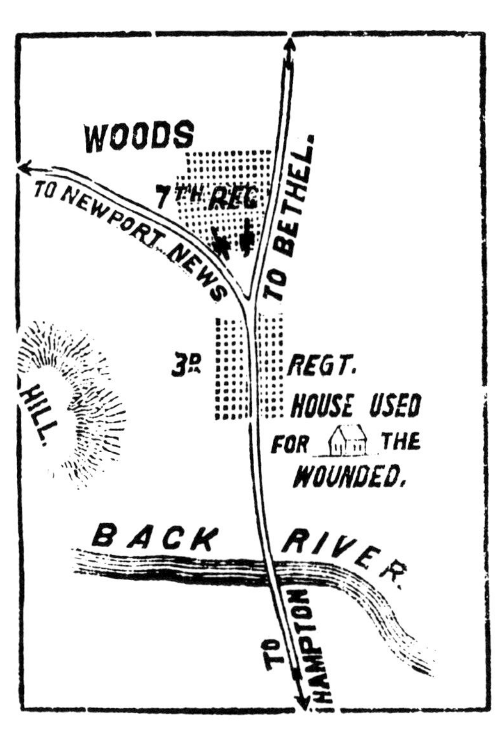
WOODS
TO NEWPORT NEWS
7TH REG.
TO BETHEL.
3D
REGT.
HOUSE USED
FOR THE
WOUNDED.
HILL.
BACK RIVER.
TO HAMPTON

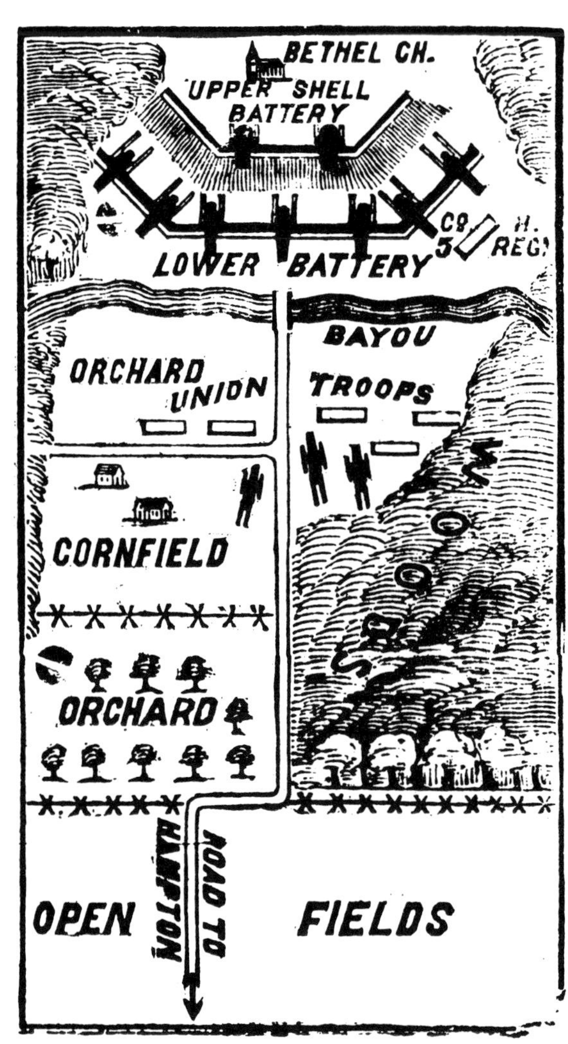
BETHEL CH.
UPPER SHELL
BATTERY
CO. 5 N.Y. REGT.
LOWER BATTERY
BAYOU
ORCHARD
UNION
TROOPS
CORNFIELD
ORCHARD
WOODS
ROAD TO HAMPTON
OPEN
FIELDS

MAP 1

The Battle of Big Bethel, Virginia

Published in the New York *World*, June 17, 1861

(Originals 8 × 6 cm. and 11 × 6 cm.)

BENJAMIN BUTLER INITIATED ONE OF THE WAR'S FIRST ENGAGEMENTS BY ORDERING seven regiments under his command to move against Confederate positions at the villages of Big and Little Bethel. Around 1 A.M. on June 10, Union troops advanced in two columns from Fortress Monroe and Newport News. The columns intended to rendezvous near the New Market Bridge, which crossed a branch of the Back River, then proceed together for a surprise attack. Instead, the Seventh New York Regiment mistook the Third New York for the enemy and opened fire. In addition to sustaining casualties, the demoralized Union troops had made their presence known. The united columns, continuing on, found Little Bethel deserted. At Big Bethel, Confederates under John B. Magruder waited in a strongly entrenched position around a church. Union forces arrived late in the morning and faced Magruder's troops across a deep stream. The Union attack never materialized; after an hour of skirmishing, the venture was abandoned and a retreat ordered.

Big Bethel ranks as the first land battle illustrated by newspaper maps. The *World*'s correspondent accompanied the expedition, sketching the maps "on the spot." The first shows the accidental nighttime encounter of Union regiments, represented by small dots. The second depicts the battlefield at Big Bethel. After approaching through an orchard and cornfield, Union troops were deployed along a lane off the main road and at the edge of a woods on the east side of the road. A battery of three guns commanded the road leading to the Confederate works, as shown. One company moved along a road to the east (not shown) and forded the creek, flanking Magruder's position at the point labeled "Co. H, 5 Reg." (Fifth New York). The company retired in confusion after the first volley felled the officer leading the charge, the noted author Theodore Winthrop. Winthrop's death attracted considerable public attention, making him one of the first slain war heroes.

Note that the heads of the screws used to secure the printing plate have printed at lower and upper left of the second map.

Reports in U.S. War Department, *War of the Rebellion*: ser. 1, vol. 2.
Map in U.S. War Department, *Atlas*: pl. 61, no. 4.
Other newspaper maps: *Chicago Post* (7/28/61, part of war supplement), *New York Tribune* (6/17/61).

THE BULL'S RUN BATTLEFIELD.

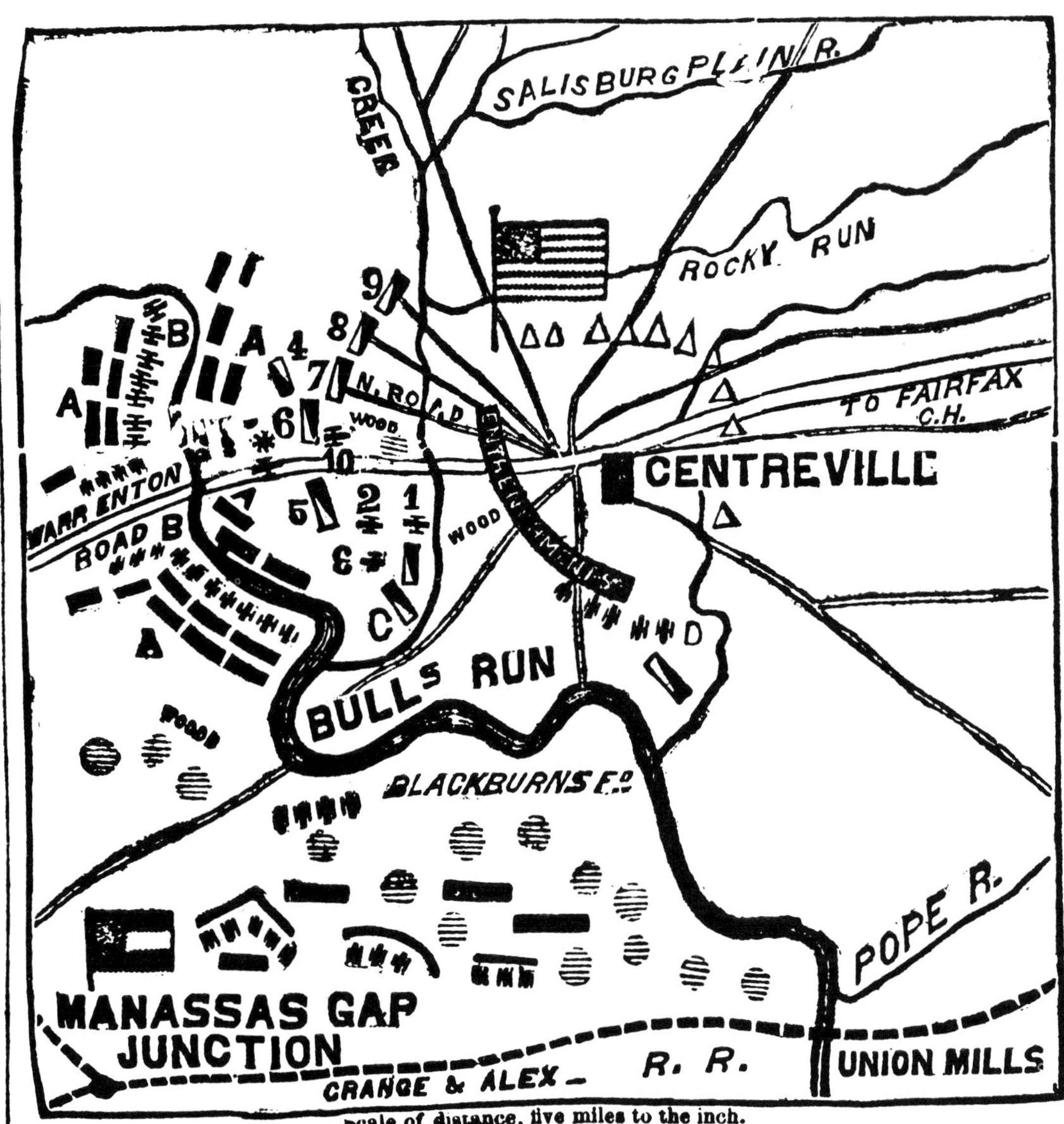

Scale of distance, five miles to the inch.

A represents the rebel camp.
B masked batteries of the secessionists.
C Col. Miles' Fifth division.
D Brig. Gen. Blenker's brigade, fortified on the heights of Centreville.
* represents Lieut. Haynes' ponderous 30-pounder Parrot gun.
1 Major Barry's Fort Pickens battery, Capt. Tidball, commanding.
2 Lieut. Green's battery.
3 Hunt's battery.
4 Tyler's division.
5 Hunter's division.
6 Heintzelman's division.
7 Franklin's division.
8 Keyes' division.
9 Porter's division.
10 Ayers' batterise.

MAPS 2A AND 2B

The Battle of Manassas, or Bull Run, Virginia

Published in the *New York Herald*, July 25, 1861, and in the *New York Tribune*, July 26, 1861

(Originals 12 × 12 cm. and 14 × 14 cm.)

IN ORDER TO PROTECT THE RAILROAD CENTER AT MANASSAS JUNCTION, CONFEDERates under Pierre Beauregard assumed a defensive position along Bull Run. Irvin McDowell's numerically superior Union army slowly moved south to engage them. Disorganization and delays prevented McDowell from attacking before Joseph E. Johnston arrived from the Shenandoah Valley with additional troops. McDowell's plan to strike the Confederate left while simultaneously demonstrating against the center initially met with success, on July 21. The Union flanking movement forced the hard-pressed Confederate line to a position south of the Warrenton Road. At a critical moment, reinforcements arriving by train and troops forming the Confederate right were directed into battle by Johnston. McDowell's attack stalled and began to falter. Late in the afternoon a Confederate counterattack caused the entire Union line to collapse and flee toward Centreville and beyond.

Map 2a was "drawn from actual observation" by the *Herald*'s correspondent, probably Henry Villard. Although it gives a fair account of the battlefield, it errs in depicting military data. Positions are vaguely represented with no indication of McDowell's flank movement. Confederate forces (*A*) are shown lying between Bull Run and an unlabeled creek (Cub Run), when in fact none crossed Bull Run until the Union retreat. The Confederate left extends too far north of the Warrenton Road, and the symbols for cannon (*B*) give an erroneous impression of strength in that quarter. Union forces became mixed during the battle and the map represents them rather confusingly. The right consisted of the brigades (not divisions) of William Franklin (*7*), Andrew Porter (*9*), and others within the divisions of David Hunter (*5*) and Samuel Heintzelman (*6*). Daniel Tyler's division (*4*), including the brigade of Erasmus Keyes (*8*), advanced along the Warrenton Road as shown. Dixon Miles's division (*C*) remained in reserve at Centreville, and Israel Richardson, not Louis Blencker, occupied the heights opposite Blackburn's Ford (*D*). The batteries of John Tidball (*1*) and Oliver Greene (*2*) stayed in reserve with Miles, while that of Henry Hunt (*3*) accompanied Richardson and Romeyn Ayres (*10*) to form the center with Tyler. The map's scale, given as one inch to five miles, should have read one inch to two miles.

On July 26, the *New York Tribune* published its map of the battle. Although some additional streams are included and named, the map's topography does not greatly improve on that of the *Herald*'s. Also, it provides a more limited view of military

THE BATTLE FIELD.

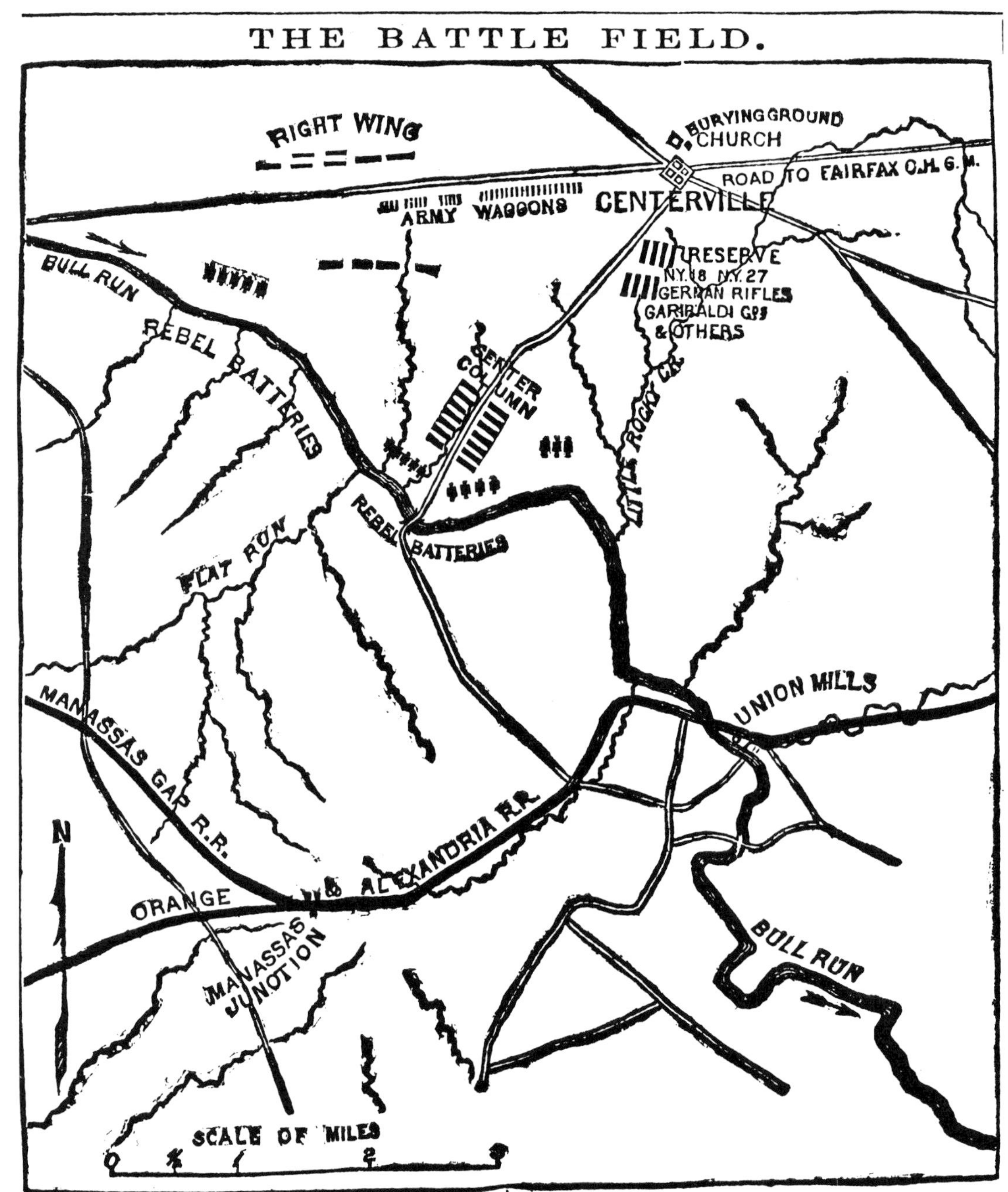

movements and positions. Across Bull Run, Confederate batteries, but no troops, are marked. Union troops on the Warrenton Road (*top*, marked "road to Fairfax") composed the center, not the right, and the map gives no indication of the flanking movement of McDowell's right wing. At Centreville some, but not all, of the units designated stayed in reserve. The "center column" moving toward Bull Run represents Richardson's division on the left. Quite possibly the mapmaker confused earlier movements involving the skirmish at Blackburn's Ford (July 18) with the main battle of the 21st.

Reports in the U.S. War Department, *War of the Rebellion*: ser. 1, vol. 2. A map of the battle appears in vol. 51, pt. 1.

Maps in U.S. War Department, *Atlas*: pl. 3, nos. 1, 2; pl. 5, nos. 1, 7.

Other newspaper maps: *Baltimore American & Commercial Advertiser* (7/24/61), *Boston Daily Journal* (7/25/61), *Chicago Post* (7/25/61), *New York Herald* (8/16 and 8/25/61), *Philadelphia Inquirer* (7/26 and 8/3/61).

The Battlefield on Wilson's Creek, near Springfield, Missouri.

POSITION OF THE UNITED STATES FORCES UNDER GEN. LYON, AND THE REBEL FORCES UNDER McCULLOCH, RAINS, PRICE, McINTOSH, &C.

FOUGHT ON THE TENTH OF AUGUST, 1861.

Drawn by Fred'k Wm. Reeder, of Co. C, First U. S. Cavalry—an eye-witness of the Battle.

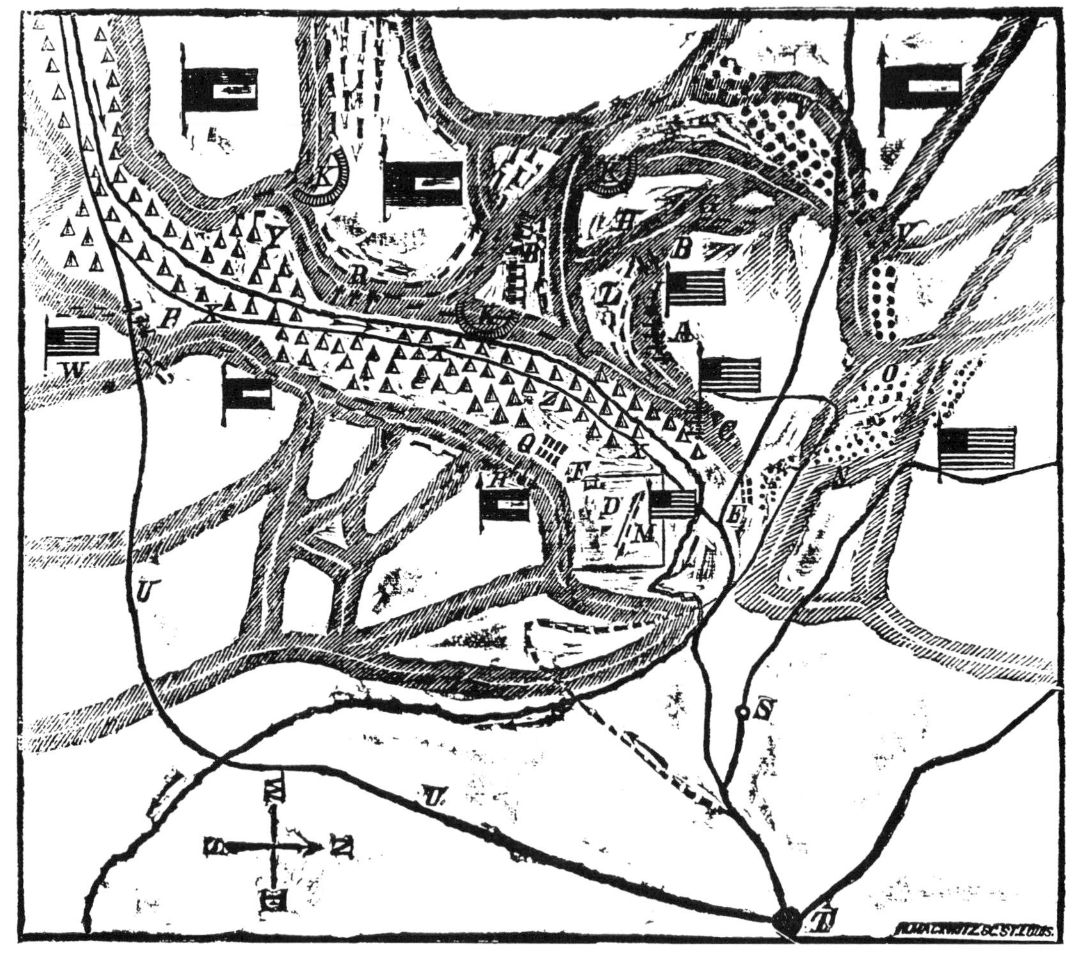

A Capt. Totten's battery
B Section of Totten's battery
C Capt. DuBois's battery
D Cornfield
E Log house
F Ambulances
G 2nd Missouri Volunteers
H 2nd Kansas Volunteers
I Spot where Lyon fell
K Masked Rebel batteries
L 1st Kansas, 1st Iowa, 1st Missouri
M Capt. Plummer's battalion
N Home guard, mounted
O Kansas Rangers, mounted
P Col. Sigel's position
Q Train of Rebels
R Rebel concealed battery
S Town of Little York
T Springfield
U Fayetteville Road, Sigel's advance
V Rebel cavalry, 1,200 strong
W 3rd and 5th Missouri
X Road through camp
Y McCulloch's headquarters
Z Rains's headquarters

MAP 3

The Battle of Wilson's Creek, Missouri

Published in the *Daily Missouri Republican*, August 25, 1861

(Original 13 × 15 cm.)

IN EARLY AUGUST, BENJAMIN MCCULLOCH'S AND NATHANIEL LYON'S ARMIES LAY twelve miles apart in southwest Missouri. Each planned an offensive, but Lyon acted first, advancing most of his army just north of the Confederate camps on Wilson's Creek. At the same time, Franz Sigel circled to the south with a smaller Union force to approach from behind. At dawn on the 10th, Union troops attacked and initially overran some Confederate positions. On the north, Lyon's thrust was checked by artillery posted east of Wilson's Creek. To the south, Sigel's artillery played havoc with the Confederate rear, then his infantry advanced toward the abandoned camps. But Benjamin McCulloch's brigade quickly re-formed and routed Sigel. The main battle occurred on a hill west of Wilson's Creek where Lyon established his line. The outnumbered Union forces repulsed three direct assaults and a cavalry attack on their flank before being forced to retire to Springfield. Lyon was killed during the second assault.

The map's author, Frederick W. Reeder, who served with Sigel, depicted the many ridges of the battlefield with hatched lines. Wilson's Creek runs nearly north to south at this site and should begin at the right side of the map, but Reeder represented it as a large bend entering at upper left (*line with arrow*) and exiting at lower left of the map. At Sigel's point of attack (*W*, *P*) a tributary enters from the west, apparently causing the confusion. Triangular tent symbols mark the Confederate camps along the creek. Lyon's final line consisted of the Second Missouri (*G*), Second Kansas (*H*), First Missouri, First Kansas, and First Iowa (*L*), and Frederick Steele's battalion of general service troops. James Totten's batteries (*A*, *B*) and John DuBois's (*C*) backed the Union position as shown. Elkanah Greer's cavalry (*V*'s *dots*), whose flank attack was repulsed by Totten's battery, numbered less than half of the 1,200 troops credited to him. Confederate artillery (*K*'s, *R*) roughly paralleled Lyon's line but are not shown operating against Sigel. Joseph Plummer's Union column (*M*) was repulsed in the cornfield (*D*) east of Wilson's Creek. Lyon's route (*dashed line*) erroneously indicates the Union advance as coming from the east, because the map places Springfield (*T*) too far to the south.

Reports in the U.S. War Department, *War of the Rebellion*: ser. 1, vol. 3.
Maps in U.S. War Department, *Atlas*: pl. 135, no. 1.
Other newspaper maps: *Chicago Post* (8/21/61), *Chicago Times* (8/20/61), *Cincinnati Daily Commercial* (8/22/61), *New York Herald* (9/1/61), *Philadelphia Inquirer* (8/31/61).

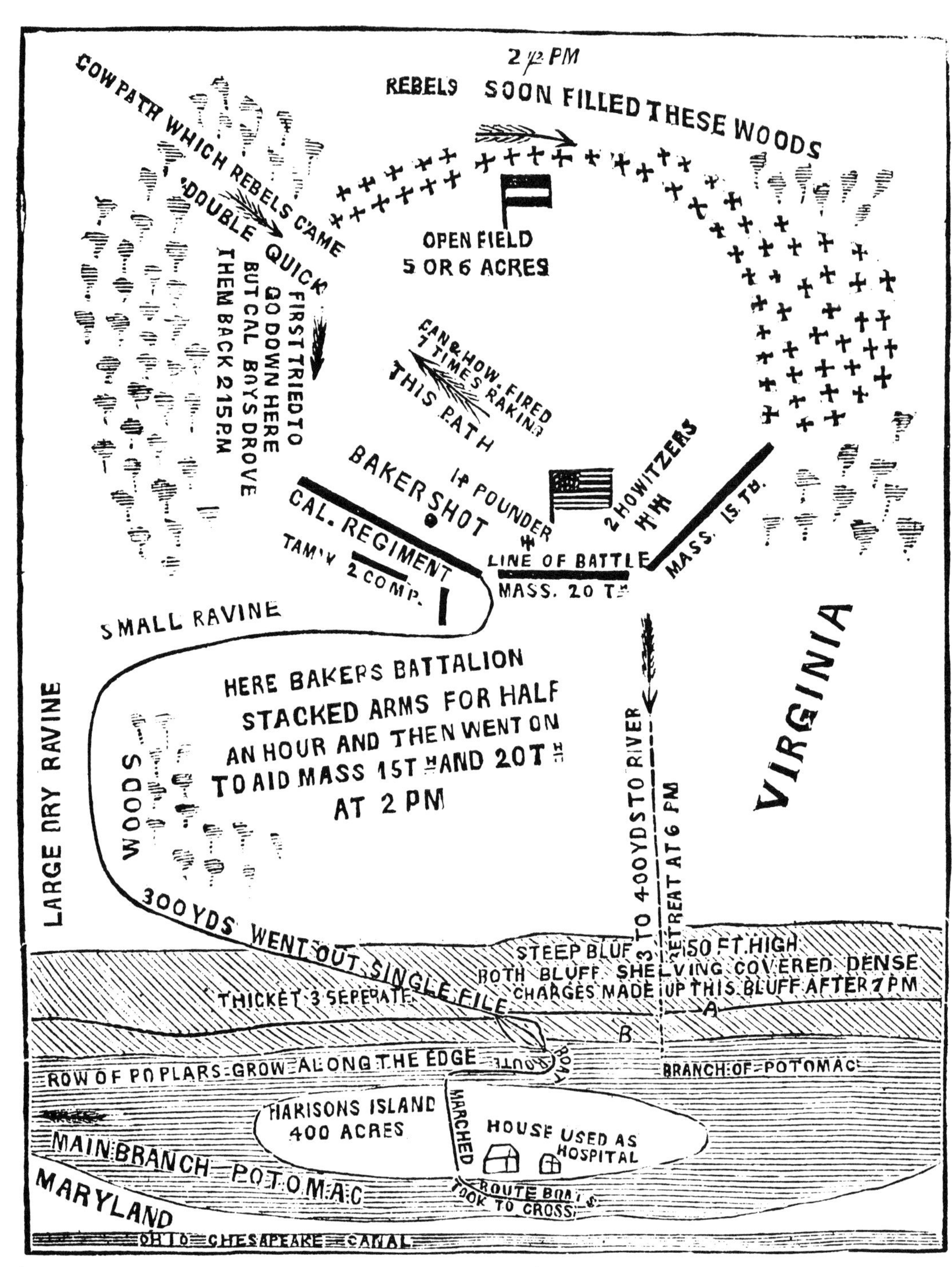

THE BATTLE FIELD OF BALL'S BLUFF, OCTOBER 21ST.

M A P 4

The Battle of Ball's Bluff, Virginia

Published in the *Philadelphia Inquirer*, October 30, 1861

(Original 18 × 14 cm.)

ON OCTOBER 21, FOUR BRIGADES UNDER THE COMMAND OF COL. EDWARD BAKER, a U.S. Senator and personal friend of Lincoln, crossed the Potomac. Baker had been directed to make a reconnaissance in the direction of Leesburg, Virginia, but little thought seems to have been given to the logistical difficulties of ferrying troops by inadequate flatboats and ascending a steep bluff. Confederates under Nathan Evans detected the movement, and skirmishing began. Baker and his brigade arrived on the field around 2 P.M., deploying Union forces in a line roughly parallel to the river. A general engagement ensued as Confederates tried to turn the Union left. Although unsuccessful in that endeavor, Evans did occupy a strategically important hill in front of the Union position. From there Confederates poured an effective fire into the Union ranks, killing Baker and others. As Union troops retreated in the early evening, they sustained many casualties, including numerous drownings, as they descended the bluffs and recrossed the Potomac.

The *Inquirer*'s map, oriented with north to the right, relies on a somewhat unusual amount of text to convey many of the battle's details. Lt. James Johnson of the Seventy-first Pennsylvania supplied much of the information for the map. His regiment, which was raised and organized by Baker, was originally known as the First California, and is so designated on the map. To reach Ball's Bluff, Union forces crossed from the Maryland shore of the Potomac to Harrison's Island, marched to the Virginia side of the island, then crossed to the Virginia shore. From there they scrambled up the bank and through a ravine. The Union line was deployed as shown. "Tam'y 2 Comp." (*center left*) refers to the Forty-second New York, known as the Tammany Regiment. The crosses (*upper right*) represent the Confederate forces scattered throughout the woods; some of them climbed into trees in order to fire at the Union position. The initial attack on the Union left and the spot in front of the lines where Baker fell while encouraging his men are indicated. The Union gunners were quickly decimated; Baker's three pieces of artillery fired only a few rounds before being rendered useless ("can & how. fired 7 times," *center*).

Reports in the U.S. War Department, *War of the Rebellion*: ser. 1, vol. 5.
Maps in U.S. War Department, *Atlas*: pl. 7, no. 1.
Other newspaper maps: *Cincinnati Daily Times* (11/2/61), *New York Times* (10/31/61).

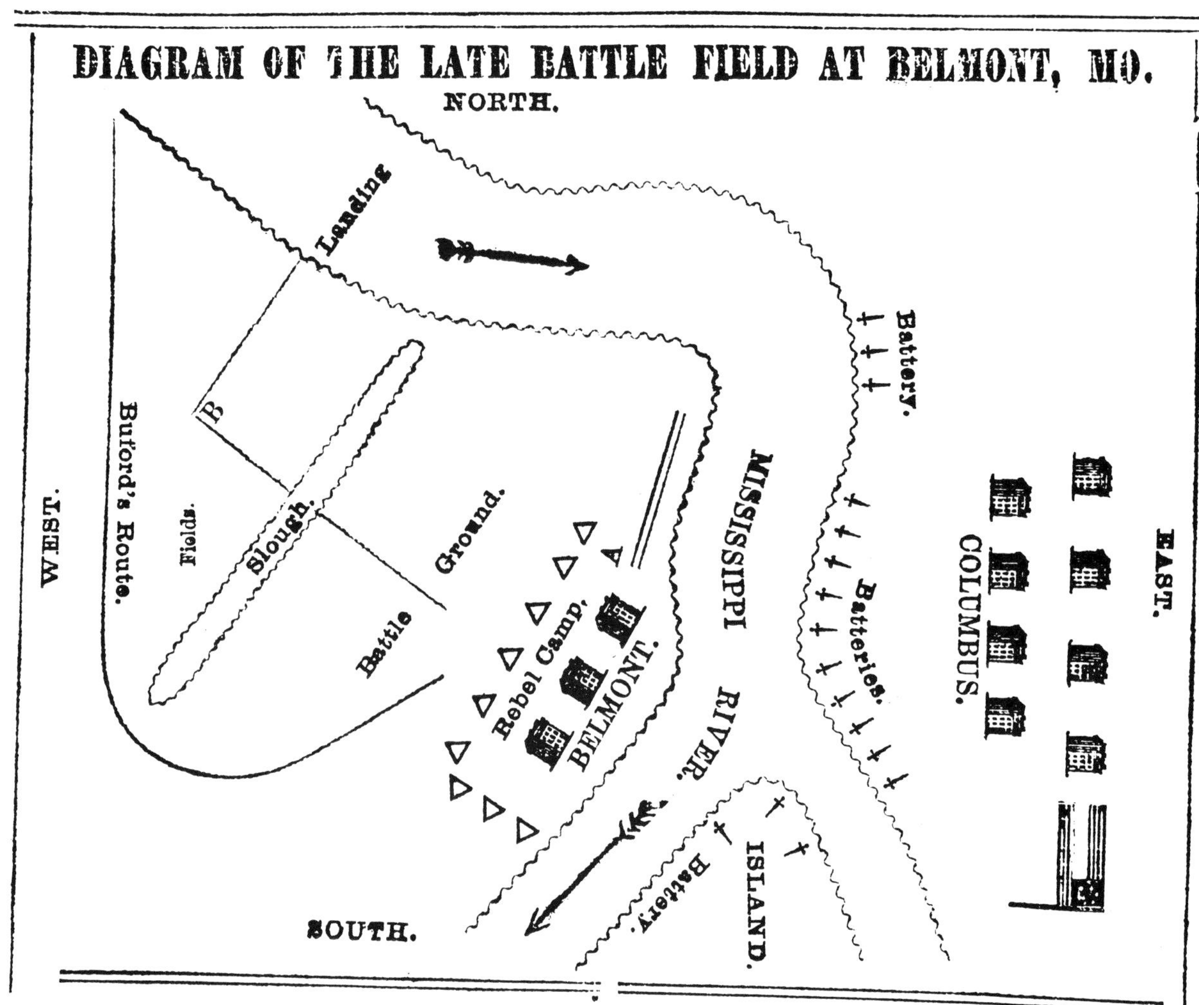
DIAGRAM OF THE LATE BATTLE FIELD AT BELMONT, MO.
NORTH.
Landing
Battery.
B
Buford's Route.
Fields.
Slough.
Ground.
Battle
MISSISSIPPI
RIVER.
Rebel Camp.
BELMONT.
A
Batteries.
COLUMBUS.
WEST.
EAST.
Battery.
ISLAND.
SOUTH.

MAP 5

The Battle of Belmont, Missouri

Published in the *Daily Missouri Republican*, November 14, 1861

(Original 10 × 12 cm.)

IN ONE OF THE WAR'S FIRST JOINT ARMY AND NAVY OPERATIONS, UNION FORCES successfully demonstrated against the Confederate stronghold at Columbus, Kentucky. Accompanied by two gunboats, two brigades of infantry and a detachment of cavalry under Ulysses S. Grant proceeded down the Mississippi from Cairo, Illinois. Grant elected to attack Camp Johnston at Belmont on November 7, while the gunboats engaged the Columbus batteries directly across the river. Landing upriver, Grant advanced to within a mile of the Confederate position, where he encountered Gideon Pillow's pickets. Union troops slowly pushed their way toward the river as Confederate ammunition and resistance dwindled. But instead of continuing to press the attack and securing victory, Grant's troops stopped to loot the captured camp. This allowed Confederates time to regroup under the shelter of the riverbank and begin a flanking movement, to get between the Union troops and their transports. As Confederate reinforcements arrived from Columbus, Grant ordered a hasty retreat and retired upriver.

William Webb wrote the *Republican*'s account of the battle and claimed authorship of the map, one of the few printed from type rather than engraved. Printer's rules and letters depict topography and troop movements, while pictures of houses denote the towns (Belmont being greatly exaggerated). Despite its simplicity, the map accurately represents most major features of the battlefield. The place where Union troops disembarked is shown near the top of the map ("landing"), and *B* (*left*) indicates the road over which they advanced. After crossing a low swampy area ("slough"), Grant deployed his command in a line of battle and began skirmishing with Confederates. The curved line to the west indicates the flank attack of Napoleon Buford's regiment, which traveled the same road as the other troops until reaching the slough. Webb's account stated that the Confederate retreat occurred along a sunken road (*A*, *center*) rather than below the riverbank. The map shows the river bending too sharply above Belmont and enlarges Wolfe Island below.

Reports in U.S. War Department, *War of the Rebellion*: ser. 1, vol. 2.
Maps in U.S. War Department, *Atlas*: pl. 4, no. 3.
Other newspaper maps: *Chicago Post* (11/9/61), *New York Herald* (11/19/61).

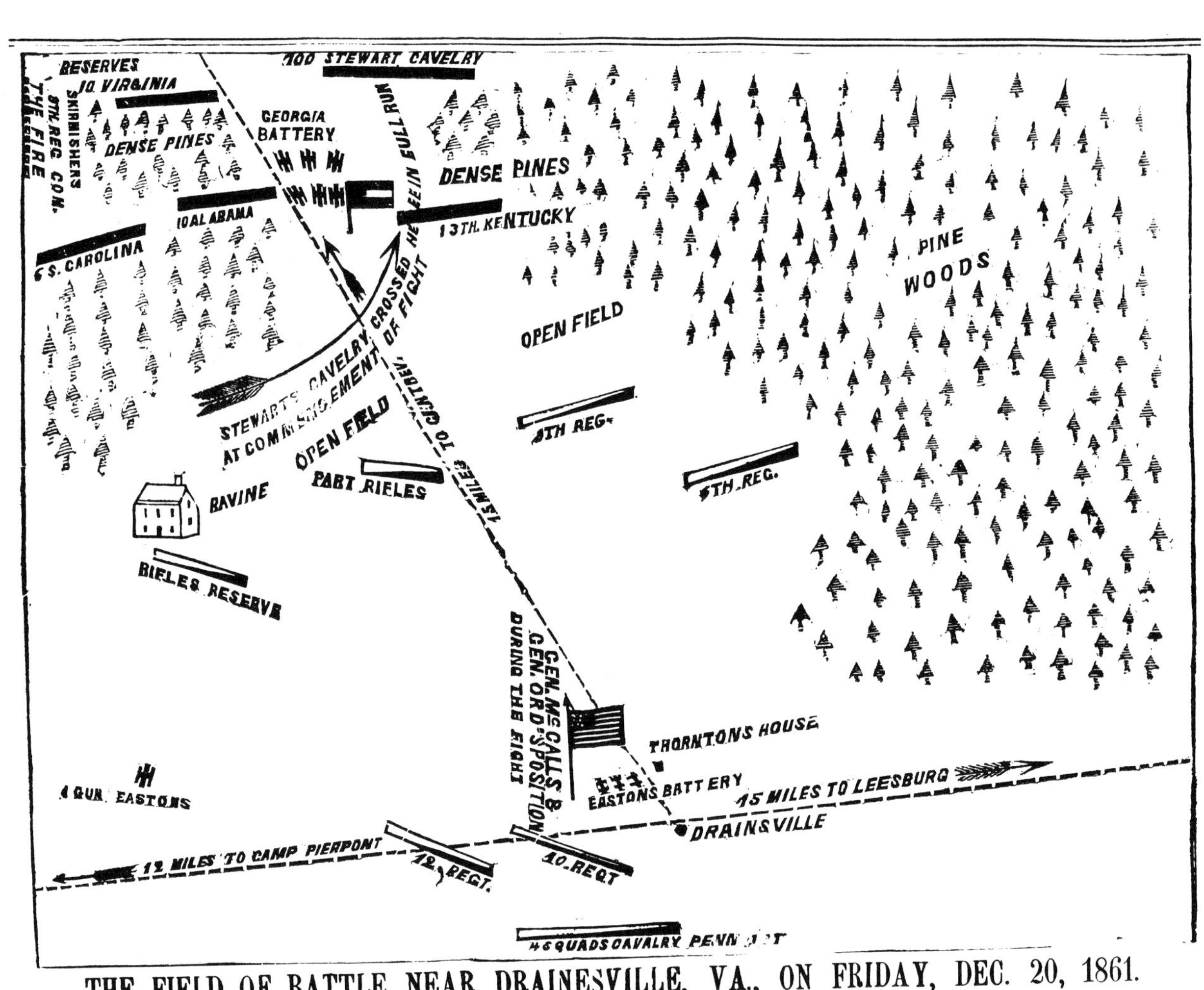

THE FIELD OF BATTLE, NEAR DRAINESVILLE, VA., ON FRIDAY, DEC. 20, 1861.

MAP 6

The Battle of Drainsville, Virginia

Published in the *Philadelphia Inquirer*, December 25, 1861

(Original 18 × 23 cm.)

As the first Union victory in Virginia, Drainsville contributed significantly to Northern morale. The affair began when Union forces on a foraging expedition encountered Confederate troops commanded by J. E. B. ("Jeb") Stuart, on December 20. After becoming aware of the presence of Stuart's cavalry, Union general Edward Ord formed a line of battle across open fields near Drainsville. Four regiments of Confederate infantry occupied a much stronger position in a densely wooded area on either side of the Centreville Road. Although both forces had cavalry at their disposal, the wooded terrain severely limited its use. In a brief artillery duel, Hezekiah Easton's battery silenced the Confederate guns of A. S. Cutt. The Sixth and Ninth Pennsylvania regiments then moved forward to engage the Confederate right. Stuart's troops offered limited resistance before being driven from their wooded hillside and retreating in disorder toward Centreville.

The *Inquirer*'s map is oriented from the Union perspective of the action, with south at the top. The map provides a distinct and accurate impression of the nature of the battlefield. The opposing batteries faced each other on the Centreville Road with one cannon on the Union left. Most of the Pennsylvania regiments are named, the two units on the left ("rifles") being the Thirteenth Pennsylvania, also known as the Bucktails. With the exception of the Twelfth Pennsylvania, which formed to the right of Easton's battery, all are correctly located in relation to the Centreville Road. Ord's position at the crossroads and that of George McCall, Ord's superior, who arrived near the end of the fight, are marked. The map mislabels two of the Confederate units involved. They should be the First Kentucky (marked "13th") and the Eleventh Virginia (marked "10th"). The map indicates the opening attack by Union skirmishers of the Ninth Regiment against the Confederate right (*upper left*) but places it too far south. The initial movement of Stuart's cavalry, carelessly noted along the large arrow, signaled the start of the affair.

Reports in U.S. War Department, *War of the Rebellion*: ser. 1, vol. 5.
Maps in U.S. War Department, *Atlas*: pl. 13, no. 5; pl. 41, no. 2.
Other newspaper maps: *Cincinnati Daily Times* (12/31/61).

NEAR SOMERSET. KY., JANUARY 9, 1862.

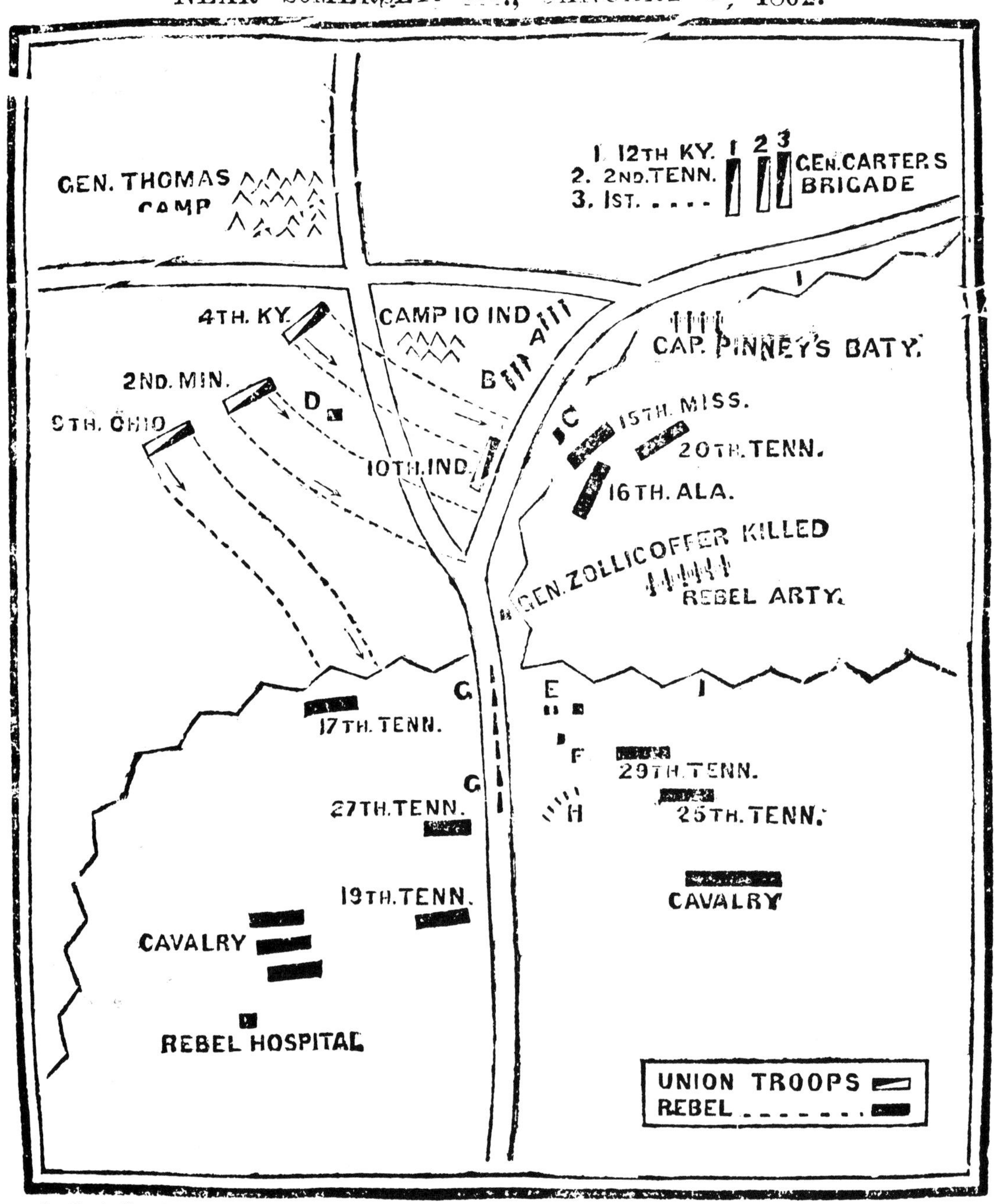

A—Capt. Standart's (Union) Battery.
B—Capt. Wetmore's (Union) Battery.
C—Place where Baillie Peyton was killed.
D—Logan's house.
E—Gen. Crittenden and Staff.
F—Position of Gen. Carroll.
G—Capt. McClarg's (Rebel) Battery.
H—Pickets of Wolford's (Rebel) Kentucky Cavalry.
I—Fences.

M A P 7

The Battle of Logan's Cross Roads, or Mill Springs, Kentucky

Published in the *New York Tribune*, February 3, 1862

(Original 13 × 12 cm.)

LATE IN 1861, CONFEDERATES COMMANDED BY FELIX ZOLLICOFFER ESTABLISHED entrenchments north of the Cumberland River opposite Mill Springs. Ordered to secure southern Kentucky for the Union, George Thomas advanced his army to Logan's Cross Roads, nine miles from the Confederate camp, on January 17. George Crittenden, the new Confederate commander, realized that he could not hold the position chosen by Zollicoffer and decided to attack Thomas before Union reinforcements arrived from Somerset. At dawn on the 19th, Crittenden's force struck, driving back Union cavalry pickets. Other Union troops hurried from their camps at the first sounds of battle and formed a line across Mill Springs Road. Confederates threatened to flank the Union left, but the arrival of Samuel Carter's brigade checked that movement. Thomas then committed additional forces on the Union right, which led to the decisive charge of the Ninth Ohio. Crittenden's left gave way and his regiments retreated to Mill Springs.

The *Tribune*'s map appeared six days after the paper's first printed account of the battle, when its Kentucky correspondent filed an additional report. Only two of the several Union camps are shown, with the main encampment ("Gen. Thomas camp") actually to the left (west) of the crossroads. The map provides a good portrayal of the battlefield, but most of the fighting occurred farther south along Mill Springs Road (not labeled). Dennis Kenny's battery (mislabeled as Pinney's) operated to the right, not the left, of those of William Standart (*A*) and Stephen Wetmore (*B*). A more glaring error identifies Frank Wolford's cavalry, which formed the Union picket, as "rebel." Other Union troop positions are accurate in relation to one another. On the Confederate side, Hugh McLung's battery (*G*, misidentified as McClarg's) and the various regiments, all correctly identified, formed a relatively continuous line of battle perpendicular to the Mill Spring Road. Noted are the sites where Zollicoffer (*center*) and Ballie Peyton, Jr., Confederate son of the pro-Union Tennessee politician (*C*), were killed.

Reports in U.S. War Department, *War of the Rebellion*: ser. 1, vol. 7.
Maps in U.S. War Department, *Atlas*: pl. 6, no. 3.
Other newspaper maps: *New York Tribune* (1/29/62).

THE PORK POINT BATTERY.

Diagram Showing the Scene of the Gallant Charge of the Twenty-first Massachusetts, the Fifty-first New-York, and Hawkins' Zouaves.

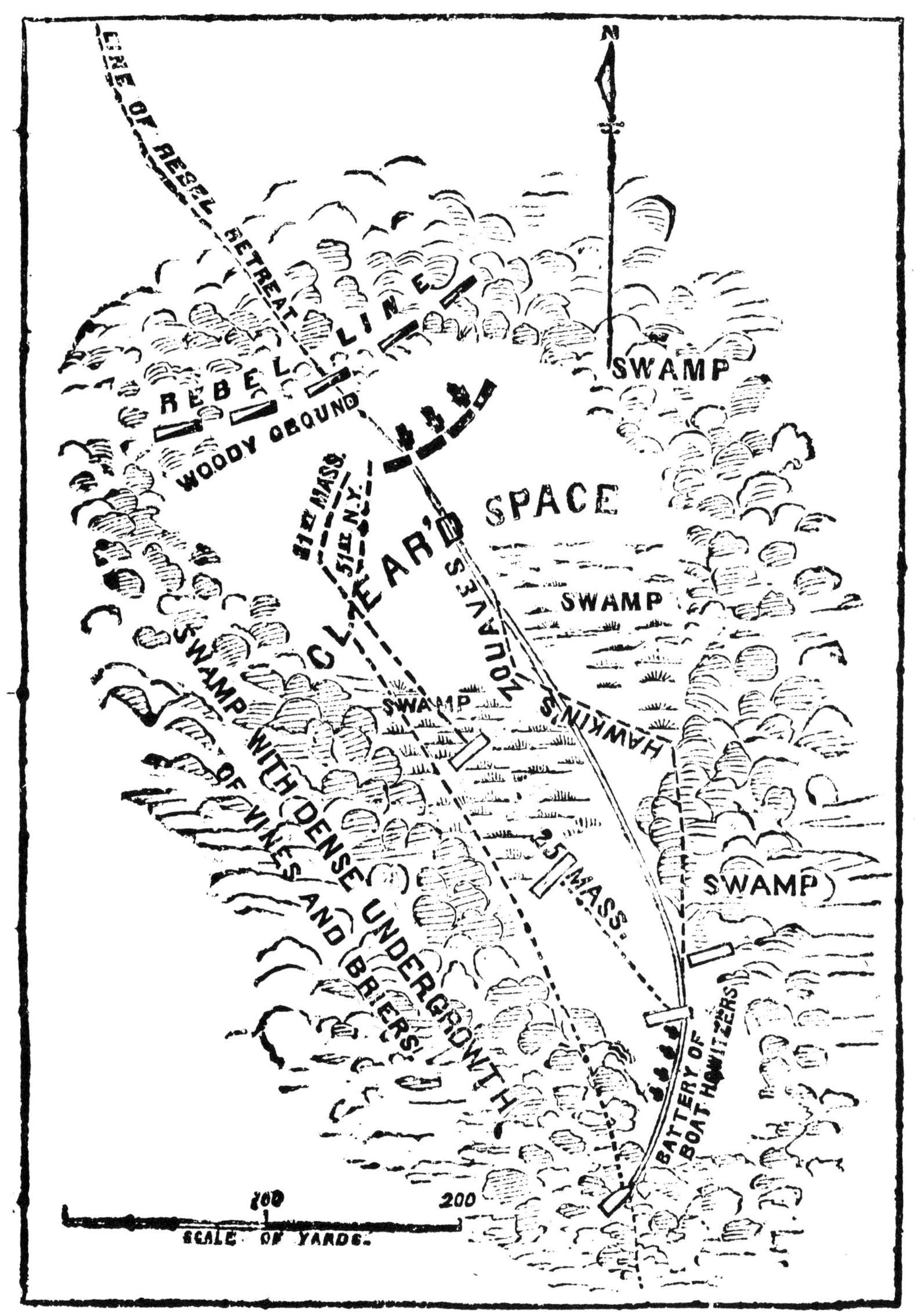

MAP 8

The Battle of Roanoke Island, North Carolina

Published in the *New York Times*, February 16, 1862

(Original 16 × 11 cm.)

AMBROSE BURNSIDE'S EXPEDITION TO THE NORTH CAROLINA COAST ENTERED Croatan Sound on February 7. While Union vessels engaged the small Confederate fleet and coastal fortifications, some 7,500 Union infantry and a gunboat battery landed to the south on Roanoke Island. The following day they moved against inland defenses commanded by Henry Wise. In a clearing surrounded by woods and swamps, a battery of three guns supported by entrenched Confederate infantry sat astride the island's main road. Union artillery took up a position opposite the battery, and two columns of infantry made their way through the woods to strike both Confederate flanks. Due in part to the difficult nature of the ground, little headway could be made against the strong Confederate position. Late in the morning additional Union troops arrived and a frontal assault broke through just as the flanking parties emerged from the swamps to join the attack. The Confederate line collapsed, and approximately 2,500 of the island's defenders were pursued and captured.

The map provides a good portrayal of the wooded and swampy terrain of the battlefield and is essentially correct in most particulars. With regard to troop positions, it fails to note the flanking movement of the Twenty-third and Twenty-seventh Massachusetts regiments against the left of the Confederate line and of the Ninth New Jersey against the right. The battery of three cannon formed the center of the Confederate line, not the advance as shown, and an infantry reserve waited to the rear. The decisive flank attack of the Fifty-first New York and Twenty-first Massachusetts, and the frontal attack of Hawkins's Zouaves (Ninth New York) are, however, indicated. Although no credit appeared in the *Times*'s account, Elias Smith covered the campaign for the paper and may be the map's author. More likely he copied a map prepared by Lt. W. S. Andrews of Hawkins's Zouaves. Andrews drew a similar map, at virtually the same scale, that was later published in the *Atlas to Accompany the Official Records of the Union and Confederate Armies*.

Reports in U.S. War Department, *War of the Rebellion*: ser. 1, vol. 9, with one map.
Maps in U.S. War Department, *Atlas*: pl. 12, no. 6.
Other newspaper maps: *Cincinnati Daily Times* (2/18/62), *Philadelphia Inquirer* (2/15/62).

THE SIEGE OF DONELSON.

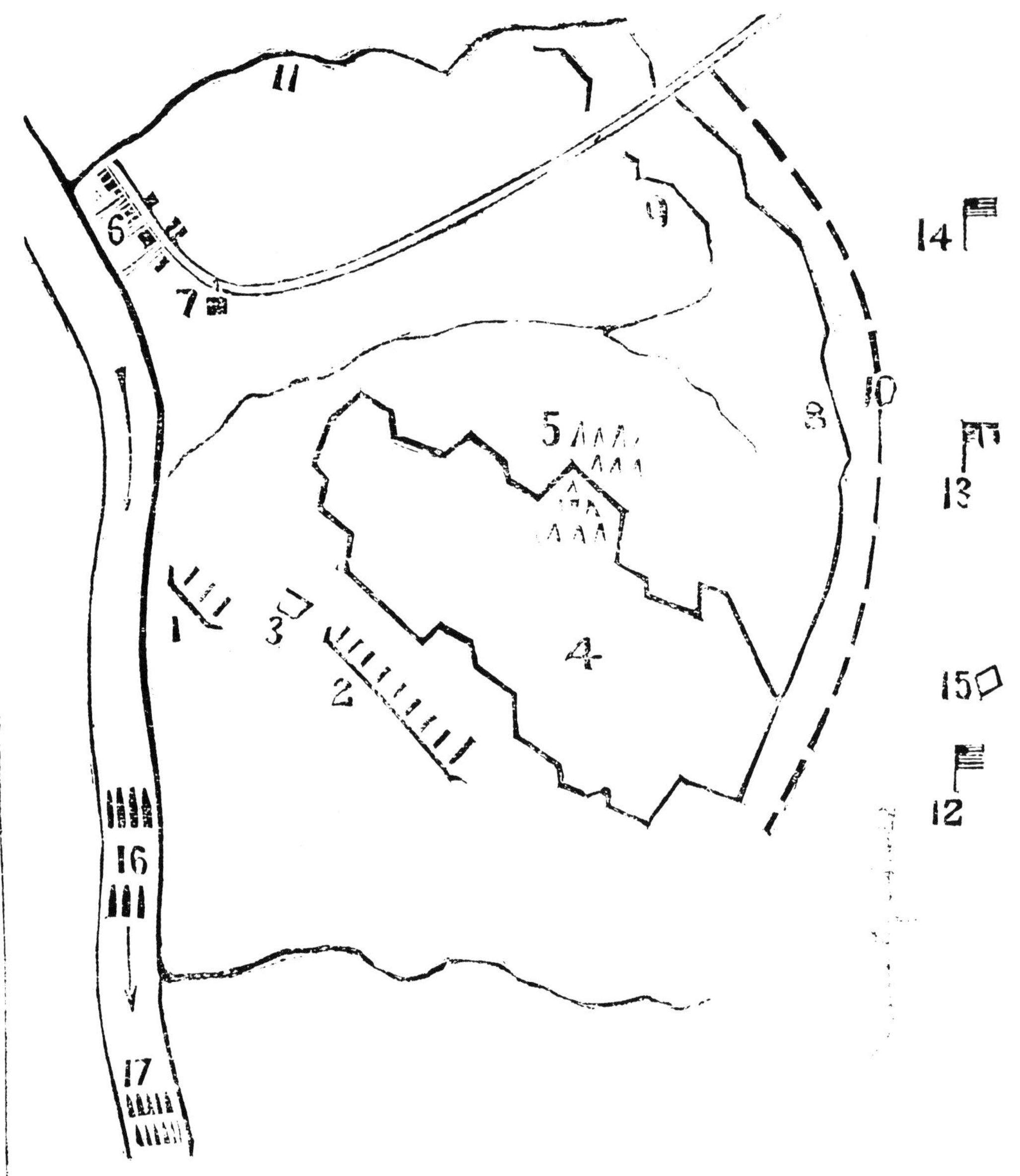

1. Lower Battery.
2. Side Hill.
3. Magazine.
4. Fort.
5. Rebel Camp.
6. Dover.
7. C. H.
8. Main line of rear defence.
9. Inner line of rear defence.
10. Rifle Pits.
11. Small Creek.
12. Gen. Smith's Division.
13. Gen. Wallace's Division.
14. Gen. McClernand's Division.
15. Gen. Grant's Headquarters.
16. Gunboats.
17. Transport fleet.

MAP 9

The Battle of Fort Donelson, Tennessee

Published in the *Chicago Daily Tribune*, February 19, 1862

(Original 16 × 12 cm.)

FORCES UNDER ULYSSES S. GRANT, ACCOMPANIED BY A GUNBOAT FLEET, ADVANCED up the Tennessee River and against Fort Henry in early February. Most of the garrison withdrew, and on February 6 the fort was surrendered after a brief battle with Union gunboats. Grant next moved overland to Fort Donelson, on the Cumberland River. Union troops deployed around the fort and the nearby town of Dover on the 12th. Two days later Union gunboats arrived, but the fort's batteries easily drove them off. To open a route of escape, troops of Gideon Pillow and Simon B. Buckner moved against the Union right at dawn on the 15th. Their attack breached the Union line, but John B. Floyd, who had assumed overall command, indecisively ordered a return to the fort's entrenchments. Grant restored and extended his position, completely ensnaring the fort. Although some Confederates, including Floyd and Pillow, slipped away, Grant demanded and received the unconditional surrender of 12,000 troops on February 16.

As its title suggests, the *Tribune*'s map illustrates the situation before the nearly successful Confederate breakthrough on the 15th. Andrew Foote's river fleet and transports (*16*, *17*) are shown in the Cumberland, but they later retired downstream (the map is oriented with south at the top). The divisions of Lew Wallace (*13*) and Charles F. Smith (*12*) formed the Union left and center, but that of John McClernand (*14*) was across the Wynn's Ferry Road (not labeled) and much closer to the river on the Union right. The map enlarges the size of Fort Donelson (*4*), an irregular-shaped bastion, and incorrectly places it closer to the outer Confederate line than to the river. The fort's two river batteries are mislabeled and slightly mislocated. The lower battery (*1*), actually the larger of the two, stood near Hickman Creek (shown without name near the bottom of map), while the upper battery (*2*) occupied a hillside approximately at the site labeled *1*. Of the numerous camps situated between the fort and the town of Dover, only one (*5*) is indicated. The "C. H." designated by *7* refers to a Confederate hospital.

Reports in U.S. War Department, *War of the Rebellion*: ser. 1, vol. 7.
Maps in U.S. War Department, *Atlas*: pl. 11, nos. 3, 5, 6, 7.
Other newspaper maps: *Cincinnati Daily Gazette* (2/22/62), *New York Herald* (2/22/62), *New York Times* (2/18 and 2/22/62), *New York Tribune* (2/22/62), *World* (2/22/62).

ISLAND No. 10 AND ITS APPROACHES.

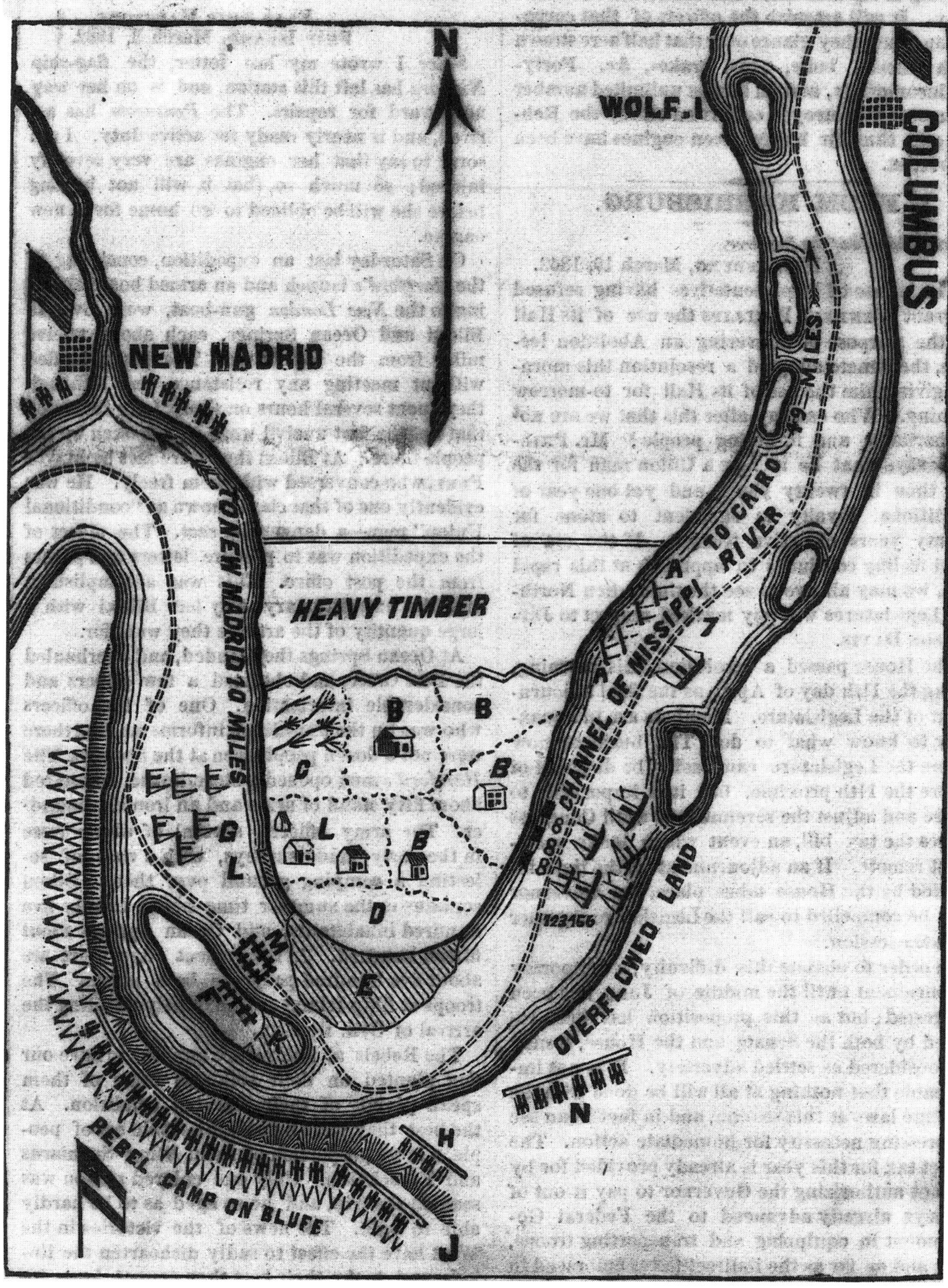

MAP 10

The Siege of Island Number 10

Published in the *Philadelphia Inquirer*, March 21, 1862

(Original 15 × 12 cm.)

IN THE SPRING OF 1861, CONFEDERATES CONSTRUCTED BATTERIES AND REDOUBTS AT Island Number 10 and New Madrid, Missouri, to obstruct passage along the Mississippi. Joint infantry and naval operations began against these works early in March of 1862. When John Pope's army appeared in front of New Madrid, Confederates abandoned the town in order to consolidate their position at Island Number 10 and on the narrow peninsula to the west formed by a bend in the river. Pope occupied New Madrid and the west bank of the river, and a flotilla of gun and mortar boats commanded by Andrew Foote moved into position upstream of the island. For weeks the Union boats shelled Confederate positions, then they finally ran past the batteries, the first such feat of the war. Once downstream of the island, the gunboats silenced Confederate batteries, allowing Union troops to cross the river. On April 7, the island's outnumbered defenders fled south, but the majority surrendered to Pope's troops, who cut off their escape at Tiptonville.

The map depicts the early stages of the siege, prior to when the Union vessels joined forces with the troops at New Madrid, whose location is shown by a United States flag and symbols for cannon. The Confederate positions are indicated by symbols and letter references: *G*, Confederate gunboats (eight in all) that did not participate in the action and retired downstream; *J*, bluff battery; *H*, *N*, water batteries; and *M*, floating battery, actually located at the downstream end of Island Number 10 (*F*). The position of the Union fleet is essentially accurate: *1–6* and *7* (*lower right, in river*) designate gunboats (only six were in fact present), *8* designates mortarboats (eleven present), and dashes and *A*'s represent transports. The letters *C*, *D*, *E*, and *K* refer to natural features such as towheads and shoals. Farms are indicated by the *B's*, and *L* marks the hamlet of Tipton Landing. The double line across the peninsula represents the boundary between Missouri and Kentucky. The map correctly portrays the double bend of the river but places Columbus, Kentucky, nearly thirty miles downstream of its true location.

Reports in U.S. War Department, *War of the Rebellion*: ser. 1, vol. 8, with 4 maps.
Maps in U.S. War Department, *Atlas*: pl. 10, no. 1.
Other newspaper maps: *Chicago Daily Tribune* (3/19 and 3/21/62), *Chicago Times* (3/21/62), *Cincinnati Daily Commercial* (3/22/62), *New York Herald* (3/18 and 3/24/62), *New York Times* (3/28/62), *New York Tribune* (3/24 and 3/27/62).

THE BATTLE GROUND OF MARCH 7.

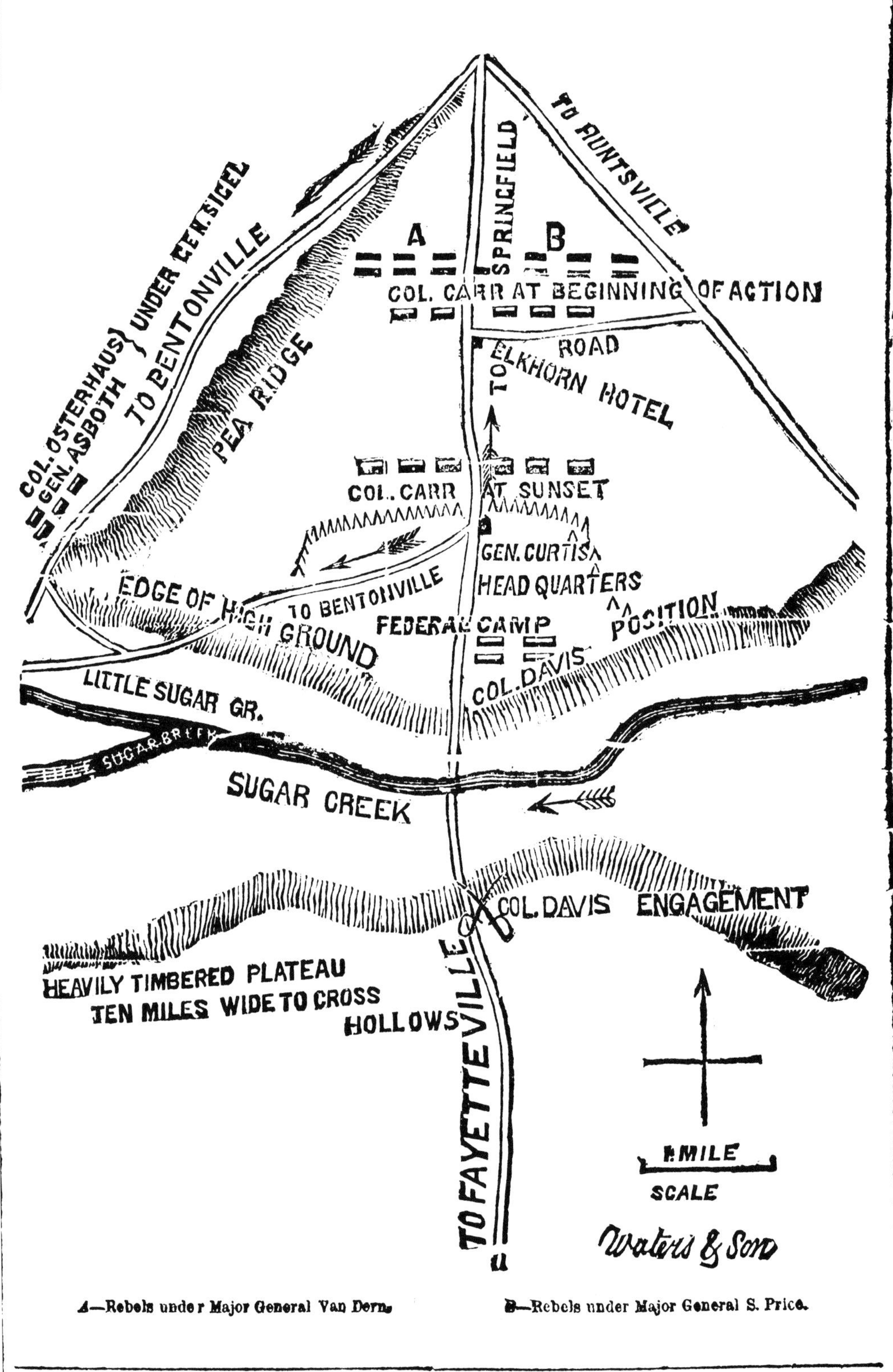

A—Rebels under Major General Van Dorn.

B—Rebels under Major General S. Price.

MAPS 11A AND 11B

The Battle of Pea Ridge, or Elkhorn Tavern, Arkansas

Published in the *New York Herald*, March 21, 1862, and the *New York Tribune*, March 20, 1862

(Originals 18 × 12 cm. and 14 × 12 cm.)

FOUGHT ON TWO DAYS AND ON TWO DIFFERENT FRONTS, PEA RIDGE COMPRISED TWO separate battles. On March 7, Confederates led by Benjamin McCulloch, and later James McIntosh, engaged the Union flank near Leetown, some two miles southwest of Elkhorn Tavern. Union forces lost several cannon before the Confederate advance was checked by the divisions of Peter Osterhaus and Jefferson C. Davis. Both McCulloch and McIntosh were killed and the attack was dispersed. At the same time, troops under Earl Van Dorn, overall commander, and under Sterling Price struck the Union rear after a long night march. A delay in this attack, however, allowed Eugene Carr's division to turn north and meet this threat. By nightfall, Carr's outnumbered division had been pushed back nearly a mile from its position north of Elkhorn Tavern. Samuel Curtis, the overall Union commander, reorganized his forces as troops arrived from the Leetown battlefield. On the morning of March 8, artillery pounded the Confederate positions before a Union advance routed the remnants of Van Dorn's army.

Thomas Knox, one of two correspondents to cover the battle, drew the only eyewitness newspaper map of Pea Ridge (Map 11a) depicting the battle on March 7. Knox indicated the Union camp near Sugar Creek, and across the creek marked the site of a skirmish with Price's rear guard as it retreated south (the north arrow should point to the upper left), in February. Davis is shown north of Sugar Creek, a position he occupied early on the 7th, before the battle near Leetown (if marked, would appear at map's left edge). The fighting around Elkhorn Tavern ("Elkhorn Hotel") involved two lines of battle formed perpendicular to the Telegraph Road ("to Fayetteville"), as shown. Carr's final position was between the tavern and Curtis's headquarters, also as shown. The divisions of Osterhaus and Alexander Asboth, under Franz Sigel's command, actually advanced over the lower road marked "to Bentonville" to join the Union left on the evening of the 7th. Knox or an editor in New York added "Little Sugar Creek"; the same stream was known by both names.

Junius Browne composed the *Tribune*'s map while receiving reports of the battle. Despite certain errors, Browne succeeded in creating a fairly creditable map. The geography is basically correct, although Bentonville and Osage Spring should be farther south. As might be expected, troop positions display less accuracy. Browne recognized that Confederate forces had divided, but he depicted three nearly continuous Union

SUGAR CREEK—THE BATTLE FIELD.

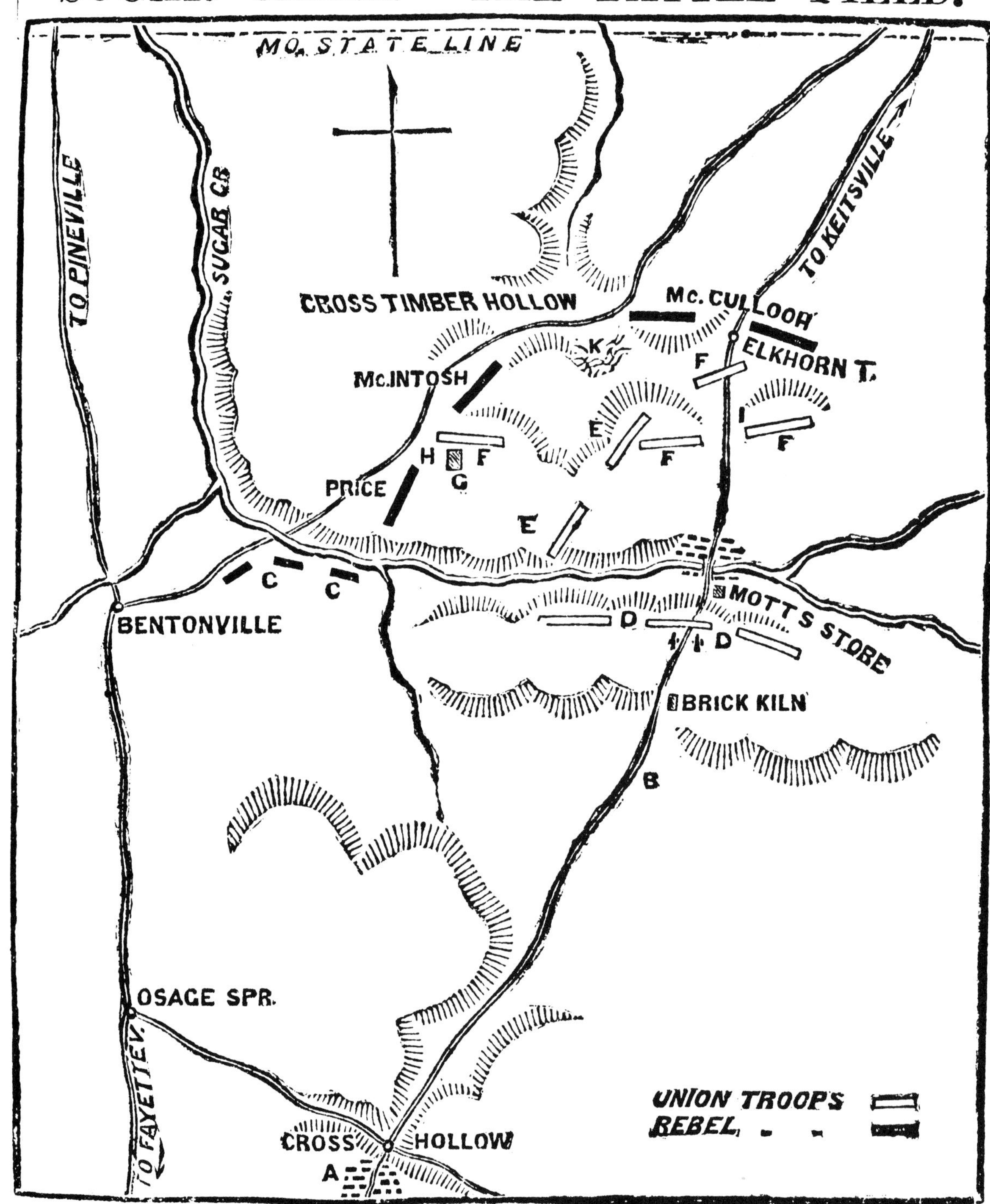

REFERENCES TO MAP.

A—Rebel Barracks at Cross Hollows.
B—Spot where the Cavalry Skirmish took place on the 20th.
C C—First Attack on Sigel on Thursday.
D D—First Line of Battle.
E E E—Second Line of Battle.
F F—Third Line of Battle and Final Charge.
G—Section.
H—Miser's Farm—Desperate Cavalry Charge.
I—Battery Captured by Rebels and Retaken by Union Troops—McCulloch fell.
K—Fallen Timber, by hurricane.

lines. The "first" (*D*) is entirely fictitious, but nearly corresponds with the Union line of March 6, north of the creek. *E* marks the approximate scene of the Leetown battle, and *F* (*near road*) shows Carr's position on the night of the 7th. Pratt's Store, incorrectly called Mott's, which served as Curtis's headquarters, should be north and west of where it is shown. The map also reverses the positions of Price and McCulloch and mislocates the site of the latter's death at *I*, just south of Elkhorn Tavern, instead of near *H*. *K* (fallen timber) denotes the efforts of Union troops to obstruct the roads, not of a hurricane, as map's key claims. However, the map correctly notes the location of Sigel's rear guard skirmish on the 6th (*C*), when his forces joined Curtis from Bentonville.

Reports in U.S. War Department, *War of the Rebellion*: ser. 1, vol. 8.
Maps in U.S. War Department, *Atlas*: pl. 10, nos. 3, 5, 6, 8; pl. 79, no. 6.
Other newspaper maps: *Chicago Daily Tribune* (3/23/62), *Cincinnati Daily Times* (3/17/62), *Daily Missouri Republican* (4/3/62), *World* (3/21/62).

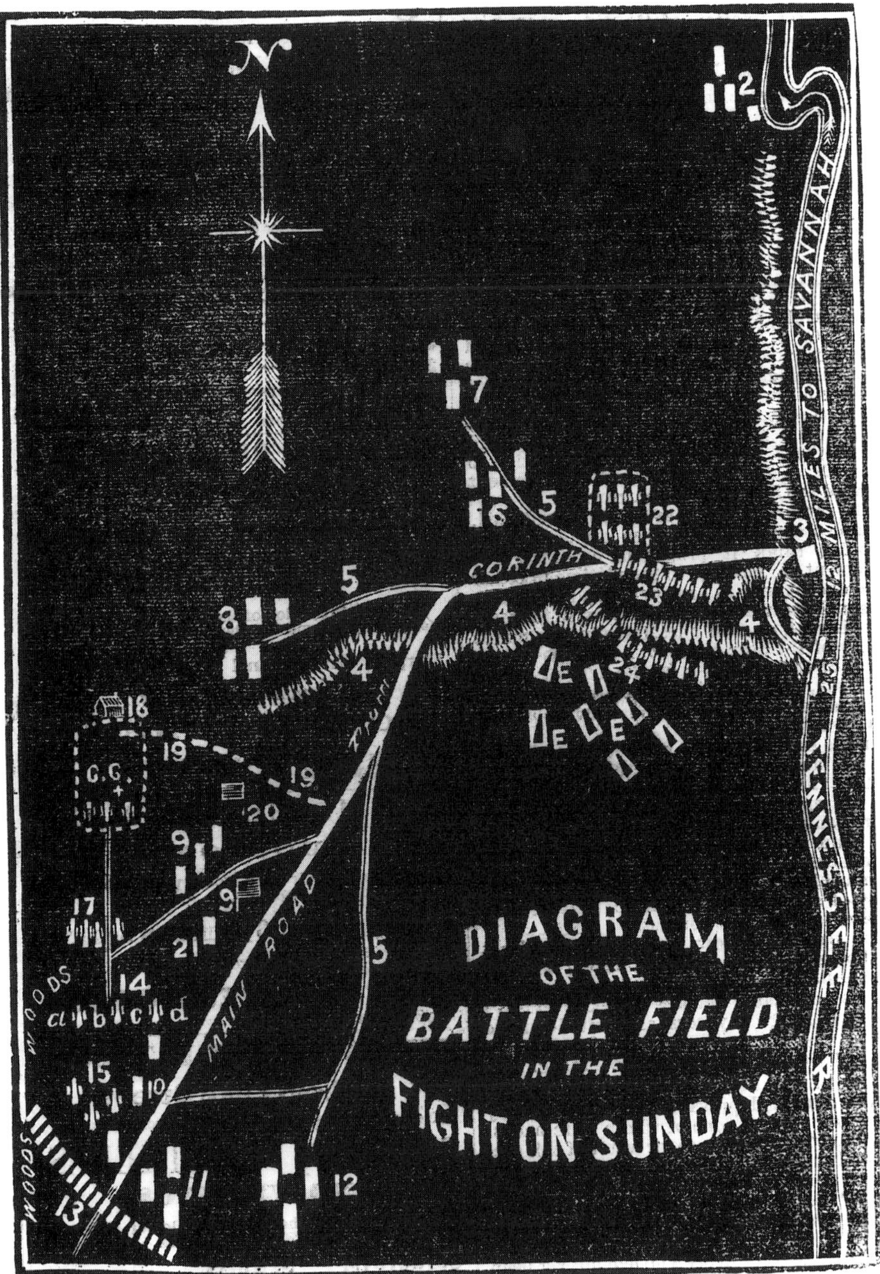

2 Crump's Landing
3 Pittsburg Landing
4 Ravine
5 Branch roads
6 Gen. Sweeny's brigade
7 Gen. McArthur's brigade
8 Gen. Wallace
9 Gen. McClernand
10 Gen. Sherman
11 Gen. Prentiss
12 Gen. Hurlbut
13 Enemy's line of attack
14 First line of battle
a 70th Ohio *c* 77th Ohio
b 23rd Illinois *d* 53rd Ohio
15 Rebel rifled guns
17 Rebel battery blown up by Taylor's battery
18 Log hut at north end of parade ground
19 Union second line of battle
20 First repulse of the enemy by Col. Marsh's brigade
21 The brigade cut off by a flank movement of the enemy
22 Artillery reserve
23 Line of artillery at 5 P.M.
24 Enemy's artillery
25 Gunboats Lexington and Tyler
E Enemy at sunset
G.G. Gen. Grant's and the writer's position at noon

MAPS 12A AND 12B

The Battle of Shiloh, or Pittsburg Landing, Tennessee

Published in the *Chicago Daily Tribune*, April 14, 1862,
and in the *New York Tribune*, April 16, 1862

(Originals 16 × 11 cm. and 16 × 12 cm.)

AFTER THE CAPTURE OF FORT HENRY AND FORT DONELSON, UNION FORCES UNDER Ulysses S. Grant and Don Carlos Buell pushed up the Tennessee River toward the railroad center at Corinth, Mississippi. Albert Sydney Johnston and Pierre Beauregard determined to strike Grant's army while it was encamped near Pittsburg Landing before Buell's arrival. The Confederates mounted a surprise attack along the Corinth Road at dawn on April 6, overrunning several Union camps. After falling back, Union troops offered stiff resistance, especially in the center, where Benjamin Prentiss's division held its position until cut off and forced to surrender. By then Johnston had been killed, and the increasingly disorganized Confederate attack made slower progress. At the end of the day, however, the Union line had been pushed back nearly three miles toward the river. The arrival of four fresh divisions overnight allowed Grant to counterattack on April 7 and to drive Beauregard's overwhelmed army from the field.

The author of the *Tribune*'s report, and presumably the map, witnessed the engagement from a position (*G.G.*) on the Union right. Perhaps for this reason the initial Union line does not extend as far to the right on the map as it should, and there is no indication of fighting in that sector. The Confederate attack (*13*, *lower left*) along the Corinth Road struck divisions of William T. Sherman (*10*) and John McClernand (*9*) near Shiloh Church (not shown). Soon after, Prentiss (*11*), in the center of the Union left, and Stephen Hurlbut (*12*) to his left, both of whose locations are shown too far from the river, were under attack. Symbols and letters at *14* mark a line of battle organized by Sherman and McClernand, but by early afternoon both had been driven back to the line marked *19*. *G.G.* indicates the spot from which Grant and the correspondent witnessed this part of the battle. On the Union right, the map notes an artillery duel between Ezra Taylor's Chicago battery (symbols below *G.G.*) and Confederate artillery (*17*). William Wallace's division (*8*) advanced to bolster the Union center, not the right as shown. As Confederates advanced toward Pittsburg Landing (*3*) they encountered the enfilading fire of gunboats in the river (*25*) while trying to cross a deep ravine (*4*; Dills Branch, exaggerated in length). Grant massed cannon (*22*, *23*) on the left of a line formed late in the day. John McArthur's brigade (*7*) fought on the Union left, not the right. At the end of the first day, after failing to cross the ravine, the Confederate line (*24*, *E*'s) extended from near the river to across the Corinth Road.

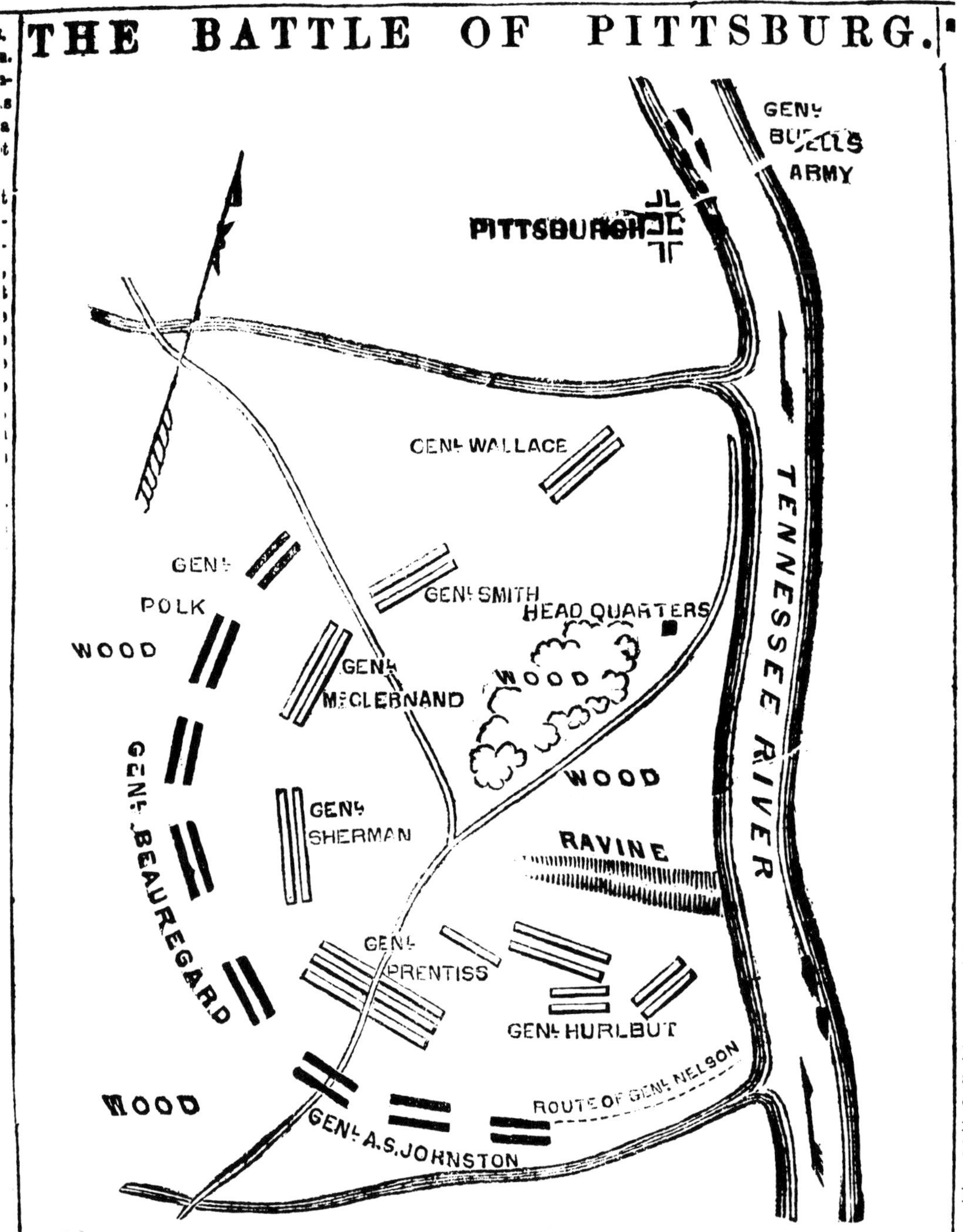

This Map shows the disposition of the opposing forces at the Battle of Pittsburg. It was carefully drawn on the spot by one familiar with the ground and the position of the two armies, and who was present at the battle.

On April 16, the *New York Tribune* published a map of Shiloh "drawn on the spot by one familiar with the ground and the positions of the two armies." Like the Chicago paper's map it illustrates only the first day's action, but it does so quite differently and provides fewer details. Topographical inaccuracies include the location of Pittsburg Landing (actually south of Snake Creek, the unnamed tributary at top of map) and the ravine (shown too far south). The Union positions are somewhat confused. Prentiss and Hurlbut operated east of the Corinth Road (not labeled), and to their right were the divisions of Wallace, McClernand, and Sherman, in that order. The notation *Genl. Smith* may have referred to Charles F. Smith who temporarily replaced Grant at the beginning of the campaign but did not command on the field. One brigade of Gen. William Nelson's Union division did cross the river, late in the day, but they did so at Pittsburg Landing, not where shown. Johnston led forces on the Confederate left, and Leonidas Polk directed a corps near the Corinth Road.

Reports in U.S. War Department, *War of the Rebellion*: ser. 1, vol. 10, pt. 1, with 2 maps.

Maps in U.S. War Department, *Atlas*: pl. 10, no. 10; pl. 12, no. 4; pl. 13, no. 1; pl. 14, no. 2; pl. 98, no. 4.

Other newspaper maps: *Boston Daily Journal* (4/15/62), *Chicago Times* (4/16/62), *Cincinnati Daily Commercial* 4/24/62), *Cincinnati Daily Gazette* (4/14/62), *Cincinnati Daily Times* (4/19/62), *Daily Missouri Republican* (4/12/62), *Daily Ohio State Journal* (4/14/62), New York Herald (4/16/62).

NAVAL TRIUMPH ON THE MISSISSIPPI.

Scene of the Splendid Naval Engagement between the Union and Rebel Gun Boats, near Fort Wright, May 10.

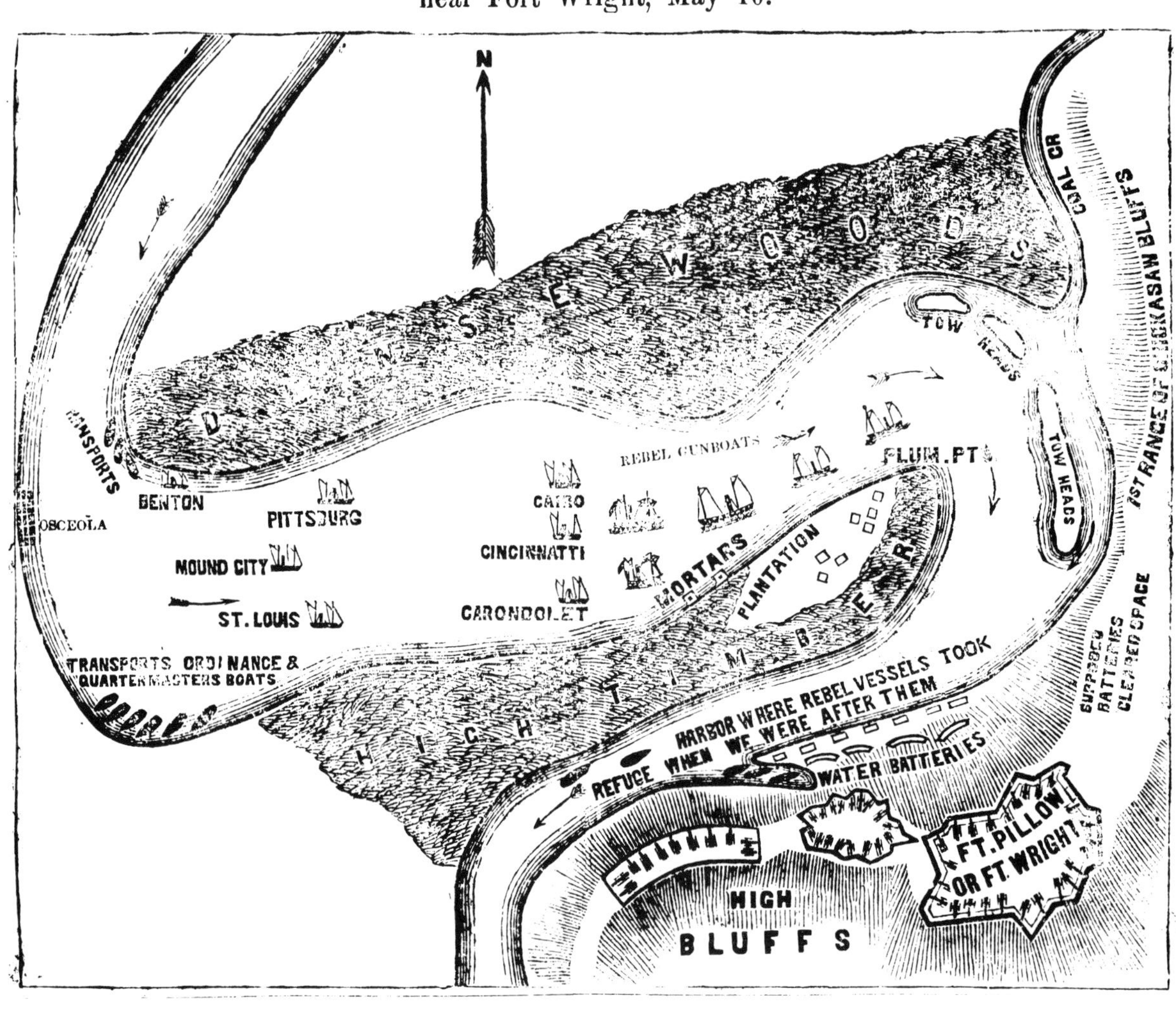

MAP 13

The Battle of Plum Run Bend, Tennessee

Published in the *Philadelphia Inquirer*, May 13, 1862

(Original 18 × 23 cm.)

AFTER THE CAPTURE OF ISLAND NUMBER 10, UNION ARMY AND NAVAL FORCES continued down the Mississippi River to operate against Fort Pillow, Tennessee, high above the river. The campaign became one of attrition when the majority of Union infantry were detached for other duty. The seven gunboats of the Western Flotilla could not engage the fort directly, but they maintained their position upstream beyond Plum Point, which was opposite the fort. The gunboats regularly towed mortar boats to a location behind the point from which they could safely bombard Fort Pillow. On the morning of May 10, the Confederate river fleet, consisting of eight poorly refitted commercial vessels, suddenly steamed around the point and engaged the Union ships. With little in the way of armament, the Confederate ships rammed their opponents and sank the *Cincinnati* and the *Mound City*. The superior firepower of the Union ships soon forced the Confederate fleet to retire to the protection of the fort.

The *Inquirer*'s map provides a rather vague depiction of the engagement but correctly portrays most of the major details. Union mortar boats rest just above Plum Point, while infantry transports are moored farther upstream. On the Tennessee shore, Fort Pillow and its formidable water battery served as the base from which the small Confederate fleet operated. The map takes certain liberties by introducing variations in the river's width, apparently to accommodate the number of vessels, and compressing the Mississippi into an exaggerated S-curve. Arrows indicate the direction of the river's current. Five of the eight attacking Confederate ships are indicated, a somewhat uncharacteristic devaluation of Confederate strength possibly caused by space constraints. All Union ships are named and represented. Only the *Cincinnati*, *Carondolet*, *Mound City*, and *Benton* took part in the action. The erroneous upstream location of the latter two ships may indicate earlier positions. Osceola, Arkansas (*left*), squeezed in as an afterthought, is shown sitting in the river. Both *Osceola* and *Rebel gunboats* are typeset lettering which suggests that these were late additions.

Reports in the U.S. Naval War Records Office, *Official Records*: ser. 1, vol. 23.
Maps in U.S. War Department, *Atlas*: None.
Other newspaper maps: *New York Herald* (5/18/62).

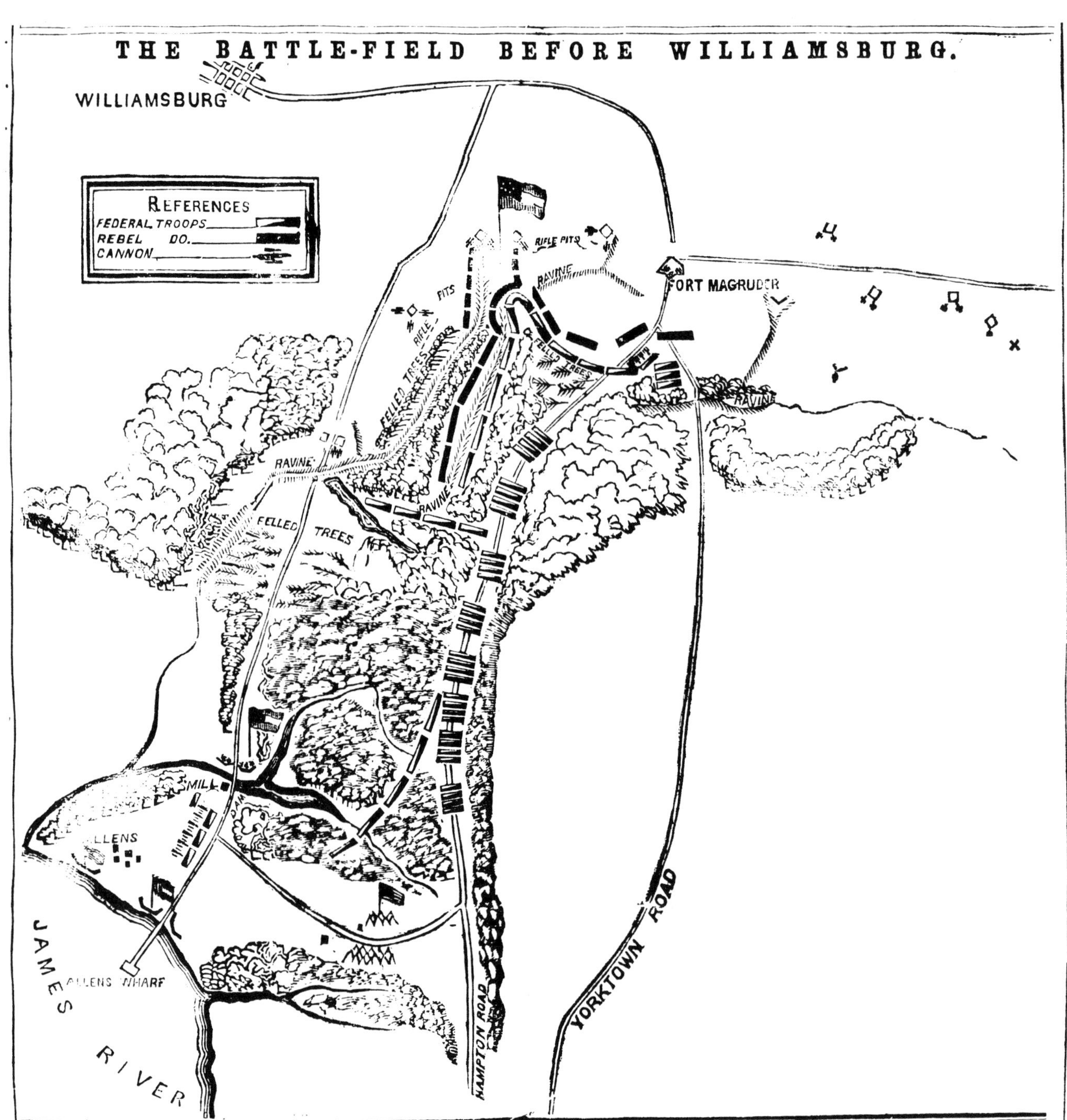
THE BATTLE-FIELD BEFORE WILLIAMSBURG.
WILLIAMSBURG
REFERENCES
FEDERAL TROOPS
REBEL DO.
CANNON
RIFLE PITS
RAVINE
FORT MAGRUDER
PITS
RIFLE
FELLED TREES
RAVINE
FELLED TREES
RAVINE
RAVINE
FELLED
TREES
MILL
ALLENS
JAMES RIVER
ALLENS WHARF
HAMPTON ROAD
YORKTOWN ROAD

MAP 14

The Battle of Williamsburg, Virginia

Published in the *New York Tribune*, May 13, 1862

(Original 25 × 25 cm.)

ALMOST AS SOON AS IT BEGAN, GEORGE MCCLELLAN'S PENINSULAR CAMPAIGN WAS halted by the Confederate defenses at Yorktown. On the night of May 3, after delaying the Union advance for nearly a month, John B. Magruder's small army abandoned Yorktown. Union forces caught up with the retreating rear guard, which had fallen back to old defensive works near Williamsburg. On the morning of May 5, Joseph Hooker's unsupported division attacked the Confederate line at Fort Magruder but could not carry the position. James Longstreet, the ranking Confederate commander on the field, organized a counterattack against Hooker's left flank. The arrival of Philip Kearny's division arrested this movement. Operations on the Confederate left proved more conclusive. In the afternoon, Winfield S. Hancock's troops took possession of several unoccupied redoubts, from which they turned the Confederate flank. Several attacks attempted to dislodge Hancock, but all failed. That night the Confederates continued their withdrawal toward Richmond.

The *Tribune*'s map bears a strong resemblance to one by Miles McAlester later printed in the *Atlas to Accompany the Records of the Union and Confederate Armies.* McAlester served as a topographer with Hooker at Williamsburg. Most of the map's detail concerns that sector, while giving no indication of Hancock's activity on the right. The Confederate line of redoubts and rifle pits stretched from east of Fort Magruder, vaguely indicated at upper right, to a mill pond near Allen's plantation (*lower left*). Hooker's attack on the morning of the 5th, shown by an inverted V-shaped line of symbols below the Confederate flag at the top, hit the center of the position. A ravine through which Longstreet's troops moved to attack Hooker's flank appears between the Union and Confederate lines. Before being reinforced, Hooker's division was pushed back as far as the Hampton Road. Symbols on the Hampton Road indicate Kearny's approach. Surprisingly, the map fails to designate either Union commanders or their units by name. Symbols at the bottom of the map represent the advanced guard's camp on the night of the 4th, and the location of William Emory's brigade (near the mill).

Reports in U.S. War Department, *War of the Rebellion*: ser. 1, vol. 11, pt. 1.
Maps in U.S. War Department, *Atlas*: pl. 20, nos. 2, 3, 4.
Other newspaper maps: *New York Herald* (5/9 and 5/24/62).

River Plan of the Scene of the Naval Victory on the Morning of April 24, 1862.

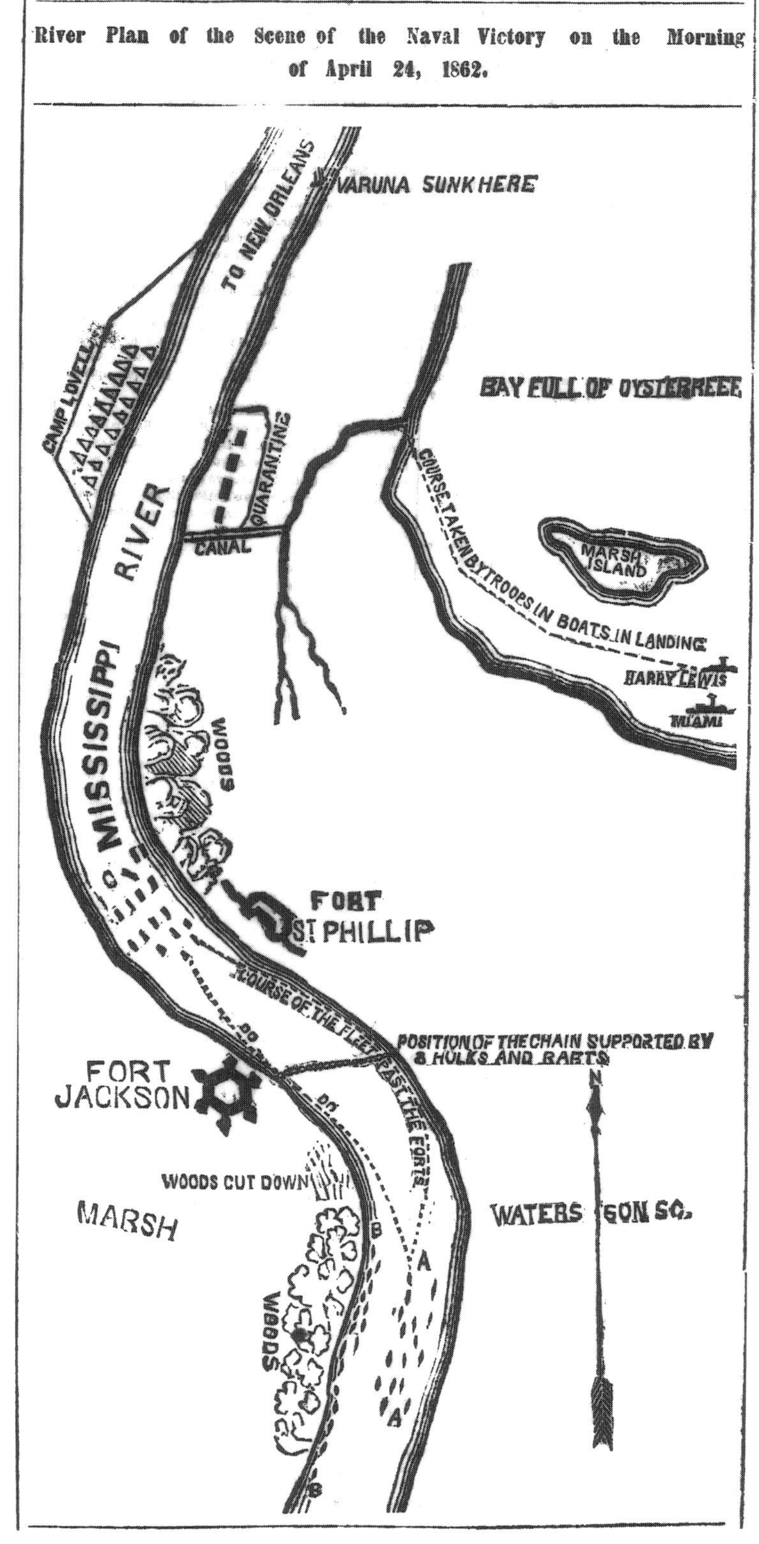

MAP 15

The Battle of New Orleans, Louisiana

Published in the *New York Herald*, May 14, 1862

(Original 23 × 12 cm.)

THE BATTLE FOR THIS IMPORTANT INLAND PORT TOOK PLACE SOME NINETY MILES downriver, where two forts and a small river fleet obstructed Union passage up the Mississippi. In mid-April, a Union fleet commanded by David Farragut began operations on the river. For six days mortar boats bombarded the forts, concentrating on Fort Jackson. In preparation for the attack, on the night of April 20 Union sailors had broken a chain that the Confederates had strung across the river. In the early hours of the 24th, Farragut's fleet started toward New Orleans, encountering a terrific cannonade when it reached the forts. Confederate ships joined in the battle but had limited success against the Union vessels' superior armament. In four and a half hours, fourteen of the seventeen Union vessels had passed the forts, crippling the vulnerable Confederate fleet in the process. The next day, the Union fleet reached New Orleans and Farragut accepted the city's surrender from civil authorities.

Publication of the *Herald*'s map was delayed while its correspondent, Bradley Osbon, sailed back to New York, arriving more than two weeks after the battle. Osbon, who witnessed the affair from Farragut's flagship, served as the fleet's signal officer during the battle. The position of the Union fleet during the bombardment of the forts is indicated by the *A*'s. Nineteen mortar boats, identified by the *B*'s, operated from behind sheltering trees below the river's bend. The river actually bends to a greater extent than shown, forming a nearly east-to-west course between the forts. *C* marks the Confederate flotilla of fourteen vessels, many of which carried a single gun, if any. Dashed lines in the river near the forts depict the course of the Union fleet upstream. The map correctly locates the final position of the *Varuna*, the only Union ship sunk during the battle, near the top of the map. As part of the operation, Benjamin Butler's Union troops landed on the Gulf coast (*upper right*) then marched to the quarantine camp. Across the river the garrison of Camp Lovell, also called the Chalmette Camp, surrendered to Union vessels on their way upstream to New Orleans.

Reports in U.S. Naval War Records Office, *Official Records*: ser. 1, vol. 18.
Maps in U.S. War Department, *Atlas*: None.
Other newspaper maps: *Chicago Daily Tribune* (5/11 and 5/12/62), *Daily Missouri Republican* (5/11 and 5/12/62), *New York Times* (5/8/62), *Philadelphia Inquirer* (4/30/62).

THE ATTACK ON GENERAL BANKS.

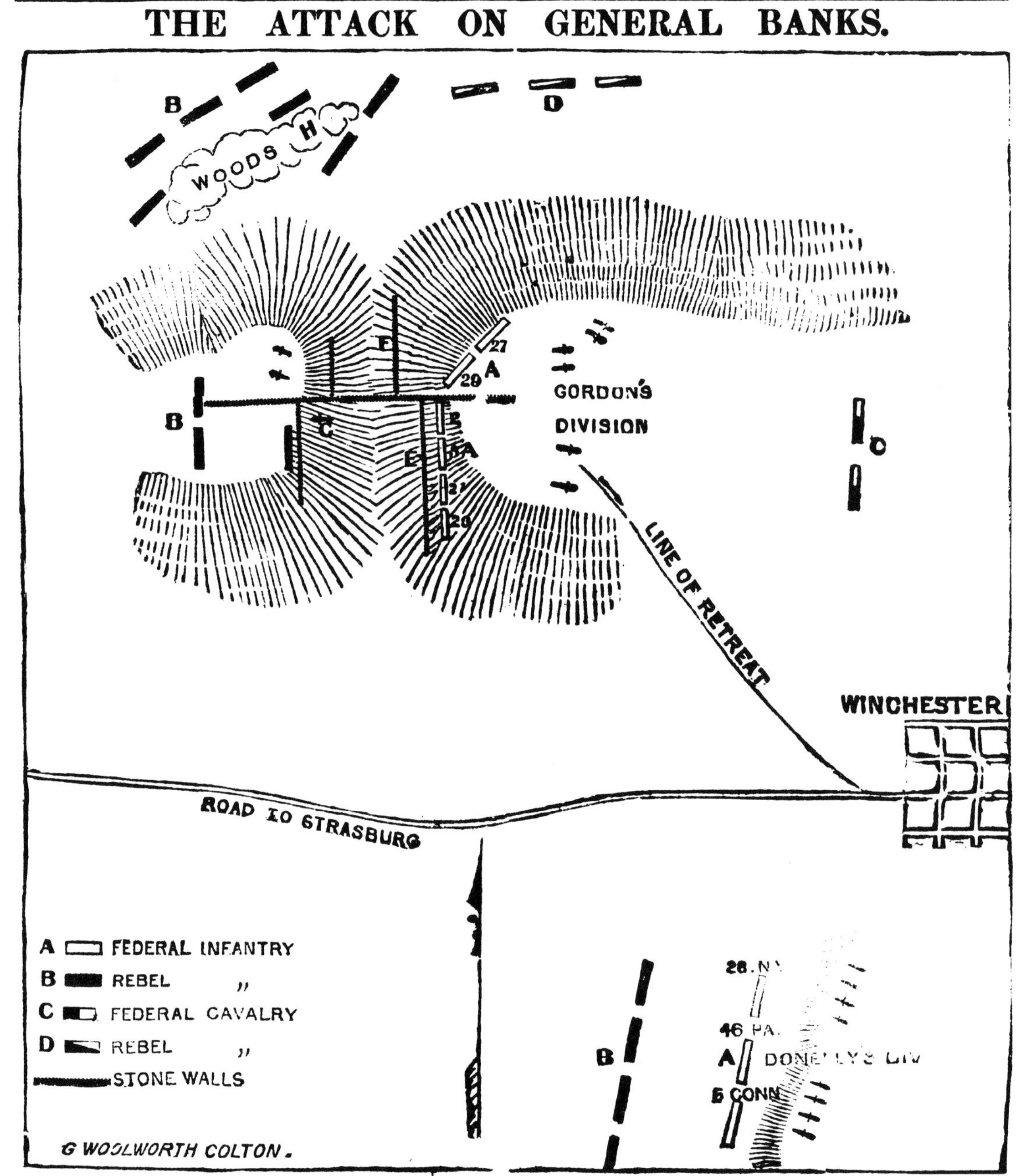

MAP 16

The Battle of Winchester, Virginia

Published in the *New York Tribune*, May 31, 1862

(Original 18 × 16 cm.)

WINCHESTER WAS ONE OF SEVERAL ENGAGEMENTS COMPOSING THOMAS J. "STONE-wall" Jackson's strategically important Shenandoah Valley campaign, which prevented additional Union troops from operating against Richmond. On the heels of his victory at Front Royal on the 23rd, Jackson tried to intercept the scattered Union army of Nathaniel P. Banks as it retreated to Winchester. Banks won the race to the town and deployed his forces in two wings on hills just to the south. At dawn on May 25, Jackson's numerically superior army attacked. Most of the action occurred on the Union right, where George Gordon's division, strongly posted and supported by artillery, held their ground. After fighting that continued throughout the morning, the Confederates turned Gordon's right flank and shattered his position. The hard-pressed Union forces broke and fled through the town in what quickly became a rout.

The map's orientation puts west, not north, at the top. The brigade of Dudley Donnelly, designated as a division, consisted of the regiments indicated as well as the First Maryland. These troops formed the Union left, basically facing southeast along the banks of Abraham's Creek (not shown) so that its line nearly paralleled the road rather than forming a right angle to it. On the right, Gordon formed his division behind stone fences (*E*, *F*) on the crest of a hill. *G* (looks like *C*, on hill, *upper left*) marks the location of one of the Confederate batteries. Behind Gordon's line Union cavalry acted as the reserve as shown. Gordon anticipated an attack on his right and shifted troops in that direction. The map indicates this somewhat confusingly by the numbers *27* (Indiana Regiment) and *29* (Pennsylvania Regiment), repeated to indicate their first and second positions. The numbers *2* (Massachusetts Regiment) and *3* (Wisconsin Regiment) represent that part of the Union line which maintained its position until the retreat. The Confederate flank attack originated from behind a wooded area (*H*), as shown by symbols at the top of the map. The map depicts only one road, the Valley Turnpike (marked "road to Strasburg"), the route over which Banks's army traveled to Winchester.

Reports in U.S. War Department, *War of the Rebellion*: ser. 1, vol. 12, pt. 1.
Maps in U.S. War Department, *Atlas*: pl. 85, no. 2.
Other newspaper maps: None.

PLAN OF THE BATTLE OF FAIR OAKS.

Sketch of the Battle-ground of "Fair Oaks," or the Seven Pines, on May 31, 1862, by Lieut. E. Walter West, A. D. C. to Brigadier-General Casey. Drawn Especially for the New-York Times.

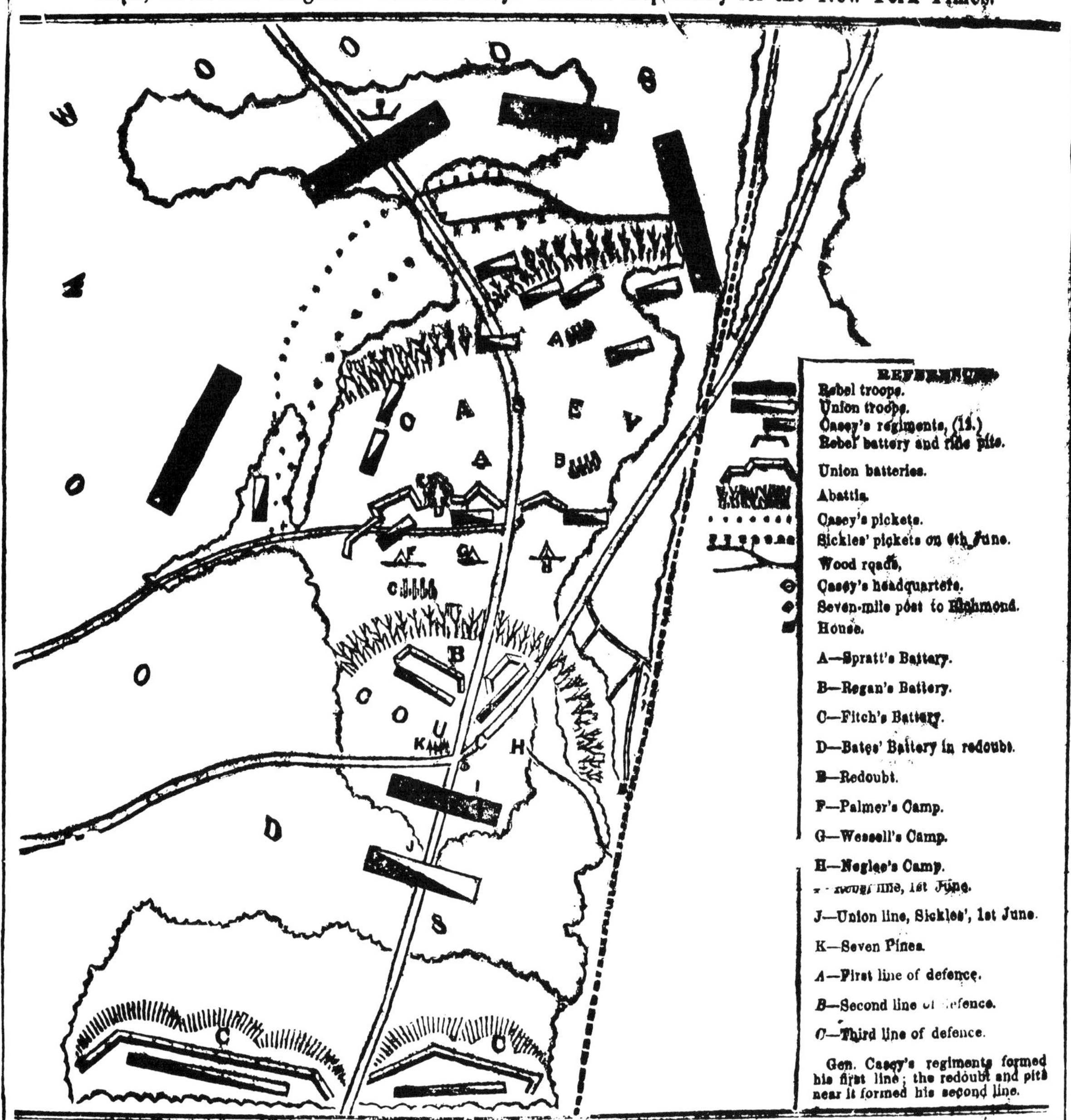

MAP 17

The Battle of Seven Pines, Virginia

Published in the *New York Times*, June 13, 1862

(Original 18 × 16 cm.)

THROUGHOUT THE SPRING OF 1862, GEORGE MCCLELLAN'S ARMY OF THE POTOMAC slowly advanced on Richmond from the east. By the end of May the army was within ten miles of the Confederate capital, but straddled the Chickahominy River. Confederate commander Joseph E. Johnston saw an opportunity to defeat the two Union corps south of the river. On May 31, Confederates struck Union positions along the Williamsburg Road and to the north at Fair Oaks Station. Confusing orders and misdirections delayed the attack, and only about a third of Johnston's forces actually cooperated in the movement. Despite this, the Confederates drove the divisions of Silas Casey and Darius Couch from their entrenched positions. The arrival of Union reinforcements late in the day and the wounding of Johnston halted the Confederate advance. On June 1, the Confederates briefly resumed the battle before retiring to their original positions.

Although its title refers to the Battle of Fair Oaks, West's map focuses on the participation of Casey's division, which was at Seven Pines. Oriented with west at the top, the map shows Union and Confederate positions at the beginning and at the end of the fighting on May 31. Johnston's army, which appears to dwarf the Union forces, held the upper hand psychologically but not numerically. The divisions of Casey and Couch formed consecutive parallel lines across the Williamsburg Road, as shown. The Union camps of Innis Palmer (*F*), Henry Wessels (*G*), and Henry Naglee (*H*) are correctly positioned. North of the Williamsburg Road the advanced batteries of Joseph Spratt (*A*) and Peter Reagan (*B*) appear in their proper places. Batteries of Butler Fitch (*C*) and Guilford Bailey (*D*, misidentified as Bates), who was killed in the redoubt (*E*), formed the second line. The map makes no indication of the fighting at Fair Oaks, where the road and railroad (*dashed line*) intersect. The final Union and Confederate lines on the 31st (*I* and *J*, respectively) appear near the bottom of the map, and Daniel Sickles's picket line (*large dots*) indicates the Union position after the withdrawal. The heavily forested nature of the battlefield is suggested by large areas labeled "woods" and bounded by scalloped lines.

Reports in the U.S. War Department, *War of the Rebellion*: ser. 1, vol. 11, pt. 1.
Maps in U.S. War Department, *Atlas*: None.
Other newspaper maps: *Chicago Daily Tribune* (6/5/62), *New York Herald* (6/3 and 6/5/62), *New York Times* (6/3/62), *New York Tribune* (6/5/62), *Philadelphia Inquirer* (6/4/62).

THE BATTLE OF JAMES ISLAND.

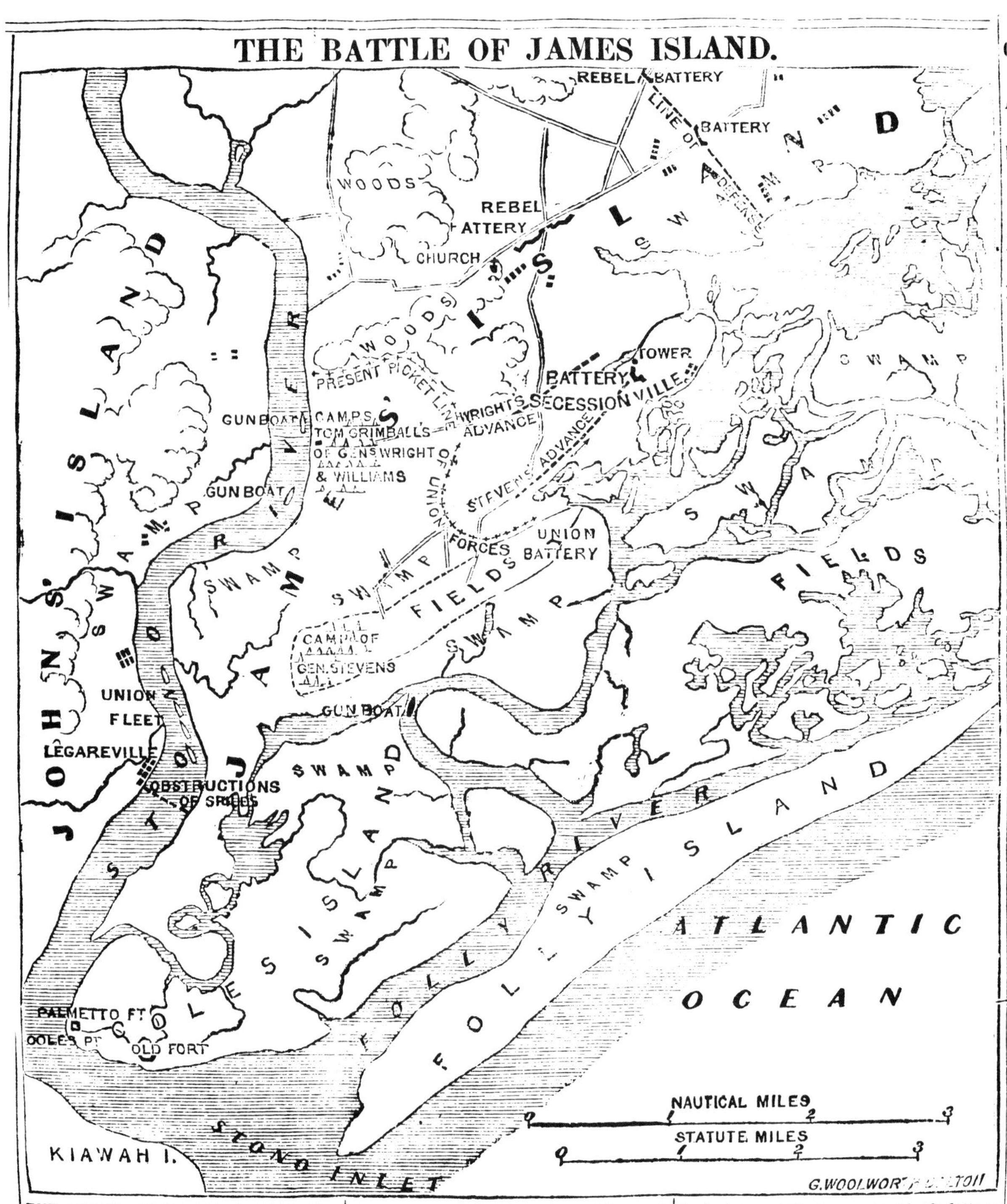

THE BATTLE-FIELD ON JAMES ISLAND.

The above map shows the battle-ground of the recent fight on James Island, before Charleston. The Fort, attacked by Gens. Benham and Stevens, is in front of the little village of Secessionville, the main body of the Rebel forces being encamped further back toward Charleston. To take the battery, from which the Rebels could shell the camps of the Union troops, was the object of the expedition.

MAP 18

The Battle of Secessionville, or James Island, South Carolina

Published in the *New York Tribune*, June 28, 1862

(Original 20 × 18 cm.)

IN THE SPRING OF 1862 UNION FORCES, PREPARING TO BEGIN OPERATIONS AGAINST Charleston, established camps on James Island within ten miles of the city. To deter an advance on Charleston from that quarter, Confederates erected earthworks near the village of Secessionville and along the road from Stono Inlet to Charleston. For several weeks the battery at Secessionville shelled Union positions. Union artillery responded but could not silence the Confederate guns. An armed reconnaissance of the position on June 10 also accomplished little. When Gen. David Hunter was called away to department headquarters, he left Henry Benham in command of Union forces. Benham ordered a direct assault against the battery despite protests by his fellow officers. On the morning of June 16, three assaults resulting in high Union casualties failed to carry the position. After the engagement Benham was relieved of command for disobeying orders forbidding him to initiate offensive operations. In early July, Union troops abandoned James Island.

The *Tribune*'s map bears a striking similarity to the pair of maps which accompanied Benham's report of the battle, later published in the *Atlas to Accompany the Official Records of the Union and Confederate Armies*. The *Tribune*'s map precisely depicts the location and movements of the Union divisions and indicates the island's defenses. Confederate troops and military works appear as lines of small rectangles and heavy wavy lines in the upper right. Union camps of Isaac Stevens, Robert Williams, and Horatio Wright are shown in their correct relationship, the latter two at Grimball's Landing ("Tom Grimball's") on the Stono River. The routes to Secessionville of Stevens and Wright (Williams's forces remained in reserve) and the final Union picket line are also marked. Benham had previously served as chief engineer in the Union army's Department of Ohio and had prepared a map of the Battle of Carnifex Ferry for the *Tribune*. He and his staff arrived in New York City on June 27 and apparently turned over a copy of his map of the James Island battle at that time.

Reports in the U.S. War Department, *War of the Rebellion*: ser. 1, vol. 14, with one map.
Maps in U.S. War Department, *Atlas*: pl. 23, nos. 6, 7.
Other newspaper maps: *New York Herald* (6/28/62), *New York Times* (6/28/62).

THURSDAY'S AND FRIDAY'S BATTLE FIELDS.

The Scene of the Late Important Military Operations on the Chickahominy River.

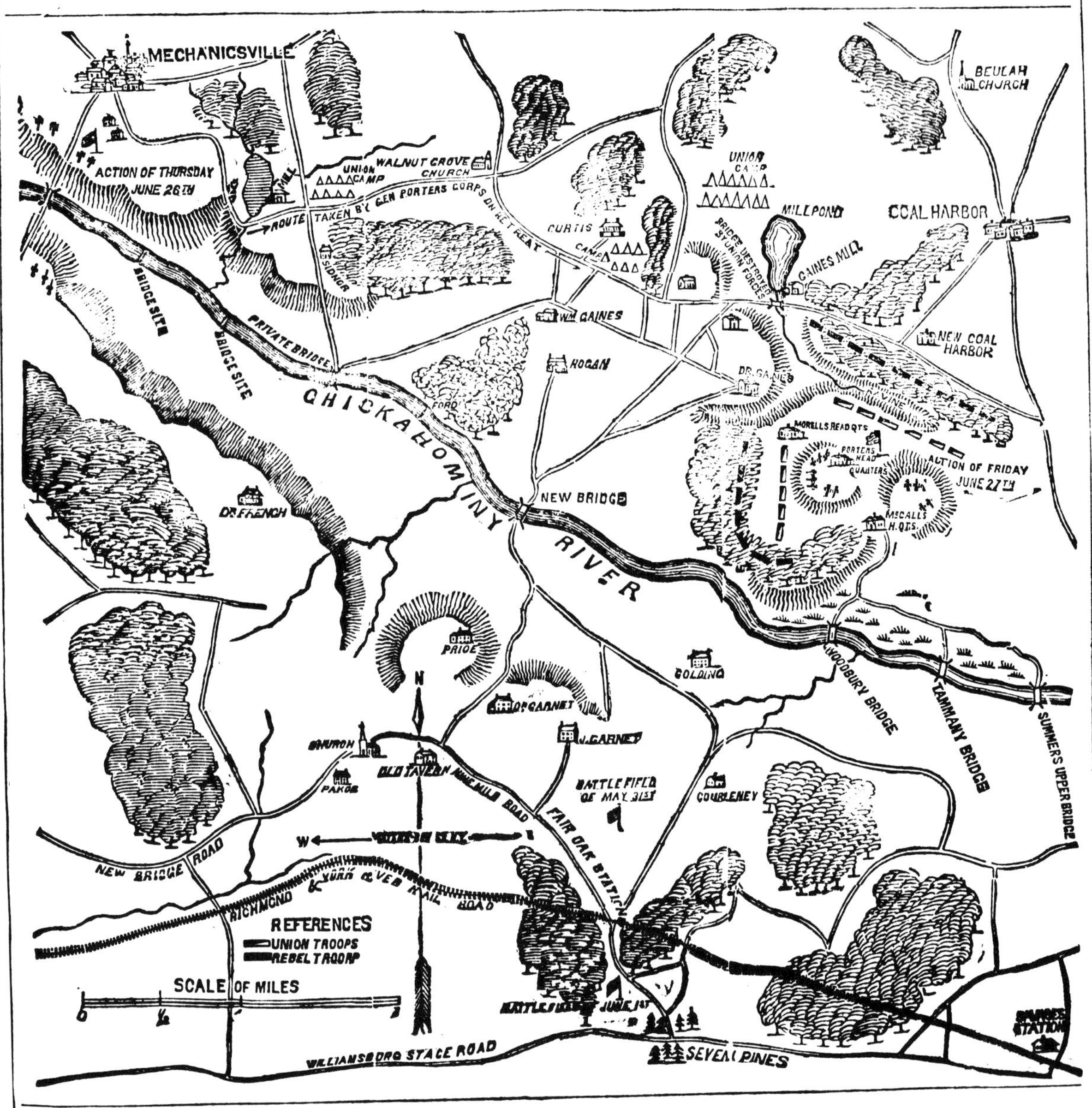

MAP 19

The Battle of Gaines's Mill, Virginia

Published in the *New York Herald*, July 1, 1862

(Original 24 × 24 cm.)

FOLLOWING THE BATTLE OF SEVEN PINES THE ARMY OF THE POTOMAC REMAINED divided by the Chickahominy River, but now the majority of the army was south of the river. To the north, Fitz-John Porter's Fifth Corps guarded essential supply lines. While George McClellan made preparations to besiege Richmond, Robert E. Lee, the new Confederate commander, recalled Thomas J. "Stonewall" Jackson from the Shenandoah Valley to reinforce his army. Lee ordered an attack against Porter at Mechanicsville on June 26, but poor execution resulted in a costly repulse. McClellan then ordered Porter to withdraw to Gaines's Mill and entrench. On June 27, Lee again attacked Porter, while simultaneously occupying the main body of McClellan's army with a demonstration. Delays prevented a coordinated movement, and Porter's troops withstood several Confederate charges. Union reinforcements arrived late in the afternoon, but just before dark a concerted assault broke the Union left and forced Porter to withdraw across the Chickahominy during the night.

The *Herald*'s unattributed map may have been the work of George Alfred Townsend, who stated that he devised a "general plan" of the battle by interviewing Porter's staff. The location of the battlefield at Mechanicsville and Porter's route eastward are marked (*upper left*). At Gaines's Mill (*right*) the Union line formed an arc, rather than the angle shown, with George Morell on its left, George Sykes on the right (not shown), and George McCall somewhat to the rear. Lee's line slightly overlapped Porter's on the Confederate right, but it neither extended as far to the south as shown nor consisted of two separate wings. Porter positioned his corps behind a wooded ravine formed by Boatswain Creek, a tributary of the Chickahominy that proved to be a significant obstacle to Confederate movements. The map shows only part of the ravine, which, instead of turning toward the Chickahominy, appears to run north. The Union camps north of the river represent earlier positions. The map fails to indicate the remainder of the opposing armies south of the river. Seven Pines and Fair Oaks, previous battlefields of the Peninsular campaign, are noted near the bottom of the map.

Reports in U.S. War Department, *War of the Rebellion*: ser. 1, vol. 11, pt. 2.
Maps in U.S. War Department, *Atlas*: pl. 42, no. 3; pl. 63, no. 8.
Other newspaper maps: None.

THE BATTLE OF CEDAR MOUNTAIN.

The Position of the Union and Rebel Forces on Cedar, Spring, Robinson's and Crooked Runs, Saturday, August 9, 1862.

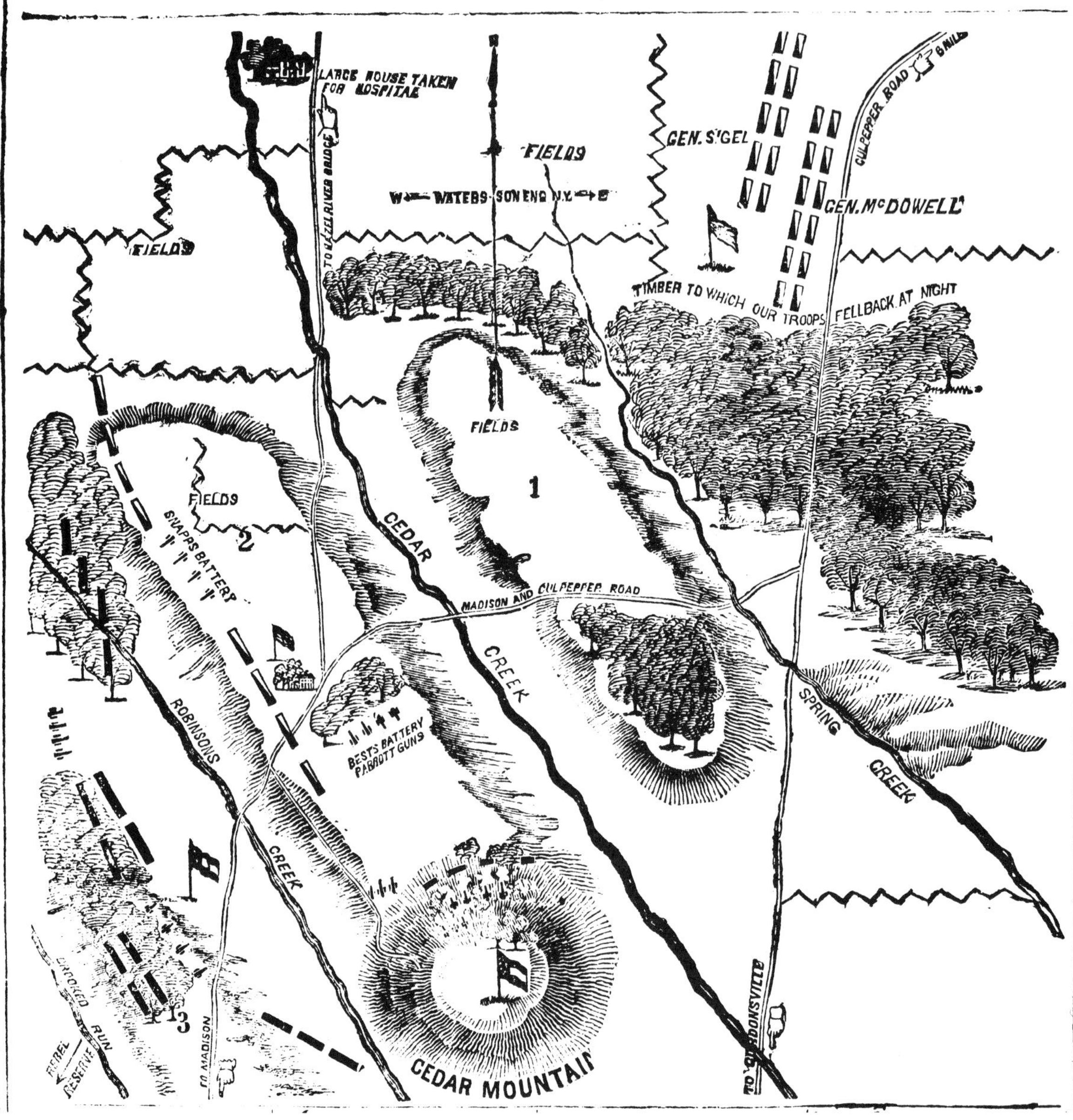

MAP 20

The Battle of Cedar Mountain, Virginia

Published in the *New York Herald*, August 13, 1862

(Original 24 × 24 cm.)

WHILE ROBERT E. LEE CONTENDED WITH GEORGE MCCLELLAN ON THE YORK-JAMES peninsula, John Pope advanced south from Washington. Lee detached Thomas J. "Stonewall" Jackson from the army defending Richmond and sent him to oppose Pope. Jackson proceeded to the vicinity of Culpeper, where he saw an opportunity to strike the isolated left wing of Pope's army. On August 9, Jackson's troops approached Union positions near Cedar Mountain and engaged in an inconclusive artillery duel. Nathaniel P. Banks, the Union commander on the field, directed two divisions to attack the Confederate left. By chance, Union forces found a gap in the Confederate line, and they exploited it. As the left gave way and retreated, Jackson arrived on the scene and personally rallied his troops. The timely arrival of reinforcements from A. P. Hill's division enabled Jackson to launch a counterattack which drove Banks's unsupported corps from the field just before dark.

George Alfred Townsend, the map's author, claimed that engravers ruined his original sketch. The confused depiction of streams may reflect changes introduced after Townsend drew the map. The stream marked "Spring Creek" actually joins Cedar Run ("Cedar Creek" on the map) south of the Culpeper Road (*center*). The map also compresses the distance between Cedar Run and Robertson's River ("Robinsons Creek") and places Crooked Run (*lower left*) west of Robertson's River, although it actually joins the river from the east. Most of the battle occurred west of Cedar Run but considerably east of Robertson's River. Union forces advanced to a point north of the eastern face of Cedar Mountain, as shown. Two of several Union batteries (Clermont Best and Joseph Knap, labeled "Snapps") are indicated somewhat beyond their true position. The map correctly shows Jackson's artillery on the mountain and in support of troops to the west. In the upper right a flag and note indicate the final Union position. Townsend's written description of the battlefield mentioned three parallel ridges, referred to by number (*1*, *2*, *3*) on the map. Townsend's account correctly identified Banks as Union commander, but no such credit appears on the map, whereas neither Franz Sigel nor Irvin McDowell (*upper right*) took part in the battle.

Reports in U.S. War Department, *War of the Rebellion*: ser. 1, vol. 12, pt. 2.
Maps in U.S. War Department, *Atlas*: pl. 22, no. 2; pl. 42, no. 2; pl. 85, nos. 3, 4; pl. 135, no. 2.
Other newspaper maps: None.

THE BATTLE AT HARPER'S FERRY.

Positions of the Union and Rebel Forces.

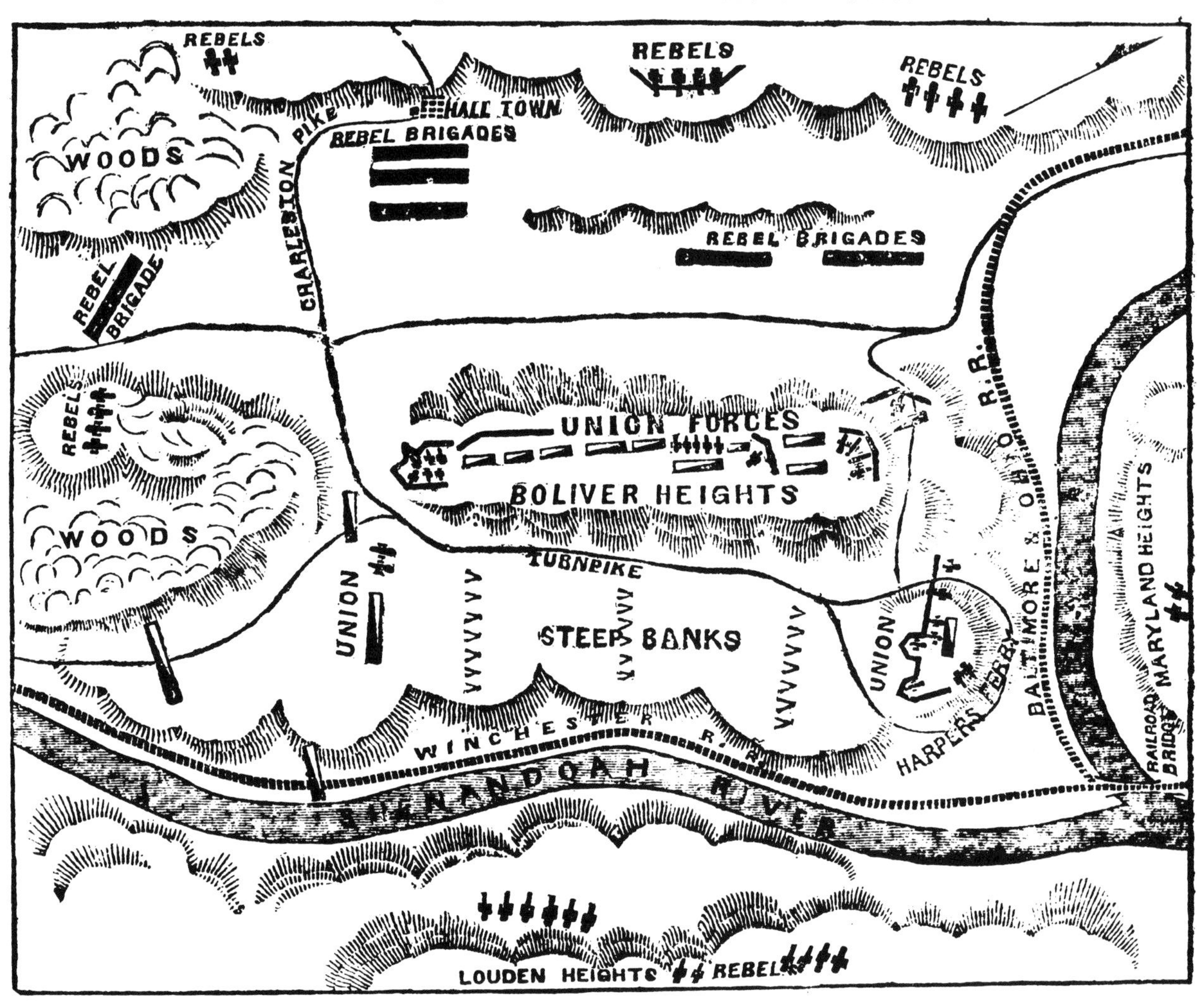

MAP 21

The Battle of Harpers Ferry, West Virginia

Published in the *New York Times*, September 18, 1862

(Original 14 × 18 cm.)

AS PART OF THE INVASION OF MARYLAND, THOMAS J. "STONEWALL" JACKSON UNDERtook the capture of the Union post at Harpers Ferry. Confederate forces moved into position on September 13 and quickly seized the virtually undefended hills around the town. Union cavalry fought their way out of Harpers Ferry that night, but some 12,000 infantry remained behind. Dixon Miles deployed these troops in defensive lines along Bolivar Heights and on some hills near the Shenandoah River. The following day Jackson's artillery began bombarding the Union positions but failed to dislodge them. Under cover of darkness Confederate troops moved onto the Union left flank in preparation for an attack on the morning of the 15th. By securing the strategically important hills around Harpers Ferry and utilizing his artillery, Jackson forced the surrender of the garrison on September 15. It was the single largest capitulation of Union troops during the entire war.

The terrain around Harpers Ferry played a critical role in the outcome of the battle, a fact recognized by the *Times*'s correspondent. Including a map with his report, he stated, "A glance at the map will enable us to understand why it [Harpers Ferry] could not be held against such powerful odds." Although depicted as nearly a ninety-degree angle, the confluence of the Potomac and Shenandoah rivers is in fact closer to a forty-five-degree angle, with Bolivar Heights ("Boliver" on the map) forming the third side of the triangle. The locations of other major topographical features, such as Loudoun ("Louden") and Maryland Heights, are approximately correct. The main Union defensive line followed Bolivar Heights and extended to the Shenandoah, as shown. Confederate divisions (called brigades on the map) stretched from near the Baltimore & Ohio Railroad (*upper right*) parallel to Bolivar Heights, crossed the Charlestown Road (labeled "Charleston Pike"), then turned east to the Winchester Railroad. The two Union troop symbols straddling the road and railroad in the map's lower left should represent A. P. Hill's Confederate division, poised to strike the Union flank on the 15th.

Reports in U.S. War Department, *War of the Rebellion*: ser. 1, vol. 19, pt. 1.
Maps in U.S. War Department, *Atlas*: pl. 29, no. 1.
Other newspaper maps: *Philadelphia Inquirer* (9/19/62).

THE GREAT BATTLE OF SHARPSBURG.

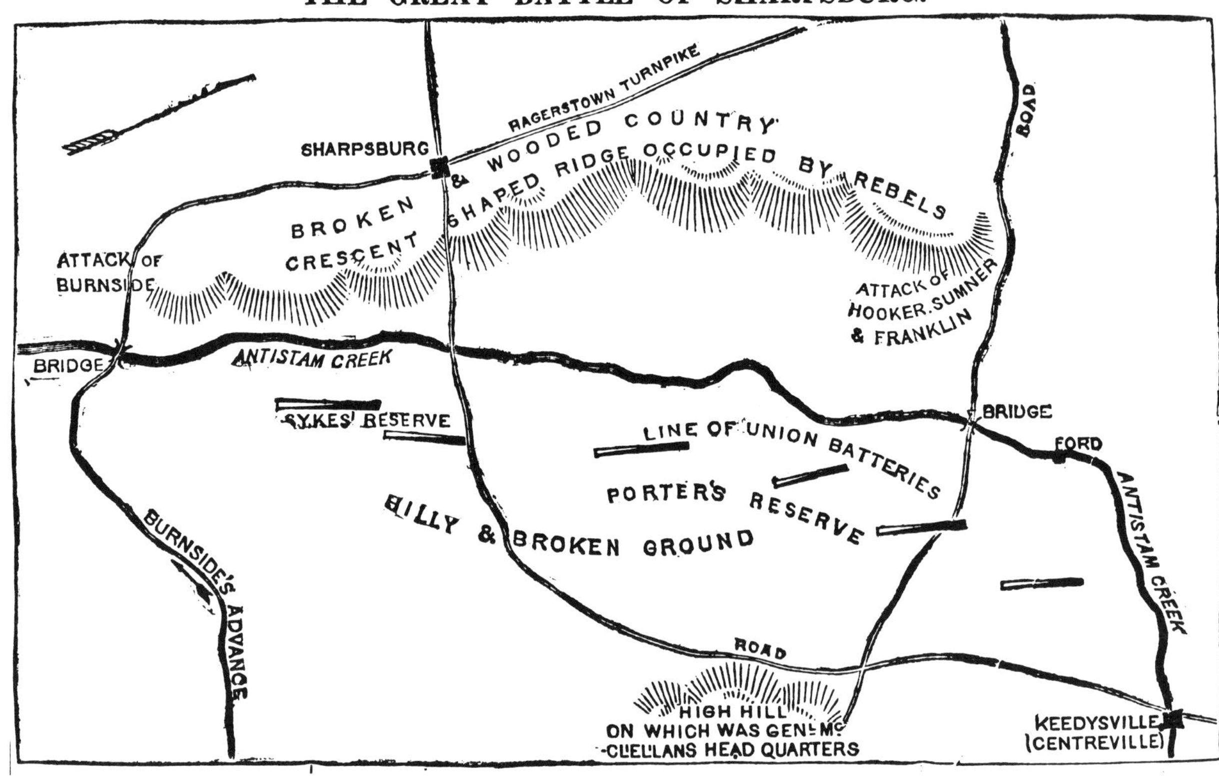

MAPS 22A AND 22B

The Battle of Antietam, or Sharpsburg, Maryland

Published in the *New York Tribune* and the *New York Herald*, September 20, 1862

(Originals 15 × 24 cm. and 20 × 24 cm.)

SENDING A PORTION OF HIS ARMY TO TAKE HARPERS FERRY AND TO PROTECT HIS lines of communication, Robert E. Lee advanced the remainder of his forces into Maryland. George McClellan cautiously moved to meet this threat. Before the Confederate army could reassemble, approaching Union troops forced Lee to deploy in a defensive position along the high ground west of Antietam Creek. At dawn on September 17, Joseph Hooker's corps initiated the battle on the Confederate left. Fighting surged back and forth with no clear advantage. The battle then shifted toward the Confederate center and right as Edwin Sumner's corps pressed the attack. In midafternoon, Ambrose Burnside's corps succeeded in forcing its way across a bridge to the south and began to drive the Confederate line toward Sharpsburg. The day ended as A. P. Hill's division arrived from Harpers Ferry and drove back Burnside's advance. The next day Lee awaited the renewal of battle, but when the expected attack never materialized, the vastly outnumbered Confederate army withdrew to Virginia.

The *Tribune*'s map can be attributed to George Smalley, but may incorporate sketches done by the three other correspondents who covered the battle for the *Tribune*. Although rather sparsely marked, the map provides an adequate depiction of the locale and an overview of the action. The stream flowing through Keedysville is actually a tributary of Antietam Creek (spelled properly in Smalley's account) just above the marked ford. An unillustrated upstream portion of Antietam Creek should run from the right edge of the map (north) to that juncture. A note indicates Joseph Hooker's initial attack on the Confederate left, although the attack occurred closer to the Hagerstown Turnpike. Sumner's corps followed and attacked to Hooker's left, approximately where noted. William Franklin's corps, like that of Fitz-John Porter (encompassing George Sykes's division) was, however, held in reserve. The Confederate right extended beyond the location of Burnside's advance and attack, while the left angled back across the Hagerstown Turnpike. Union batteries, far more extensive than shown, ranged from across Antietam Creek on the right to below what became known as Burnside's bridge on the left.

The *Herald*'s map, also published on the 20th, offers limited information on the battle itself. The Union positions shown are essentially those occupied prior to the attack on the 17th, with no indication of their movements during the battle. Lee de-

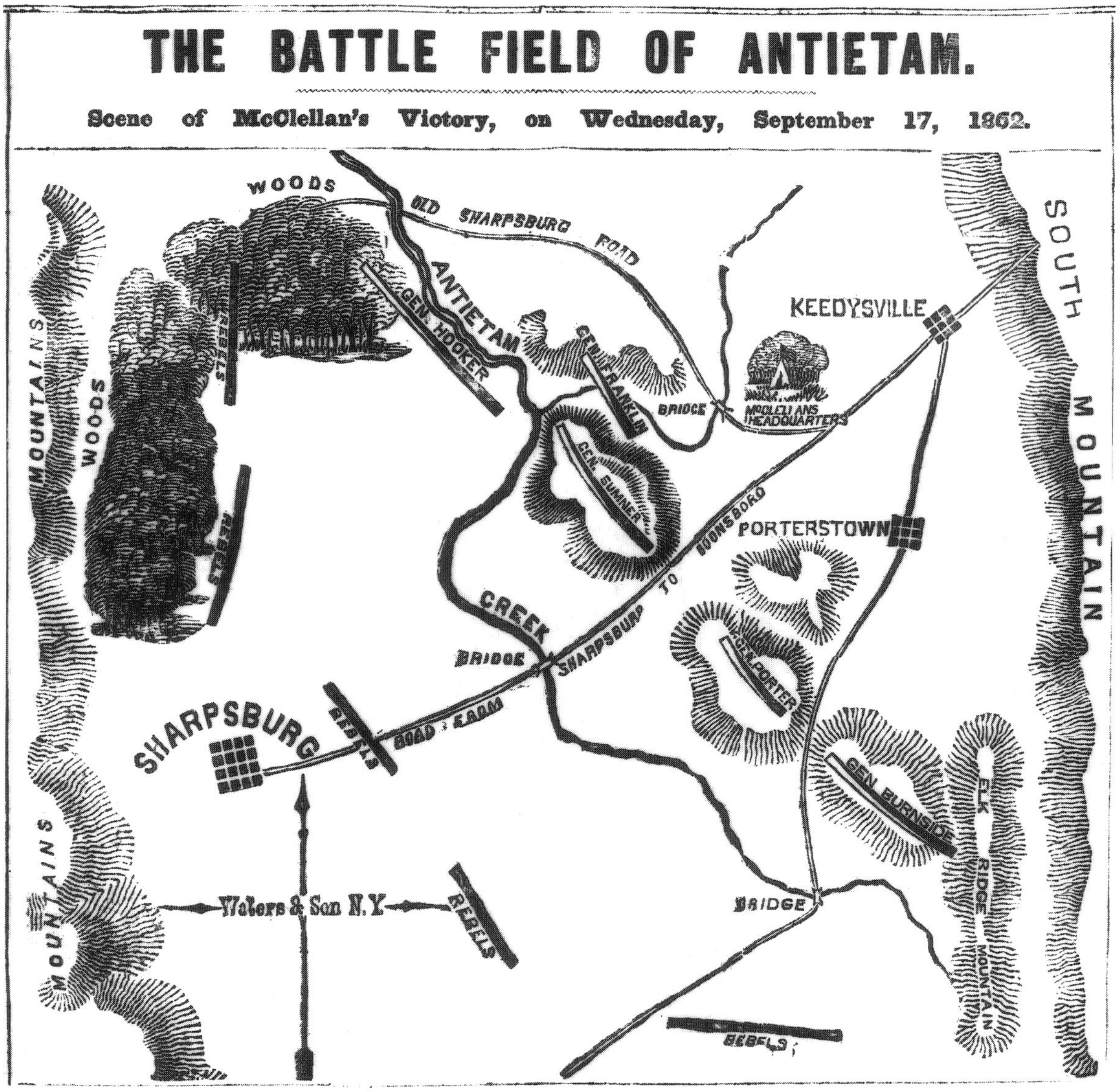
THE BATTLE FIELD OF ANTIETAM.
Scene of McClellan's Victory, on Wednesday, September 17, 1862.
WOODS
OLD SHARPSBURG ROAD
ANTIETAM
GEN. HOOKER
REBELS
WOODS
MOUNTAINS
GEN. FRANKLIN
BRIDGE
McCLELLANS HEADQUARTERS
KEEDYSVILLE
SOUTH MOUNTAIN
GEN. SUMNER
REBELS
PORTERSTOWN
SHARPSBURG TO BOONSBORO
CREEK
BRIDGE
GEN. PORTER
SHARPSBURG
REBELS
ROAD FROM
GEN. BURNSIDE
ELK RIDGE MOUNTAIN
MOUNTAINS
Waters & Son N.Y.
REBELS
BRIDGE
REBELS

ployed his army from north to south as indicated. However, several mistakes exist in the map's topography. Antietam Creek appears to run north rather than in its true course south. The Boonsboro Road correctly passes through Keedysville, but the town should be marked approximately where the Old Sharpsburg Road bridge crosses the tributary to Antietam Creek. Elk Ridge and South Mountain are slightly farther east than shown, and although hilly ground lies south and west of Sharpsburg, it in no way compares with the mountains to the east.

Reports in U.S. War Department, *War of the Rebellion*: ser. 1, vol. 19, pt. 1.
Maps in U.S. War Department, *Atlas*: pl. 28, nos. 1, 2, 6; pl. 29, nos. 1, 2.
Other newspaper maps: *Baltimore American & Commercial Advertiser* (9/25/62), *Boston Daily Journal* (9/23/62), *Philadelphia Inquirer* (9/22/62).

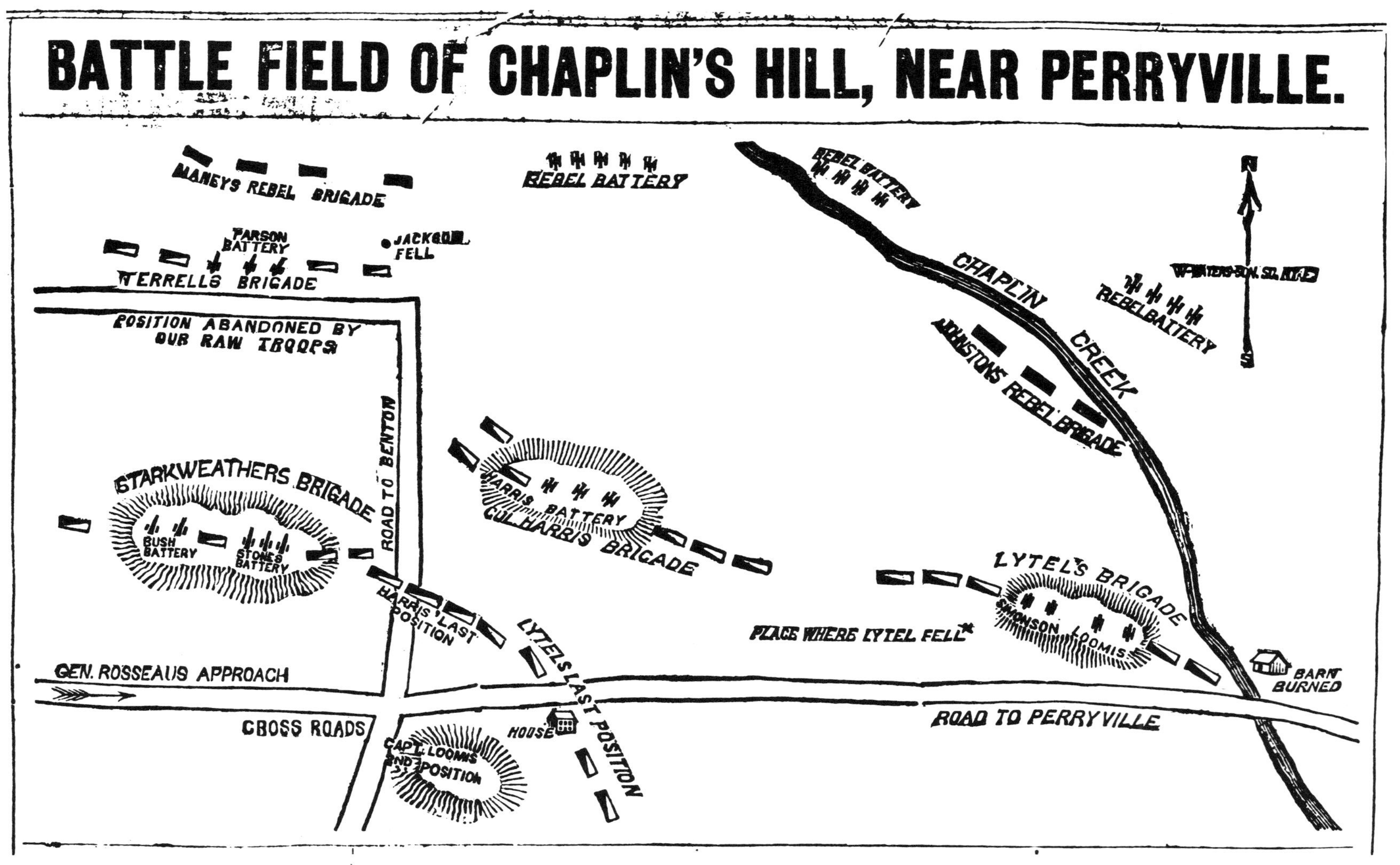
BATTLE FIELD OF CHAPLIN'S HILL, NEAR PERRYVILLE.
MANEYS REBEL BRIGADE
REBEL BATTERY
REBEL BATTERY
N
S
REBELBATTERY
PARSON BATTERY
JACKSON FELL
TERRELLS BRIGADE
CHAPLIN CREEK
JOHNSTONS REBEL BRIGADE
POSITION ABANDONED BY OUR RAW TROOPS
ROAD TO BENTON
STARKWEATHERS BRIGADE
BUSH BATTERY
STONES BATTERY
HARRIS BATTERY
COL. HARRIS BRIGADE
LYTEL'S BRIGADE
SIMONSON LOOMIS
HARRIS LAST POSITION
LYTELS LAST POSITION
PLACE WHERE LYTEL FELL
GEN. ROSSEAUS APPROACH
BARN BURNED
CROSS ROADS
HOUSE
ROAD TO PERRYVILLE
CAPT. LOOMIS 2ND POSITION

MAP 23

The Battle of Perryville, Kentucky

Published in the *New York Herald*, October 15, 1862

(Original 13 × 24 cm.)

CONFEDERATE ARMIES BEGAN OPERATIONS IN KENTUCKY LATE IN THE SUMMER OF 1862. In response, a Union column under Don Carlos Buell moved south from Louisville. On October 7, Confederate cavalry clashed with Union forces concentrating west of Perryville. Skirmishing resumed at dawn on the 8th, and the battle began in earnest later in the day, when Braxton Bragg's Confederates moved against the Union left. This attack routed a brigade of new troops commanded by William Terrill, forcing the Union line back, but two batteries supported by John Starkweather's brigade checked the advance. Farther to the right, Lew Harris's brigade retired after expending its ammunition, opening a gap in the Union line. Confederates pushed Union troops back nearly half a mile in this sector before being halted. On the right wing, Union forces repulsed an attack in the late afternoon then pursued retreating Confederates back through the town of Perryville. Unable to continue the battle, Bragg withdrew his small army into eastern Tennessee.

The map was probably drawn by William Shanks, a correspondent who served as a volunteer aide to Gen. Lovell Rousseau during the battle. Shanks's authorship may account for why the map portrays only the action on the Union left, north of the Old Mackville Pike (marked "road to Perryville"), and shows Rousseau's advance before the battle (*lower left*). Interestingly, all other officers identified are of lower rank. The brigades of Terrill (supported by Charles Parsons's battery), Harris (in reality supported by Peter Simonson's battery), and William Lytle (supported by Cyrus Loomis's battery) were arranged more north to south than as shown. Starkweather moved in support of Terrill with the batteries of Asahel Busch and David Stone. Slightly east of Russell house (*lower left*) these brigades formed a final line. George Maney's and Bushrod Johnson's (marked "Johnstons") brigades are the only Confederate troops named. Johnson attacked near the burning barn which screened his movement. The barn was actually south of the Perryville road. Also marked are the site of Union general James Jackson's death (*upper left*) and the spot where Lytle fell wounded (*lower right*).

Reports in U.S. War Department, *War of the Rebellion*: ser. 1, vol. 16, pt. 1.
Maps in U.S. War Department, *Atlas*: pl. 24, nos. 2, 4.
Other newspaper maps: None.

THE SCENE OF SATURDAY'S ACTION.

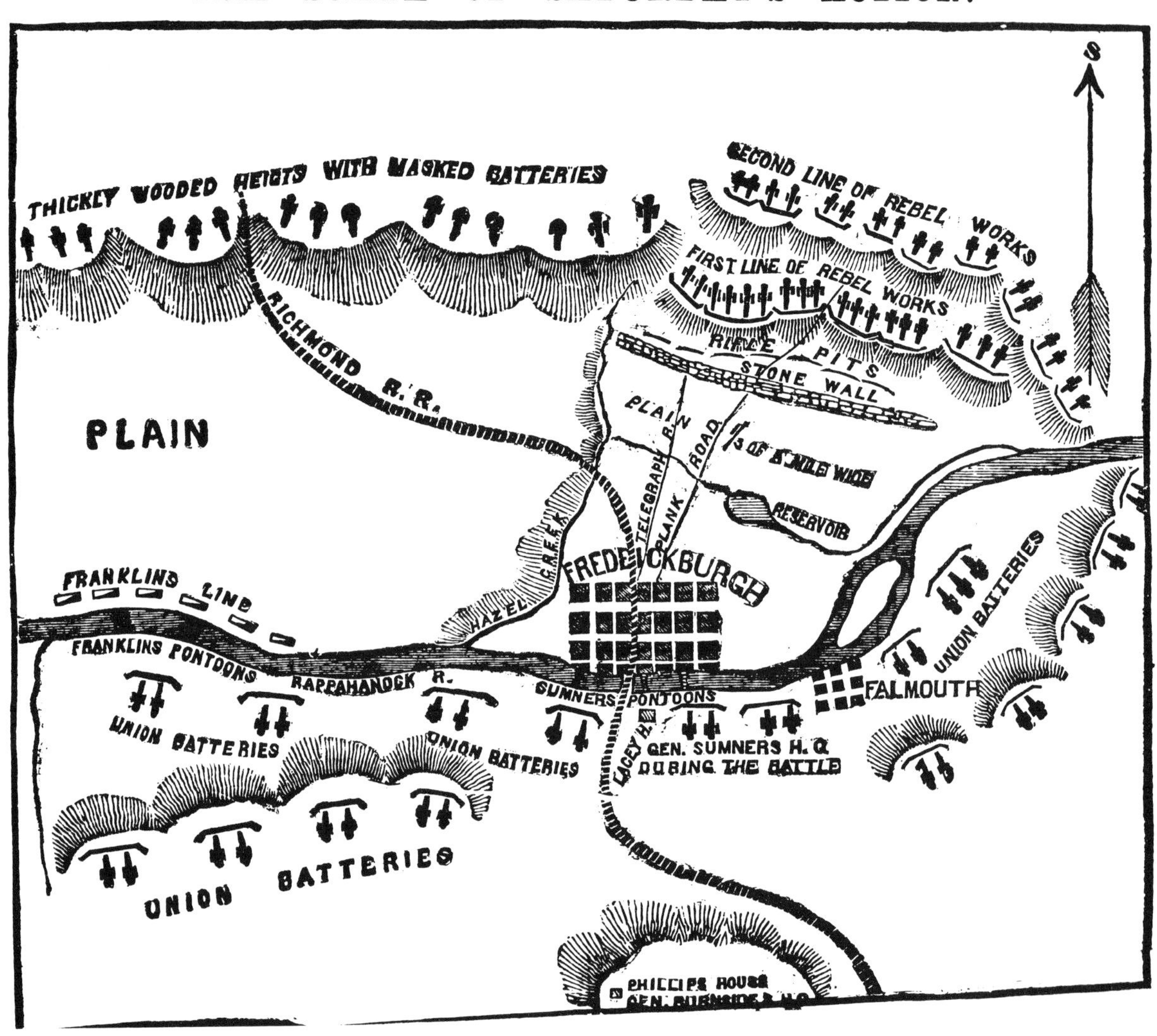

MAP 24

The Battle of Fredericksburg, Virginia

Published in the *New York Times*, December 17, 1862

(Original 20 × 23 cm.)

AMBROSE BURNSIDE, THE NEW COMMANDER OF THE ARMY OF THE POTOMAC, PROposed to march on Richmond by crossing the Rappahannock River at Fredericksburg. While Burnside waited for pontoon bridges to arrive, Robert E. Lee gathered his army and prepared strong defensive positions on the heights west of the city. After considerable difficulty, Union troops crossed the river and faced their adversaries across open fields. The battle commenced on December 13 with an attack on the Confederate right. After a single battery thwarted their advance, William Franklin's corps eventually broke through a gap in the Confederate line, only to be repulsed by a counterattack. At the same time, Burnside ordered a series of frontal assaults against the Confederate center and left. Each Union charge up the Fredericksburg slopes met with a bloody repulse. Despite terrible losses among his forces, Burnside proposed renewing the battle the following day, but he was persuaded to withdraw across the river on the night of December 15.

William Swinton prepared the *Times*'s map, probably in collaboration with the six other correspondents the paper had fielded there. The map gives a good impression of the terrain of the battlefield and the formidable nature of the Confederate position. Behind the stone wall Lee arranged his infantry with supporting lines of artillery. Parallel to the wall and some four hundred yards in front of it, a drainage ditch, following a hollow (marked "reservoir"), offered the only cover for Union troops advancing to the attack. Union batteries reached from above Falmouth to below the location of Franklin's pontoons, but Burnside also massed artillery west of the river (west, not south, is actually at the top of the map), below Fredericksburg. On the Union left, the initial position of Franklin's division and the line of the Richmond & Fredericksburg Railroad, along which they attacked, are shown. The divisions of Edwin Sumner and Joseph Hooker formed the Union right and center, respectively, but only Sumner's headquarters are indicated.

Reports in U.S. War Department, *War of the Rebellion*: ser. 1, vol. 21, with two maps.
Maps in U.S. War Department, *Atlas*: pl. 25, no. 4; pl. 30, nos. 3, 4; pl. 31, no. 4; pl. 32, no. 3; pl. 33, no. 1; pl. 63, no. 7.
Other newspaper maps: *Boston Daily Journal* (12/17/62), *Chicago Daily Tribune* (12/19/62), *Philadelphia Inquirer* (12/17/62).

THE BATTLE OF CHICKASAW BAYOU.

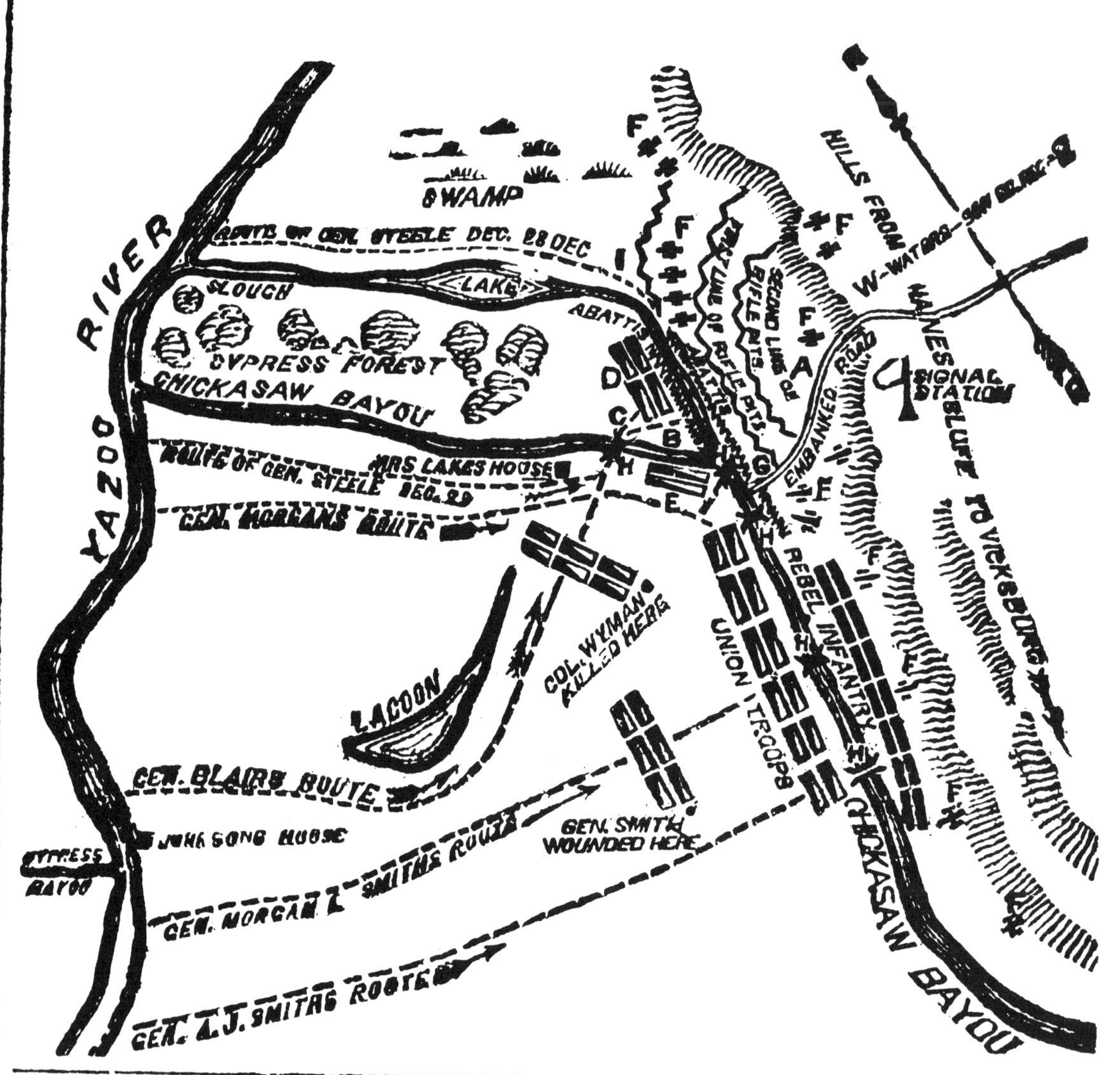

REFERENCES.

A—Willow copse reached by the Thirteenth Illinois and Twenty-ninth Missouri regiments.

B—General Thayer's route in the assault.

C—General Blair's route in the assault.

D—Blair's brigade before the assault.

E—Thayer's brigade before the assault.

F—Heavy batteries of the enemy.

G—Point reached by Colonel De Courcey.

H—Bridges over Chickasaw Bayou

I—Causeway swept by the rebel batteries

MAP 25

The Battle of Chickasaw Bluffs, or Bayou, Mississippi

Published in the *New York Herald*, January 18, 1863

(Original 12 × 12 cm.)

IN AN EARLY ATTEMPT TO TAKE VICKSBURG, UNION TROOPS UNDER WILLIAM T. SHERman moved up the Yazoo River then overland to assault Confederate defenses north of the city at Chickasaw Bluffs. Four Union divisions led by George W. Morgan, Andrew J. Smith, Morgan Smith, and Frederick Steele advanced to the bluffs. Union engineers tried to bridge a lake in front of a poorly defended section of the Confederate line, but failed. On December 29, 1862, Sherman ordered a general assault on the fortified position. Because the bayou at the foot of the bluffs could be crossed only in a few places, Union troops were forced to attack in columns. This allowed Confederate defenders, commanded by Martin Smith, to effectively concentrate their fire. Sherman's forces took some of the outer works, but eventually retired after sustaining heavy casualties. On January 2, 1863, Sherman abandoned the operation and retired to the mouth of the Yazoo, where he relinquished his command.

The map was "drawn from memory" by Thomas Knox, whose earlier report and maps were confiscated by the Union command and never reached the *Herald.* Knox's map greatly simplifies the confusing tangle of waterways forming the region in which the Union forces operated. The body of water marked "lagoon" probably represents McNutt Lake, over which Sherman attempted to lay pontoons. The lake actually connects to the bayou and should be located closer to the foot of the bluffs. Steele's reconnaissance on the 28th, halted by Confederate artillery (*I*), and his route on the 29th when ordered to support Morgan, are indicated. Knox shows the route of Francis Blair's brigade (*C*) and point of attack (*D*) as well as that of John Thayer (*B*, *E*). Letter *A* correctly indicates the farthest extent of the Union advance into the second line of works but mentions only two of the four regiments under Blair. The attack of John DeCourcey's brigade (*G*) halted at the first line of rifle pits, as shown. Although Knox's map depicts two bridges over the bayou, none are mentioned in accounts of the battle.

Reports in U.S. War Department, *War of the Rebellion*: ser. 1, vol. 17, pt. 1, with one map.
Maps in U.S. War Department, *Atlas*: None.
Other newspaper maps: *Chicago Daily Tribune* (1/14/63), *Daily Missouri Republican* (1/13/63), *New York Herald* (1/15/63), *Philadelphia Inquirer* (1/9/63).

THE CAPTURE OF FORT HINDMAN.

The Combined Military and Naval Victory on the Arkansas River.

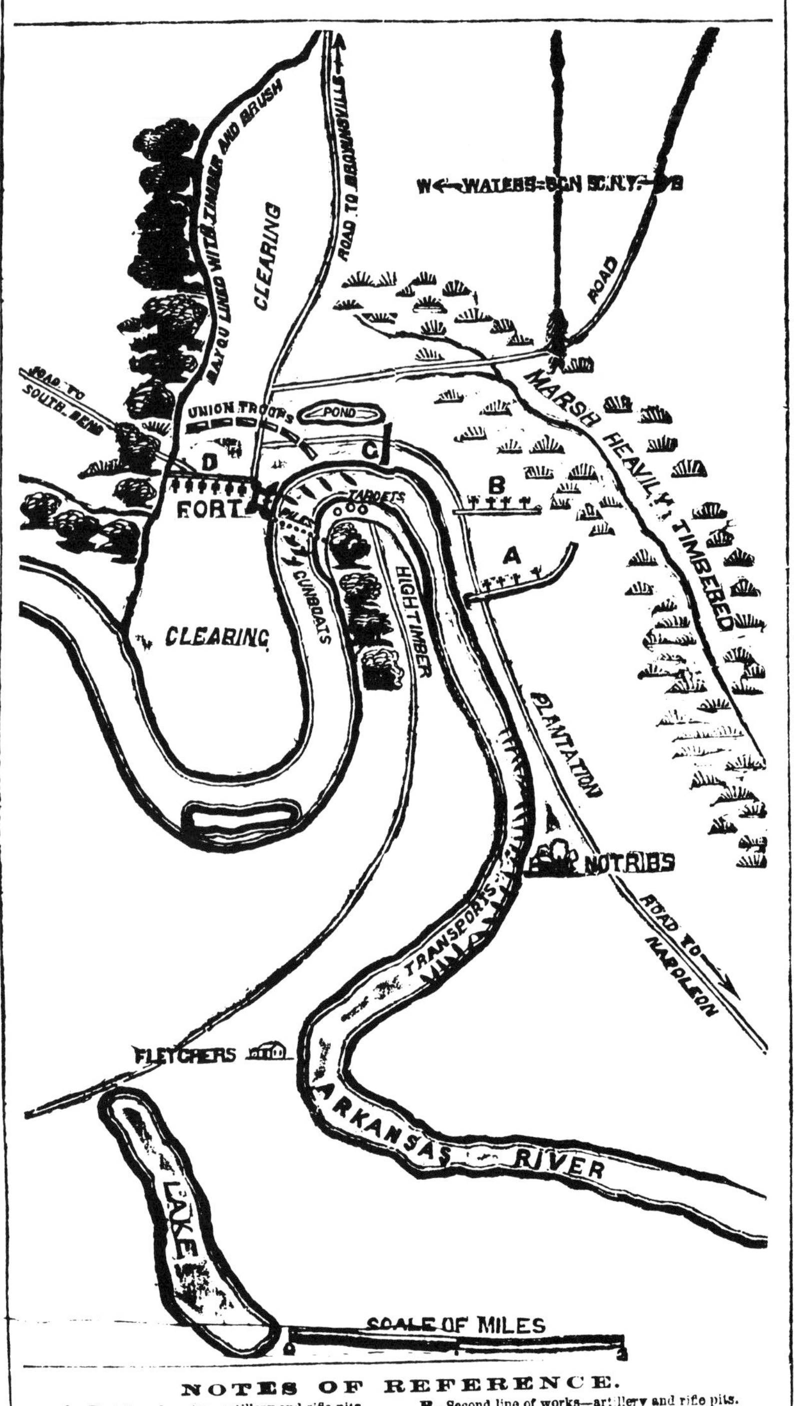

NOTES OF REFERENCE.

A—First line of works—artillery and rifle pits.
B—Second line of works—artillery and rifle pits.
C—Third line of works—rifle pits.
D—Main line of works—artillery and rifle pits.

MAP 26

The Battle of Arkansas Post, or Fort Hindman, Arkansas

Published in the *New York Herald*, January 25, 1863

(Original 20 × 12 cm.)

THROUGH POLITICAL MANEUVERING JOHN MCCLERNAND BRIEFLY RECEIVED AN INDEPendent command to operate against Vicksburg. He chose to move against Fort Hindman, a base for gunboats, about fifty miles up the Arkansas River from its junction with the Mississippi. McClernand's forces consisted of some 30,000 infantry accompanied by gunboats and transports under the command of David Porter. Troops landed on the east bank, below Hindman, and a detachment crossed the river to block a Confederate retreat. Operations began on January 10 as Porter's gunboats silenced Confederate artillery. Union infantry carried the two lines of outer defensive works, but a coordinated land and naval assault on the fort itself was delayed until the following day. On the 11th, gunboats again pounded Confederate positions prior to the attack. Four hours later, Thomas Churchill surrendered the fort's garrison of approximately 4,500 men. McClernand wished to push upstream, but Ulysses S. Grant, newly given command of all forces in the region, recalled him.

The *Herald*'s map depicts the military situation during the final assault on January 11. It closely resembles the map accompanying McClernand's official report of the battle, a copy of which may have been provided by McClernand. The *Herald*'s map includes many of the same terrain features found on the official map, including the bayou on which the Union right rested, the swamps to the east of the river, and the heavy forests near the fort. More than fifty Union transports (*dashes* in the river) tied up at Notrib's Farm. A brigade of supporting infantry (not shown) disembarked at Fletcher's Landing and operated at the tip of the peninsula across from the fort. The map indicates the Confederate works captured on January 10 (*A*, *B*, *C*), but only two outer lines existed. The Union assault concentrated on the main works (*D*) beside the fort. Seven of the actual eight Union gunboats are represented in the Arkansas River just downstream of Fort Hindman and above the pilings, where they later moved to seal the surrender of the fort.

Reports in U.S. War Department, *War of the Rebellion*: ser. 1, vol. 17, pt. 1, with eight maps of the campaign.
Maps in U.S. War Department, *Atlas*: None.
Other newspaper maps: *New York Herald* (1/21/63).

THE BATTLES ON THE RAPPAHANNOCK.

Diagram of the Relative Positions of the Rebel Army and the Forces of Generals Hooker and Sedgwick, on the South Side of the Rappahannock.

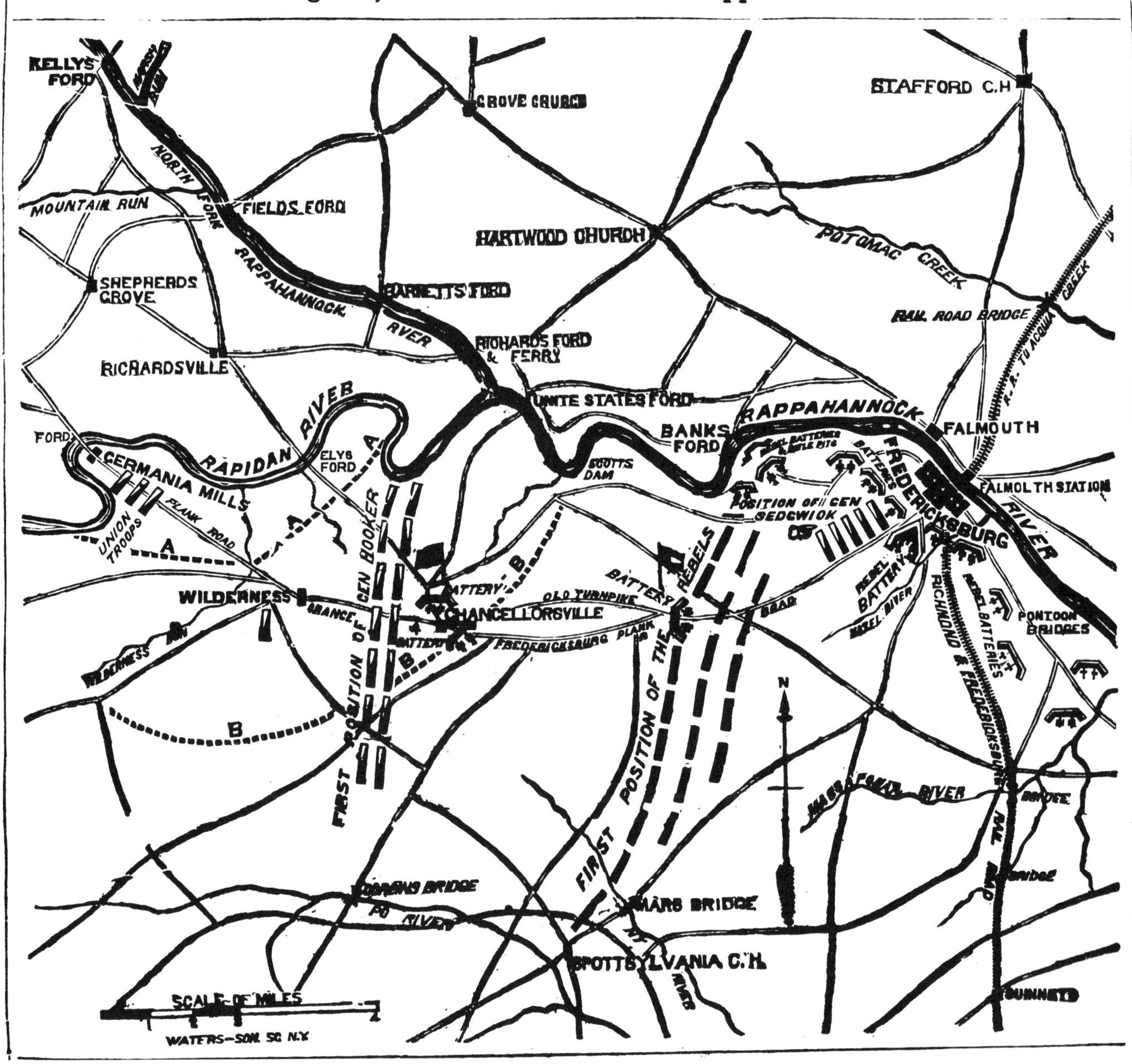

MAPS 27A AND 27B

The Battles of Chancellorsville and Fredericksburg, Virginia

Published in the *New York Herald*, May 6, 1863, and the *New York Tribune*, May 7, 1863

(Originals 21 × 24 cm. and 15 × 24 cm.)

UNABLE TO CARRY THE STRONG POSITION AT FREDERICKSBURG BY ASSAULT, UNION forces, newly under the command of Joseph Hooker, outflanked the Confederate line. Leaving a division under Jubal Early to hold the heights at Fredericksburg, Robert E. Lee's outnumbered forces moved to block Hooker. After initial skirmishing on May 1, Hooker withdrew to a defensive position near Chancellorsville. The next day Lee daringly divided his small army. Thomas J. "Stonewall" Jackson led better than half of it on a long march around the Union right. To screen this movement, Lee demonstrated against the Union center. Jackson's corps reached the Union flank by early evening, and their surprise assault crushed the Eleventh Corps. Near the end of the fighting, which continued after darkness fell, Jackson was accidentally shot by his own men. While Hooker's forces retired from Chancellorsville on the 3rd, John Sedgwick's corps gained the Fredericksburg heights after several attempts. Lee then turned east and defeated Sedgwick at Salem Church, forcing him to retreat across Banks's Ford.

Map 27a, which covers the events of May 1–3, accurately depicts the area's rivers and roads but mistakes some of the military operations. The first Union line basically faced south, not east, with the left wing stretching from Chancellorsville to near Scott's Dam and the right wing paralleling the Orange Plank Road. Troops shown near Germania Mills probably represent William Averell's cavalry, which approached Hooker's position on the morning of May 2 at Ely's Ford but did not cross the river. The Confederate line of May 1, farther to the west than marked, gives the impression of great strength when in fact Lee's army numbered only slightly more than half of Hooker's. Hooker's second position, after Jackson's successful attack, appears as the dashed line *A*, and that of the Confederates as *B*. The actual Union line resembled a V, with the right wing on the Rapidan, east of Ely's Ford, the left resting near Scott's Dam on the Rappahannock, and coming to a point just north of Chancellorsville. Lee's second position consisted of two separate wings, one on either side of Chancellorsville. The map indicates Sedgwick's corps before its defeat, on the Plank Road approximately at Salem Church (not shown).

Based on a sketch made on the battlefield on May 4, the *Tribune*'s map provides far greater detail on the Union lines. The first line (*dashes*) indicates dispositions before the battle. The corps of Darius Couch (Second) and George Meade (Fifth) formed the left, of Henry Slocum (Twelfth) and Daniel Sickles (Third) the center, and that of O. O. Howard

THE POSITION SOUTH OF THE RAPPAHANNOCK

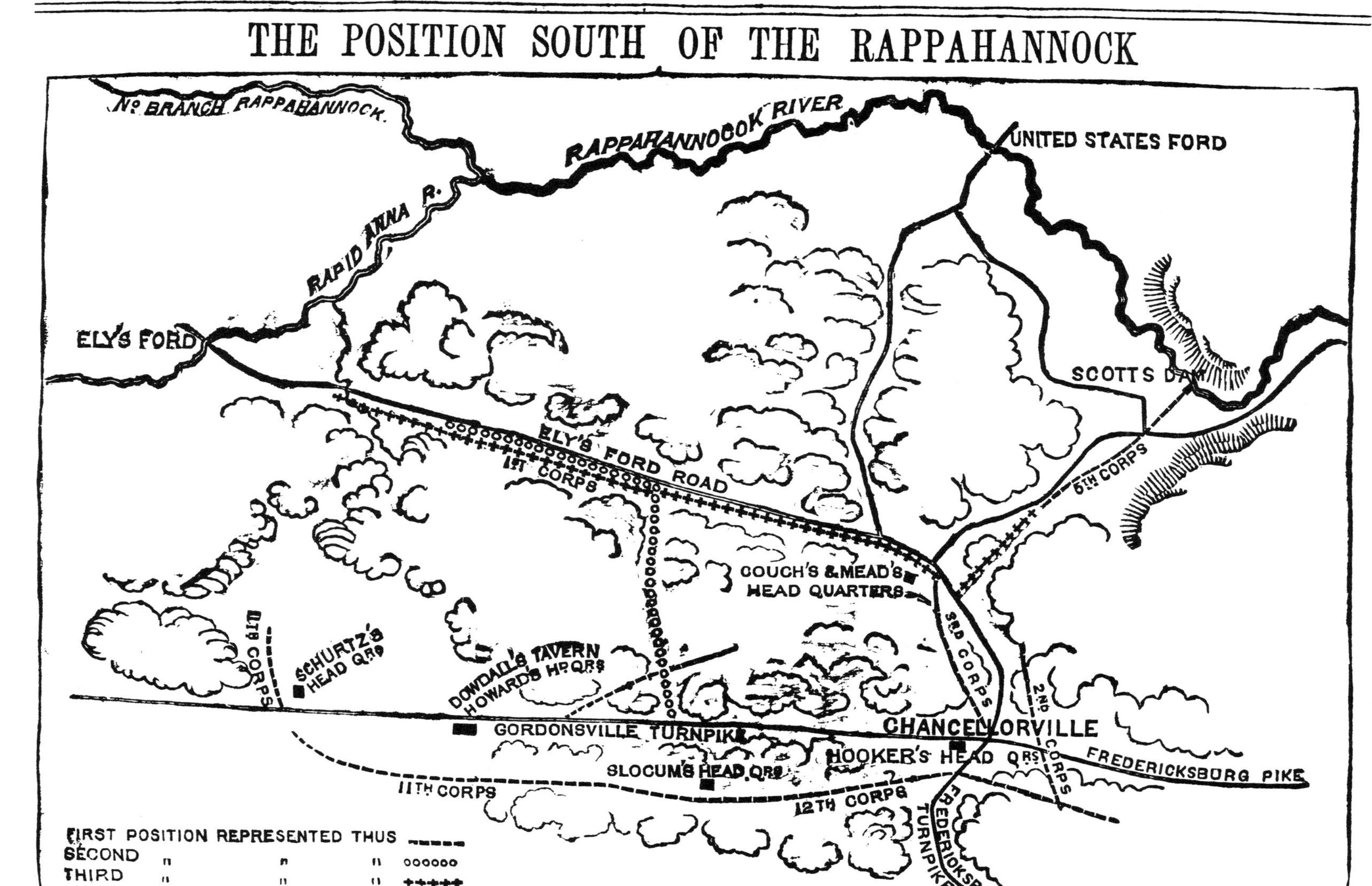

The above Map, from a sketch taken on the field on Monday morning, shows the position of Gen. Hooker's army on the several days since it crossed the Rappahannock River. The references show the changes from day to day, and the final position occupied by General Hooker at the time of the attack made upon him on Monday morning.

(Eleventh) the right. After the battle on the evening of the 2nd, John Reynolds's First Corps, then en route from Fredericksburg, moved into position on the right, as shown. Meade's corps also shifted to this new line which paralleled Ely's Ford Road to some extent but turned abruptly north toward the Rapidan River. As noted above, the final Union position roughly formed a V. The *Tribune*'s depiction greatly elongates the right wing, as a result of an exaggeration of distances east to west, in effect doubling the length of the Rappahannock from Scott's Dam to where it is joined by the Rapidan.

Reports in U.S. War Department, *War of the Rebellion*: ser. 1, vol. 25, pt. 1, with ten maps of the campaign.
Maps in U.S. War Department, *Atlas*: pl. 41, no. 1; pl. 93, no. 2; pl. 135, no. 6.
Other newspaper maps: *Boston Daily Journal* (5/9/63), *Chicago Daily Tribune* (5/7/63), *Cincinnati Daily Gazette* (5/11/63), *New York Herald* (5/7 and 5/19/63).

THE BATTLE FIELDS OF BAKER'S CREEK AND BLACK RIVER BRIDGE.

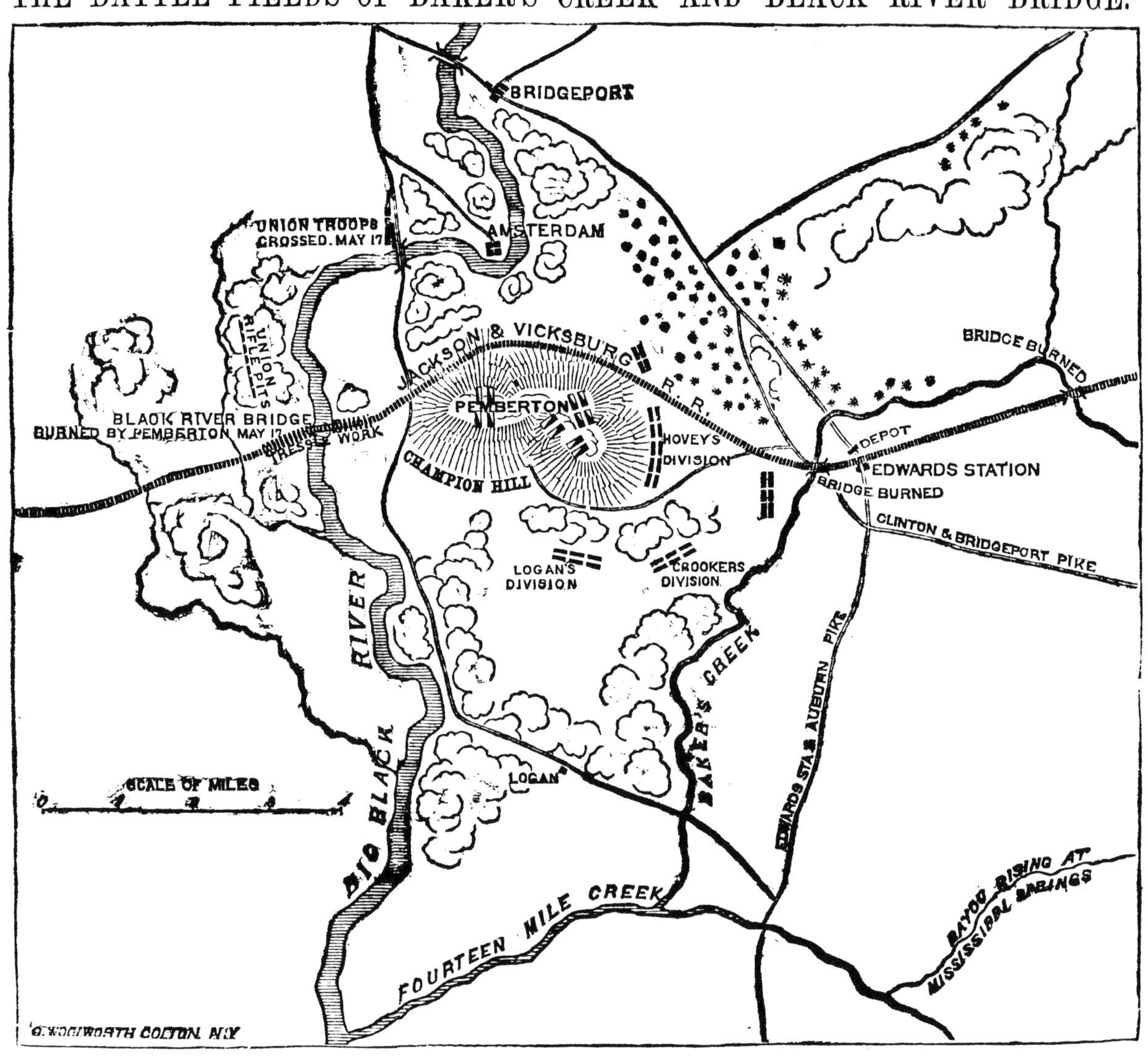

MAP 28

The Battle of Champion's Hill, or Baker's Creek, Mississippi

Published in the *New York Tribune*, May 30, 1863

(Original 21 × 24 cm.)

UNABLE TO CRACK VICKSBURG'S RIVER DEFENSES, ULYSSES S. GRANT ADOPTED THE strategy of operating against the city from the rear. His army crossed the Mississippi below Vicksburg and quickly maneuvered between John Pemberton's garrison and Confederate reinforcements assembling to the east of Jackson. Grant defeated this relief force on May 14, then turned west toward Vicksburg. Meanwhile, Pemberton belatedly moved out of the Vicksburg fortifications to strike Grant. He later retired to a defensive position at Champion's Hill. There, on May 16, the leading units of the Union column, led by Alvin Hovey's division, initiated the battle. Their attack nearly routed Pemberton's left wing, but the arrival of troops from the right drove back the Union line. Fighting surged back and forth on Champion's Hill until Union reinforcements tipped the balance. After losing control of the hill, Pemberton retreated to Vicksburg.

The *Tribune* had no representative at Champion's Hill but reprinted an account from the *Chicago Times* and printed this map with that report. The map does not faithfully record all the details as mentioned in the report, so was apparently compiled from additional written sources and maps. Big Black River, which appears where Baker's Creek should be, is actually some eight miles to the west. Baker's Creek does begin east of the battlefield, but it curls around to the north of Champion's Hill before flowing south. The map shows Edwards Station (actually west of Baker's Creek) in the place of Bolton Station, and overlooks the strategically important Raymond Road, Pemberton's escape route, just south of the hill. In regard to military positions, Pemberton's line formed an angle, the left wing on Champion's Hill roughly parallel to the railroad and the right stretching to the south along a ridge. The divisions of John Logan and Hovey, with later support from Marcellus Crocker ("Crooker" on the map), formed the Union right and fought on the hill. All of these units are identified, but Hovey's are the only troops located with any accuracy.

Reports in U.S. War Department, *War of the Rebellion*: ser. 1, vol. 24, pt. 2, with two maps.
Maps in U.S. War Department, *Atlas*: pl. 132, no. 8; pl. 135C, no. 4.
Other newspaper maps: *New York Herald* (5/29/63).

THE BATTLE-FIELD AROUND GETTYSBURG.

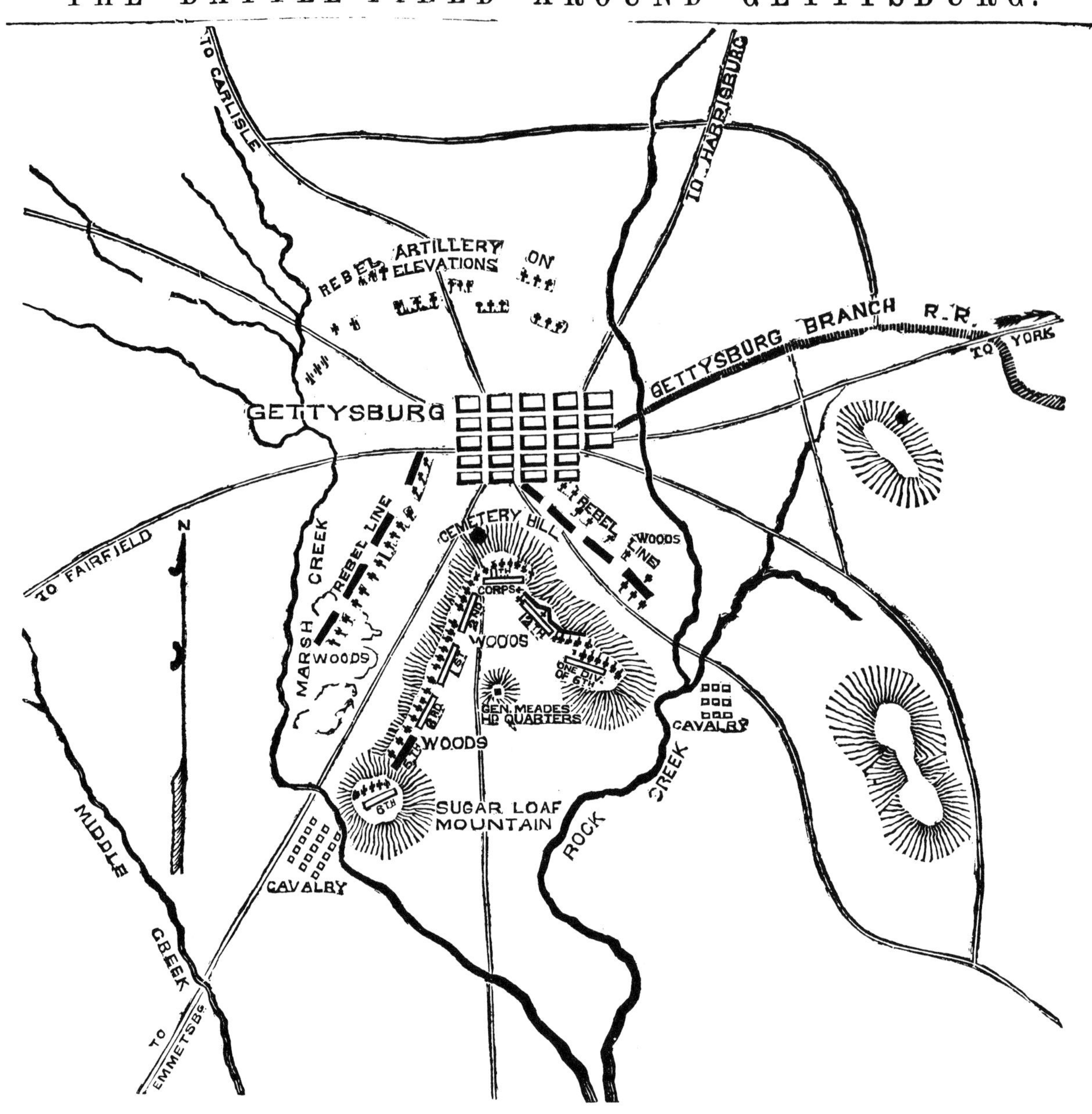

MAP 29

The Battle of Gettysburg, Pennsylvania

Published in the *New York Tribune*, July 7, 1863

(Original 23 × 25 cm.)

ROBERT E. LEE'S CONFEDERATE ARMY ADVANCED INTO PENNSYLVANIA LARGELY unaware of Union movements. When Lee discovered the approach of the Union army, he ordered a concentration of his scattered forces near Gettysburg, without intending to give battle. On July 1, skirmishing began west of the town and by evening had developed into a major engagement. After being forced back through the town, George Meade's troops established themselves along a series of hills and ridges south of Gettysburg. The next day the Confederates' attack on Culp's Hill failed, but on their right they drove Daniel Sickles's corps from its advanced position near the Emmitsburg Road. During the day's inconclusive fighting Meade's army secured a strong defensive position. Lee chose to renew the offensive on the 3rd and launched a major attack, which Union forces on Cemetery Ridge severely repulsed. On the night of July 4, the Confederate army began to withdraw south.

Five correspondents represented the *Tribune* at Gettysburg. A. Homer Byington directed the *Tribune*'s coverage and probably prepared the map, which several Union generals allegedly examined for mistakes. It depicts the situation on the final day of battle and gives a sense of Meade's formidable position. Round Top—on the map mistakenly called Sugar Loaf Mountain and actually farther from Gettysburg than shown—anchored the Union left. The center followed the crest of Cemetery Ridge, and the right extended across Cemetery Hill, southeast across Culp's Hill (shown only as location of the Twelfth Corps), to just beyond Rock Creek (the last portion of the Union right is not shown). Other than the Sixth Corps, forming the extreme left flank, which was southeast of Round Top rather than on it, Union units are correctly placed in relation to one another. Cavalry covered the Union left flank and operated nearly a mile away on the right, shown too close to the main position. The Confederate line continued as far south as Round Top, through the town, and across Rock Creek. The map only suggests the hilly terrain of the battlefield, and shortens the distance between Cemetery Hill and Round Top. Willoughby Run, mislabeled "Marsh Creek," should join Marsh Creek, mislabeled "Middle Creek," west and slightly south of Round Top.

Reports in U.S. War Department, *War of the Rebellion*: ser. 1, vol. 27, pts. 1, 2, with fourteen maps.
Maps in U.S. War Department, *Atlas*: pl. 28, no. 4; pl. 40, no. 2; pl. 43, nos. 1, 2; pl. 73, no. 6; pl. 95, nos. 1, 2.
Other newspaper maps: *Boston Daily Journal* (7/7/63), *Cincinnati Daily Gazette* (7/8/63), *New York Herald* (7/6/63), *Philadelphia Inquirer* (7/4/63).

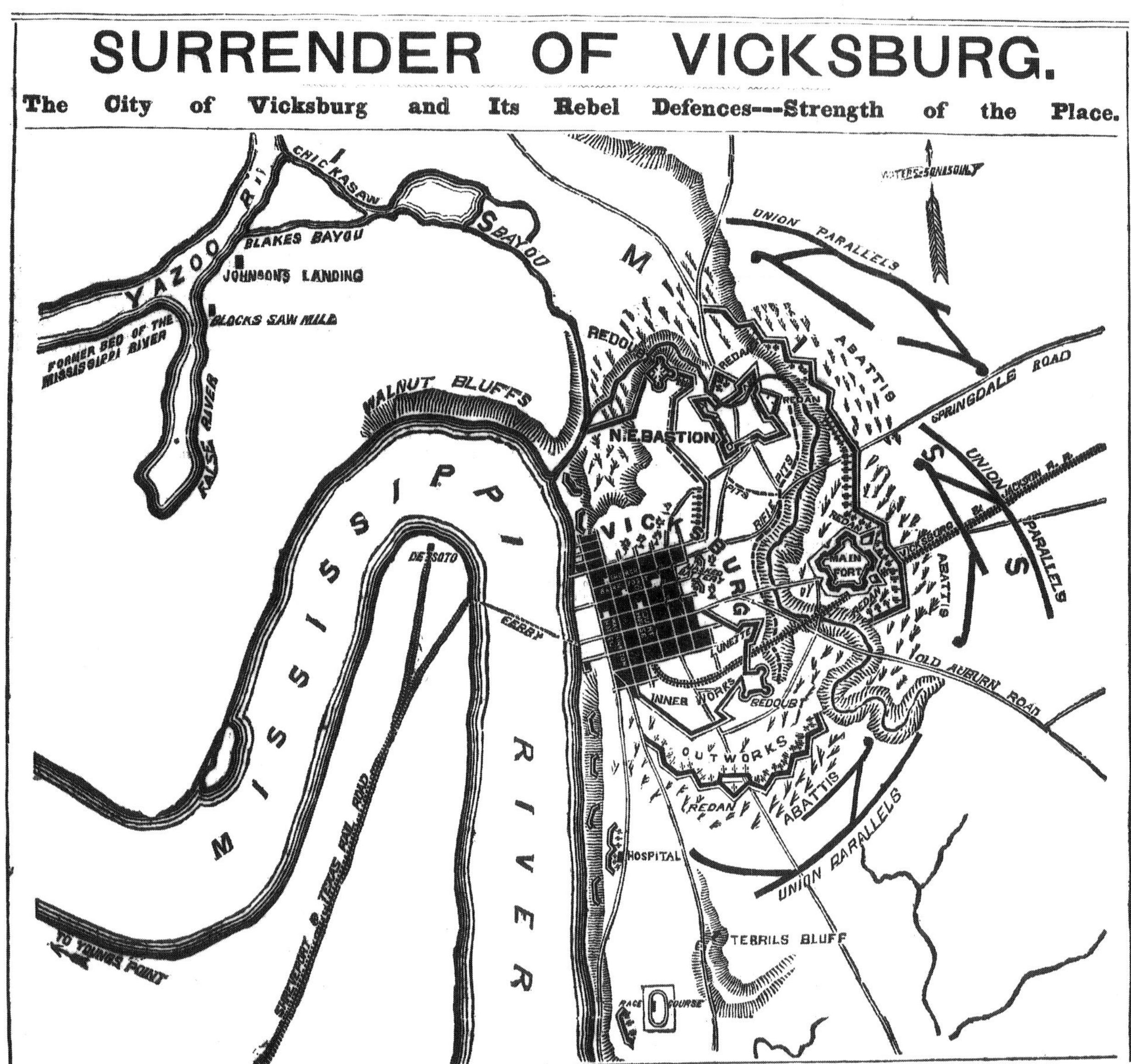
SURRENDER OF VICKSBURG.

The City of Vicksburg and Its Rebel Defences---Strength of the Place.

MAP 30

The Siege of Vicksburg, Mississippi

Published in the *New York Herald*, July 8, 1863

(Original 22 × 24 cm.)

IN A SERIES OF QUICK VICTORIES, ULYSSES S. GRANT'S ARMY DISPERSED CONFEDERATE troops attempting to relieve Vicksburg and drove the remnants of John Pemberton's garrison back into the city's defenses. Hoping to avoid a protracted siege and thinking Pemberton's forces spent, Grant moved against the Confederate left on May 19. Although this movement was strongly repulsed, Grant prepared to assault the entire Vicksburg position. Three days later artillery pounded the Confederate fortifications, but the second attack met with equally disastrous results. On May 25, Grant reluctantly began siege operations and entirely isolated the city. Union forces encircled Vicksburg and occupied positions opposite it in Louisiana, while the Union fleet controlled the river. Union engineers excavated and exploded tunnels under the city's defenses, but the line could not be breached. For six weeks the city endured a systematic bombardment. On July 4, with his army and the city's populace reduced by starvation, Pemberton surrendered Vicksburg.

The map provides little information on the Union situation during the siege but does depict a number of the defensive positions. The "main fort" was also known as the railroad redoubt, and the structure labeled "N. E. bastion" probably represents the stockade fort or redan. Confederate lines continued farther south (north is to the upper left, not where indicated), along the river beyond the race course, with the Union lines mirroring them. Union lines on the north actually reached the river. To extend their lines closer to the Vicksburg defenses, Union engineers dug a maze of tunnels and trenches ("Union parallels") that zigzagged in order to avoid direct enemy fire. Just upstream of the city, the Walnut Bluffs (actually called both Walnut Hills and Chickasaw Bluffs) were part of a ridge tending to the northeast on the Vicksburg side of Chickasaw Bayou, at the top of the map. Neither the Shreveport & Texas Railroad, which terminated at the previously destroyed village of DeSoto (directly across river from Vicksburg), nor the ferry across the Mississippi operated during the siege.

Reports in the U.S. War Department, *War of the Rebellion*: ser. 1, vol. 24, pt. 2, with two maps of the siege.
Maps in U.S. War Department, *Atlas*: pl. 36, no. 2.
Other newspaper maps: *Chicago Daily Tribune* (6/19/63), *Chicago Evening Journal* (6/18/63), *New York Herald* (6/27 and 7/15/63), *New York Times* (7/8/63), *New York Tribune* (7/8/63), *Philadelphia Inquirer* (7/8/63).

THE BATTLES AT CHATTANOOGA.

The Relative Position of the Union and Rebel Forces on the Second Day.

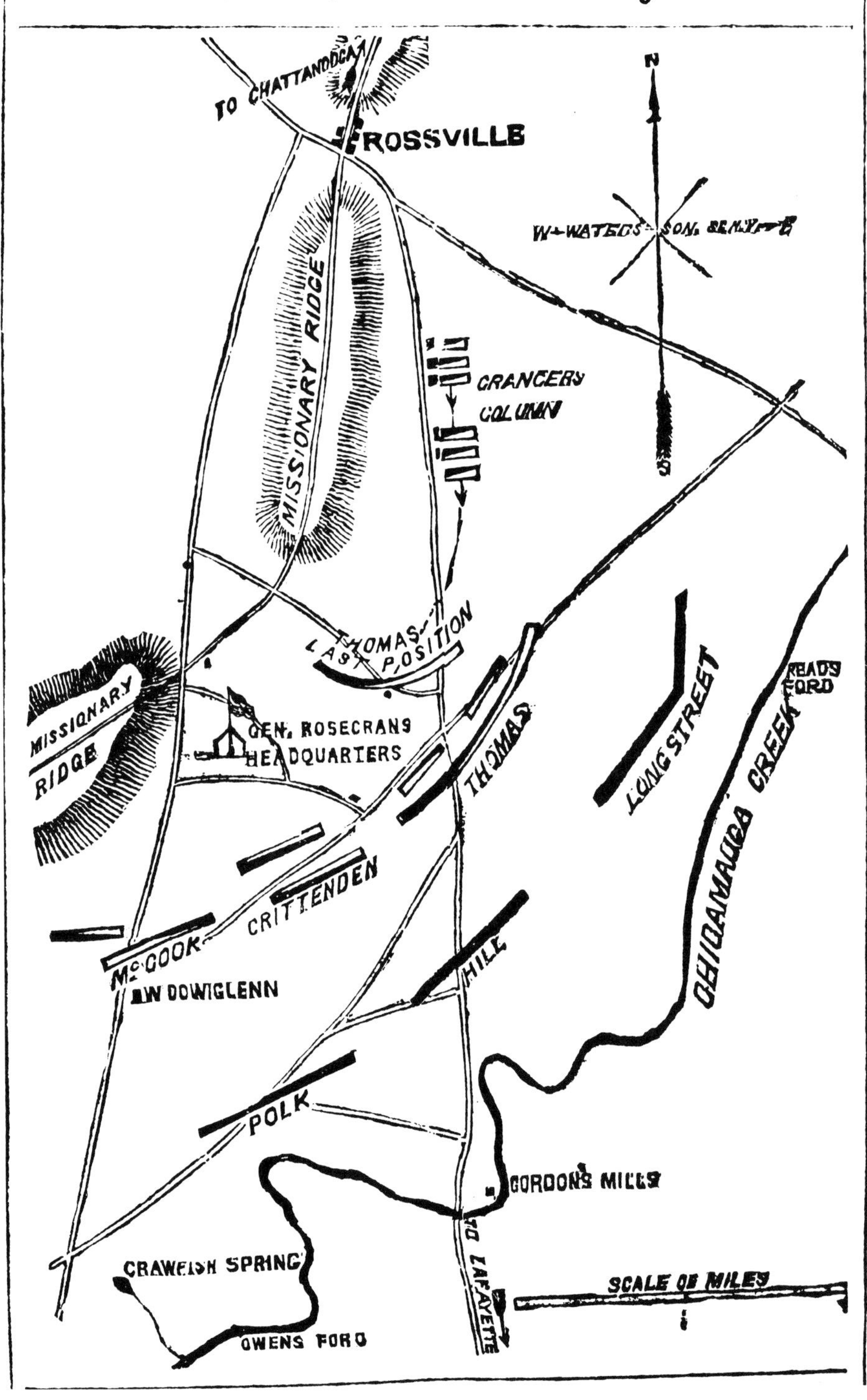

MAP 31

The Battle of Chickamauga, Georgia

Published in the *New York Herald*, September 27, 1863

(Original 19 × 12 cm.)

AFTER MANEUVERING BRAXTON BRAGG'S ARMY OUT OF CHATTANOOGA, WILLIAM Rosecrans's Union troops advanced into Georgia. This movement accomplished little, and Rosecrans decided to withdraw to his base in Chattanooga. As the scattered Union corps retired north along Chickamauga Creek, Bragg tried to trap and destroy them. Skirmishing occurred on September 18, but Union forces managed to concentrate and prevent Bragg from blocking their route to Chattanooga. The heavily forested terrain prevented either commander from recognizing the other's dispositions, and a major battle began on the 19th as the two armies collided. More and more troops became engaged, but with no clear advantage to either side. The next morning, Confederates pressed the Union left and Rosecrans shifted troops in response. This mistakenly opened a gap in the line, which Confederates poured through, causing the Union right to collapse and flee. Union general George Thomas held his position, however, and with reinforcements from Gordon Granger's corps survived repeated attacks. That night Thomas withdrew the remainder of his forces north to Rossville.

William Shanks covered the battle for the *Herald* and most likely drew the map. It depicts the situation on the morning of the 20th but also indicates positions later in the day after the rout of the Union right. Initially the Union line stretched from the Widow Glenn's north of Crawfish Springs (the actual location of Rosecrans's headquarters) to the intersection of the Lafayette Road and McFarland's Gap Road ("Thomas last position"). The Union line consisted of the corps of Edward McCook, Thomas Crittenden, and George Thomas, arranged as indicated. Opposing them, James Longstreet's troops formed the Confederate left and Leonidas Polk's formed the right (positions reversed on map). At the time of the battle, Bragg's army had been reorganized into these two wings, but Shanks also noted the position of D. H. Hill, a corps commander under Polk. Thomas's second line, reinforced from the north by Granger, formed more of an angle, with its flanks bent back to the northwest. The map fails to depict the forest cover and rugged terrain of the battlefield but includes other major topographical features.

Reports in U.S. War Department, *War of the Rebellion*: ser. 1, vol. 30, pts. 1, 2, with twenty maps.
Maps in U.S. War Department, *Atlas*: pl. 30, no. 6; pl. 46, nos. 1, 2, 4; pl. 47, nos. 2, 3, 7; pl. 96, no. 4; pl. 97, no. 3; pl. 98, no. 2; pl. 101, no. 20; pl. 111, no. 9.
Other newspaper maps: *Cincinnati Daily Commercial* (9/28/63), *Cincinnati Daily Gazette* (9/25/63), *Cincinnati Daily Times* (9/25/63), *Philadelphia Inquirer* (9/23/63).

THE VICTORY AT BRISTOE.

Map of the Battle Field of Broad Run, or Bristoe, October 14, 1863, Drawn on the Spot by Mr. F. G. Chapman.

MAP 32

The Battle of Bristoe Station, Virginia

Published in the *New York Herald*, October 19, 1863

(Original 17 × 24 cm.)

AFTER ITS DEFEAT AT GETTYSBURG, ROBERT E. LEE'S ARMY OF NORTHERN VIRGINIA retreated to a position south of the Rapidan River, slowly pursued by the Army of the Potomac. Lee remained on the defensive for the rest of the summer, but early in October Confederate forces crossed the Rapidan on a flanking movement. To prevent Lee from cutting his lines of communication, George Meade withdrew his army northward. On October 14, Confederates made contact with the rear guard of the Union column as it forded Broad Run near Bristoe Station. A. P. Hill's division hastily formed to attack the Union Third Corps, which was attempting to cross the stream. As Hill's troops approached the stream, they were fired upon by G. K. Warren's Second Corps, deployed in a line of battle along a railroad embankment. Not realizing the strength of the Union position, the Confederates turned to meet the threat on their flank and tried to carry the line by direct assault, but they were driven off with high casualties.

Frank Chapman, the senior *Herald* correspondent in Virginia, produced a highly accurate map of this engagement. Hill's route, marked "road by which Lee came in," and his first and second lines of battle are clearly marked. The left consisted of the Twenty-sixth and Twenty-seventh (labeled the Twenty-eighth) North Carolina regiments. These troops of Henry Heth's brigade sustained the highest casualties of the battle. Union divisions of John Caldwell ("Caudwell" on the map), Alexander Hays ("Hayes"), and Alexander Webb deployed behind the railroad from left to right. Batteries commanded by Bruce Ricketts and William Arnold operated from behind the Union line. T. Frederick Brown's battery, shown on both sides of the stream, fired a few rounds from behind the embankment just before the attack then crossed to the north, where it was unsupported. After repulsing the Confederate attack, Hays's troops advanced and captured a battery of five guns, as indicated. The map accurately portrays the topography of the battlefield but errs in identifying Kettle Run as Cedar Run and in placing it too close to Broad Run.

Reports in U.S. War Department, *War of the Rebellion*: ser. 1, vol. 29, pt. 1, with two maps of the campaign.
Maps in U.S. War Department, *Atlas*: pl. 45, no. 7.
Other newspaper maps: None.

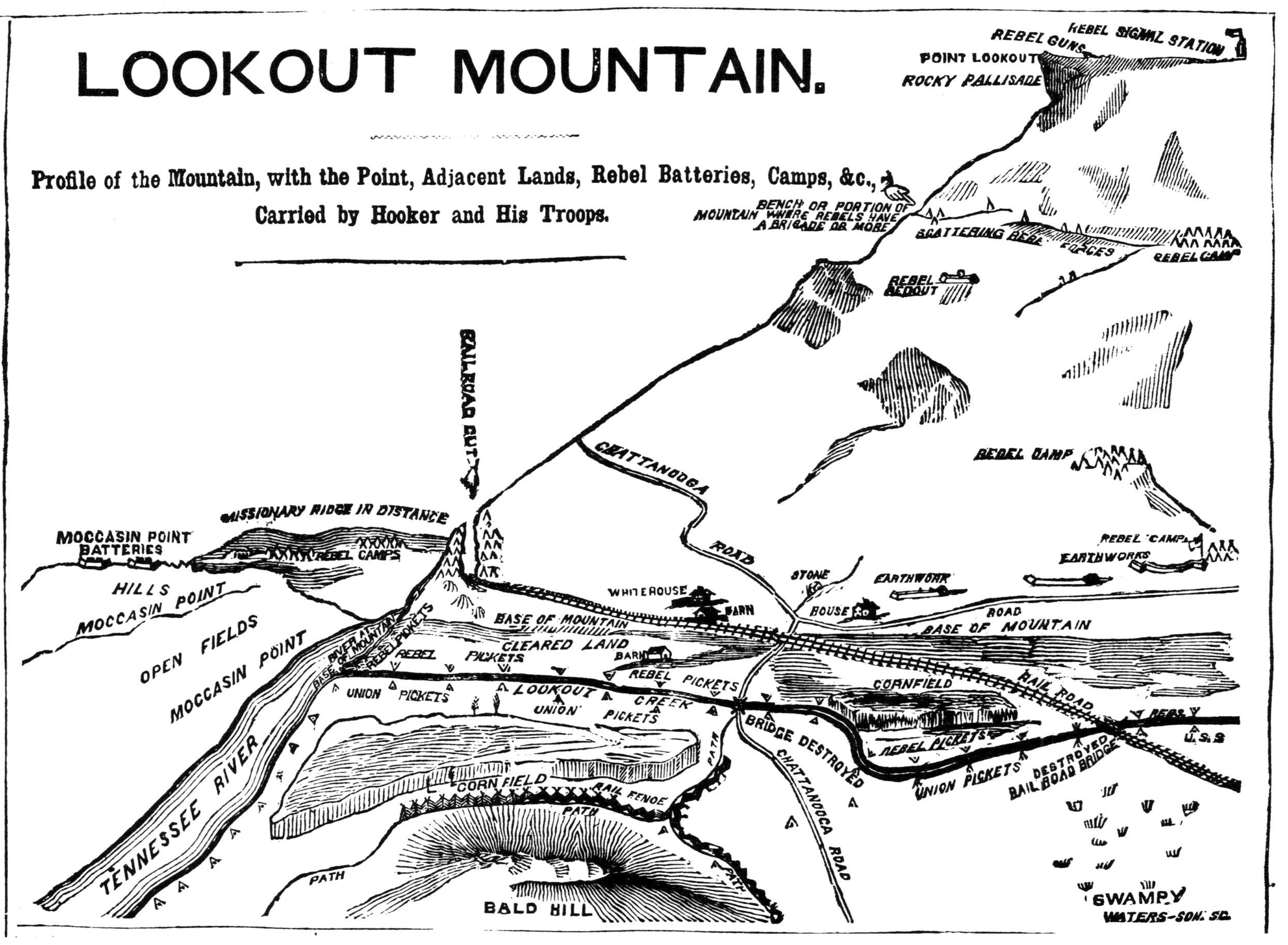
LOOKOUT MOUNTAIN.
Profile of the Mountain, with the Point, Adjacent Lands, Rebel Batteries, Camps, &c., Carried by Hooker and His Troops.
REBEL SIGNAL STATION
REBEL GUNS
POINT LOOKOUT
ROCKY PALLISADE
BENCH OR PORTION OF MOUNTAIN WHERE REBELS HAVE A BRIGADE OR MORE
SCATTERING REBEL FORCES
REBEL CAMP
REBEL REDOUT
RAILROAD CUT
REBEL CAMP
REBEL CAMP
EARTHWORKS
MISSIONARY RIDGE IN DISTANCE
MOCCASIN POINT BATTERIES
REBEL CAMPS
HILLS
MOCCASIN POINT
OPEN FIELDS
MOCCASIN POINT
CHATTANOOGA
ROAD
STONE
EARTHWORK
WHITEHOUSE
BARN
HOUSE
ROAD
BASE OF MOUNTAIN
BASE OF MOUNTAIN
CLEARED LAND
REBEL PICKETS
BARN
REBEL PICKETS
UNION PICKETS
LOOKOUT CREEK
UNION PICKETS
CORNFIELD
RAIL ROAD
REBS
U.S.S
BRIDGE DESTROYED
REBEL PICKETS
UNION PICKETS
DESTROYED RAIL ROAD BRIDGE
CHATTANOOGA ROAD
PATH
CORN FIELD
RAIL FENCE
PATH
TENNESSEE RIVER
PATH
BALD HILL
PATH
SWAMPY
WATERS-SON. SC.

MAP 33

The Battle of Lookout Mountain, Tennessee

Published in the *New York Herald*, November 28, 1863

(Original 18 × 24 cm.)

HAVING BEEN DRIVEN FROM THE FIELD AT CHICKAMAUGA, THE UNION ARMY TOOK refuge in Chattanooga. Braxton Bragg's army quickly occupied the undefended heights south and east of the city and began limited siege operations. At the end of October Ulysses S. Grant assumed command in Chattanooga. Union reinforcements eventually secured tenuous supply lines then made preparations for an offensive. On the morning of November 24, the Confederate left, anchored on Lookout Mountain, came under attack. Three divisions commanded by Joseph Hooker crossed Lookout Creek at the base of the mountain and drove back Confederate pickets. Heavy skirmishing took place near Craven's Farm where the defenders, outnumbered four to one, slowly gave way, moving up the slope to another position. With reinforcements from the summit, Confederates under Carter Stevenson held Lookout Mountain until midnight, when they were ordered to join the rest of Bragg's army on Missionary Ridge.

The *Herald*'s correspondent, Sylvanus Cadwallader, accompanied Hooker at Lookout Mountain and probably sketched this bird's-eye-view. Missionary Ridge and the "Rebel camps" sit on the horizon (east). Bald Hill is in the foreground and the battlefield in the middle ground. The profile of Lookout Mountain, rising 1,100 feet above the Tennessee River, looms over the battlefield, which is drawn in perspective. The river appears to swing around the base of Lookout Mountain from the right, but in reality it originates north of Moccasin Point, loops around the point, then flows north, away from Lookout Mountain. On either side of Lookout Creek the Union and Confederate picket lines are indicated. The majority of Hooker's forces crossed near the destroyed bridge on the Chattanooga Road and drove Confederate pickets from their rifle pits and from the railroad embankment. The most severe fighting took place near Craven's Farm ("White House"), farther up the slope. The map mistakenly places the White House too close to the railroad and on the wrong side of the road. A number of Confederate positions are shown, but no indication of troops appears in the contested areas above the railroad cut.

Reports in U.S. War Department, *War of the Rebellion*: ser. 1, vol. 31, pt. 2.
Maps in U.S. War Department, *Atlas*: pl. 50, no. 4.
Other newspaper maps: None.

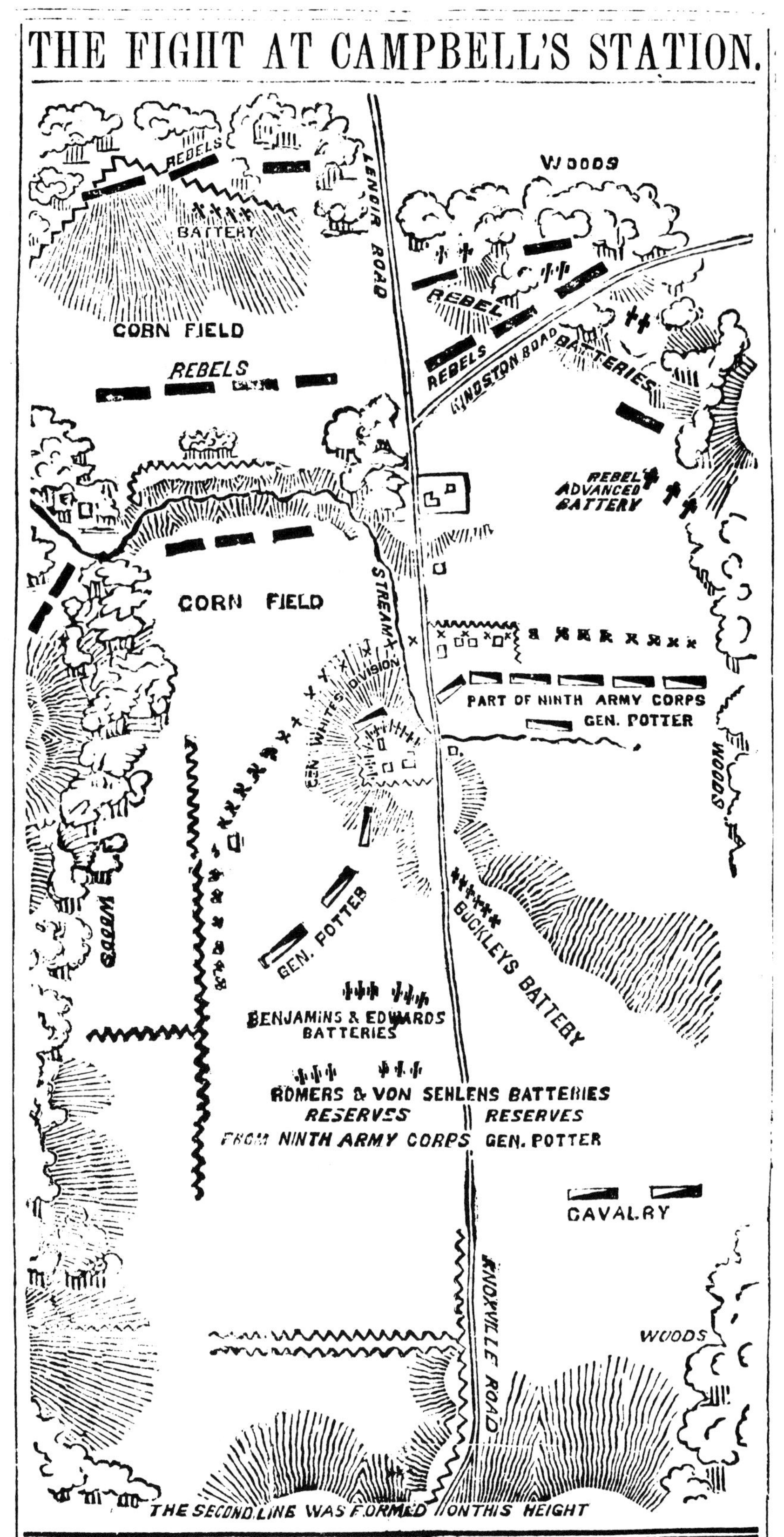
THE FIGHT AT CAMPBELL'S STATION.
REBELS
BATTERY
CORN FIELD
REBELS
LENOIR ROAD
WOODS
REBEL
REBELS
KINGSTON ROAD
BATTERIES
REBEL ADVANCED BATTERY
CORN FIELD
STREAM
GEN. WHITE'S DIVISION
PART OF NINTH ARMY CORPS
GEN. POTTER
WOODS
WOODS
GEN. POTTER
BUCKLEYS BATTERY
BENJAMINS & EDWARDS BATTERIES
ROMERS & VON SEHLENS BATTERIES
RESERVES
RESERVES
FROM NINTH ARMY CORPS
GEN. POTTER
CAVALRY
KNOXVILLE ROAD
WOODS
THE SECOND LINE WAS FORMED ON THIS HEIGHT

MAP 34

The Battle of Campbell's Station, Tennessee

Published in the *New York Tribune*, December 7, 1863

(Original 23 × 12 cm.)

LATE IN OCTOBER, CONFEDERATE OPERATIONS IN THE HOLSTON VALLEY CAUSED Ambrose Burnside to retract his lines toward Knoxville. On November 16, James Longstreet's troops attempted to reach Campbell's Station ahead of Burnside's column, to block the route north. The initial skirmishing occurred near the intersection of the Lenoir and Kingston roads, where the first of the pursuing Confederates attacked Burnside's rear guard. Once past the intersection, three Union divisions with artillery support were quickly deployed in a defensive line across the Knoxville Road. Longstreet ordered a wide flanking march, to get behind the Union left, while at the same time engaging the right. A conflict between subordinates caused a delay, however, and before his troops could execute the maneuver, Union forces retired to a stronger line along the crest of a hill to the rear. The engagement drew to a close as night fell. Burnside's column continued its withdrawal and safely reached Knoxville the next day.

The map's orientation reflects the position of the *Tribune*'s correspondent, Elias Smith, who witnessed the fighting from the Union rear, facing southwest (top of map). The important intersection of the Lenoir and Kingston roads, called Campbell's Station, appears near the top of the map, but no indication is made of the earlier skirmish to hold the intersection. Confederates approached in two columns, taking up positions on either side of the Knoxville Road. Julius White's division occupied the center of the Union line with troops of Robert Potter's corps (divisions of Edward Ferrero and John Hartranft) on the two flanks. The line essentially stretched across the narrow valley, perpendicular to the road. Smith may have depicted the Union left at an angle to indicate the Confederate movement against that flank and the subsequent withdrawal. The batteries of William Buckley, John von Sehelen, Samuel Benjamin, and Erskine Gittings (the last not shown) at first operated on the Union right, with Jacob Roemer to the left. It should be noted, however, that the batteries moved a number of times during the action. A note at the bottom of the map ("the second line") marks the Union position at the end of the engagement.

Reports in U.S. War Department, *War of the Rebellion*: ser. 1, vol. 31, pt. 1.
Maps in U.S. War Department, *Atlas*: None.
Other newspaper maps: None.

SCENE OF THE RECENT AND COMING BATTLES.

Typographical Map showing the Scene of the Great Battles of Thursday and Friday, with the Rebel Defenses on the Route to Richmond.

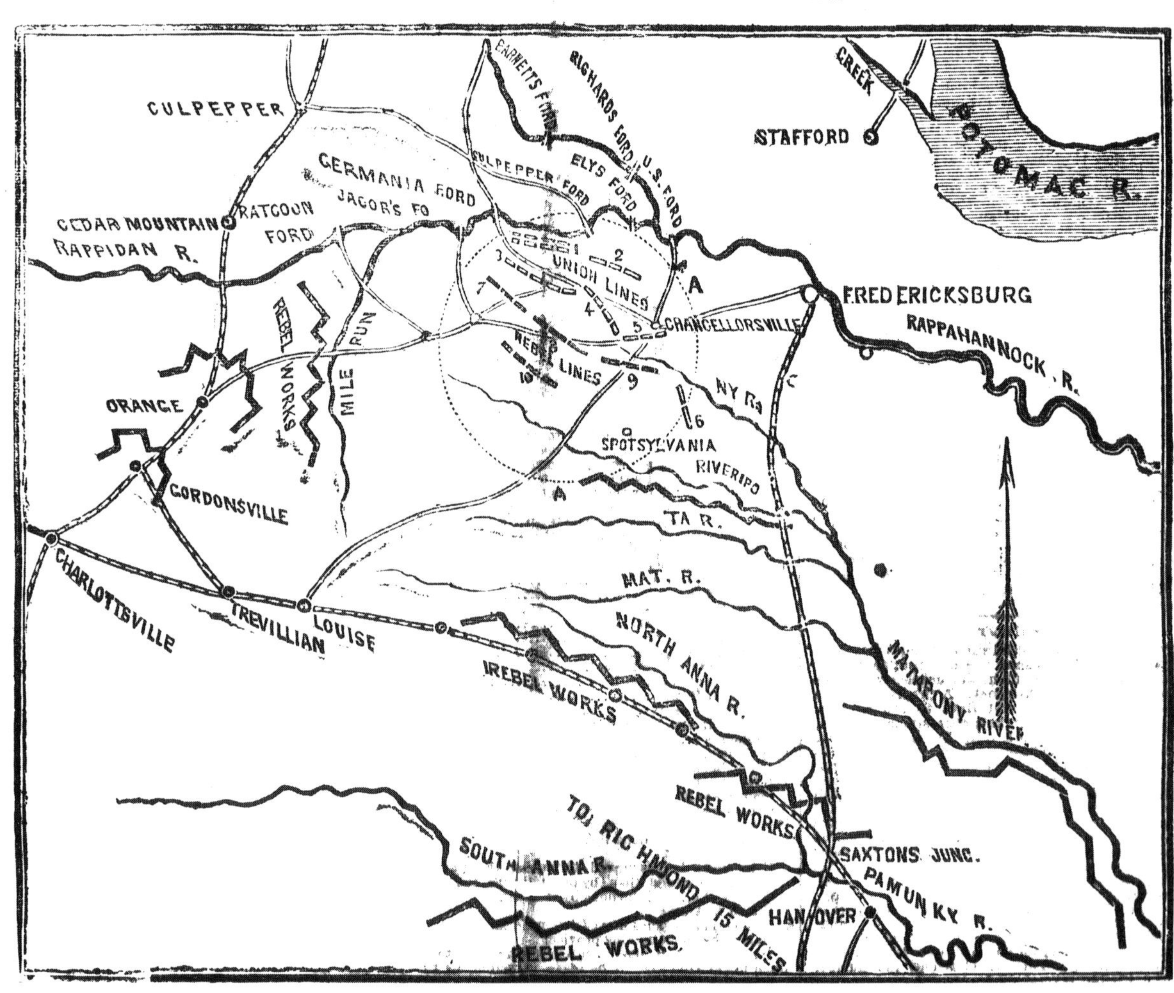

MAP 35

The Battle of the Wilderness, in Virginia

Published in the *World*, May 10, 1864

(Original 15 × 18 cm.)

ULYSSES S. GRANT'S SPRING CAMPAIGN BEGAN WITH A MOVE TOWARDS RICHMOND TO confront Lee's army. In May, Union forces crossed the Rapidan River into a densely wooded area known as the Wilderness. The difficult terrain slowed the Union columns and gave Lee an opportunity to assume the offensive. On the morning of May 5, his troops encountered the Union right wing and the battle began. Largely because of limitations imposed by the nature of the battlefield, only portions of each army engaged in the first day's fighting. As more troops entered into the battle the opposing lines shifted, but without clear advantage. Fighting continued the next day and extended farther to the southeast. Just as the Confederate right appeared to crumble, James Longstreet's corps arrived. Longstreet's flank attack hurled back the Union line, nearly breaking it. Although vastly outnumbered, Lee's army inflicted heavy casualties while holding its ground until maneuvered out of the Wilderness on May 7.

Like the battle itself, the *World*'s map exhibits a certain degree of confusion. A dotted line labeled *A* encircles the battlefield of May 5 and 6. Important fords on the Rappahannock and Rapidan are indicated, along with some of the Wilderness roads. West of Chancellorsville the Union lines roughly paralleled the Germanna Plank Road, as shown. Winfield S. Hancock's corps (*5*) comprised the Union left, John Sedgwick's corps (*2*) the right, and G. K. Warren's corps (*3*) the center. The latter two are out of place and Ambrose Burnside's corps (*1*), also in the center, appears in the position it initially held, on the 5th. George Getty's division (*4*) became attached to Hancock's troops. Union cavalry under Phil Sheridan (*6*) saw limited action, but they did skirmish with J. E. B. ("Jeb") Stuart's cavalry at Todd's Tavern (not shown), southeast of the battlefield on the 6th. Richard Ewell's corps (*10*, incorrectly shown in reserve) formed the Confederate left. The map notes Robert Rodes's division (*8*), one of three under Ewell's command, in the center. A. P. Hill (*9*) and Longstreet (*7*, misplaced) formed the right of Lee's line.

Reports in U.S. War Department, *War of the Rebellion*: ser. 1, vol. 36, pts. 1, 2, with eight maps.
Maps in U.S. War Department, *Atlas*: pl. 55, no. 1; pl. 83, nos. 1, 2; pl. 94, no. 6.
Other newspaper maps: *New York Herald* (5/11/64).

GENERAL BUTLER'S OPERATIONS

The Rebel Defences at Drury's Bluff--·The Position of the Union Forces.

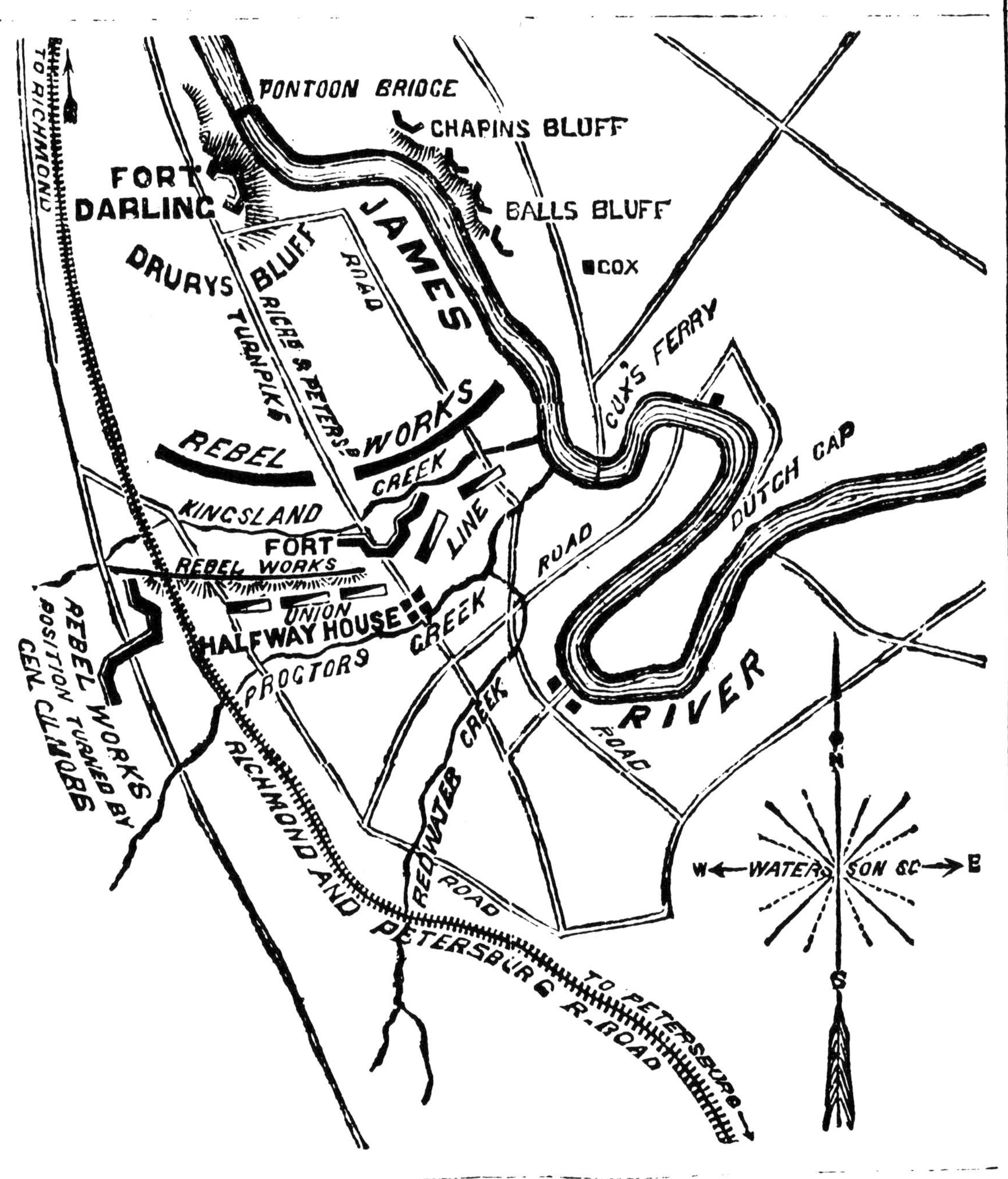

MAP 36

The Battle of Drewry's Bluff, Virginia

Published in the *New York Herald*, May 19, 1864

(Original 13 × 12 cm.)

AS PART OF THE JOINT OPERATIONS AGAINST RICHMOND, BENJAMIN BUTLER'S ARMY of the James moved south of the James River and constructed a defensive line in the vicinity of Bermuda Hundred. Butler conducted several raids and reconnaissances in early May before moving in force against Drewry's (sometimes Drury's) Bluff. On May 13 and 14, heavy skirmishing drove Confederate troops from the outer works into the main defenses. Butler, however, failed to follow up on this success. Pierre Beauregard assumed command at Drewry's Bluff and, with reinforcements from Petersburg, seized the initiative. Beauregard believed that he could destroy Butler's army by cutting it off from Bermuda Hundred. Early in the morning of May 16, Confederate forces pushed back Butler's right and nearly succeeded in turning it, while gaining some ground on the Union left and center. To protect his flank Butler retired to the Bermuda Hundred entrenchments, closely followed by Beauregard, who effectively contained the Union army there.

Charles Hannam, the *Herald* correspondent attached to Butler's army, may have supplied details for the map. It illustrates the situation on or about May 15, just before Beauregard's attack. By then Union forces had occupied about two miles of the abandoned outer line of Confederate works north of Proctor's Creek. Fortifications on Wooldridge Hill ("position turned by Gen. Gilmore") are correctly shown just west of the railroad. Quincy Gillmore's corps secured this position, after heavy skirmishing on the 13th drove out the Confederate defenders. William F. Smith's corps (not designated) formed the Union right. The map depicts a limited amount of the engagement but provides a good overview of the battlefield and troop locations. It includes many of the area's roads and streams but places Kingsland Creek too far south. Proctor's Creek and a ridge along it formed a natural defensive line and was used as such by Union troops falling back before the Confederate attack. The final Union line passed in front of the Halfway House on the Richmond and Petersburg Turnpike.

Reports in U.S. War Department, *War of the Rebellion*: ser. 1, vol. 36, pt. 2.
Maps in U.S. War Department, *Atlas*: None.
Other newspaper maps: *Philadelphia Inquirer* (5/20/64).

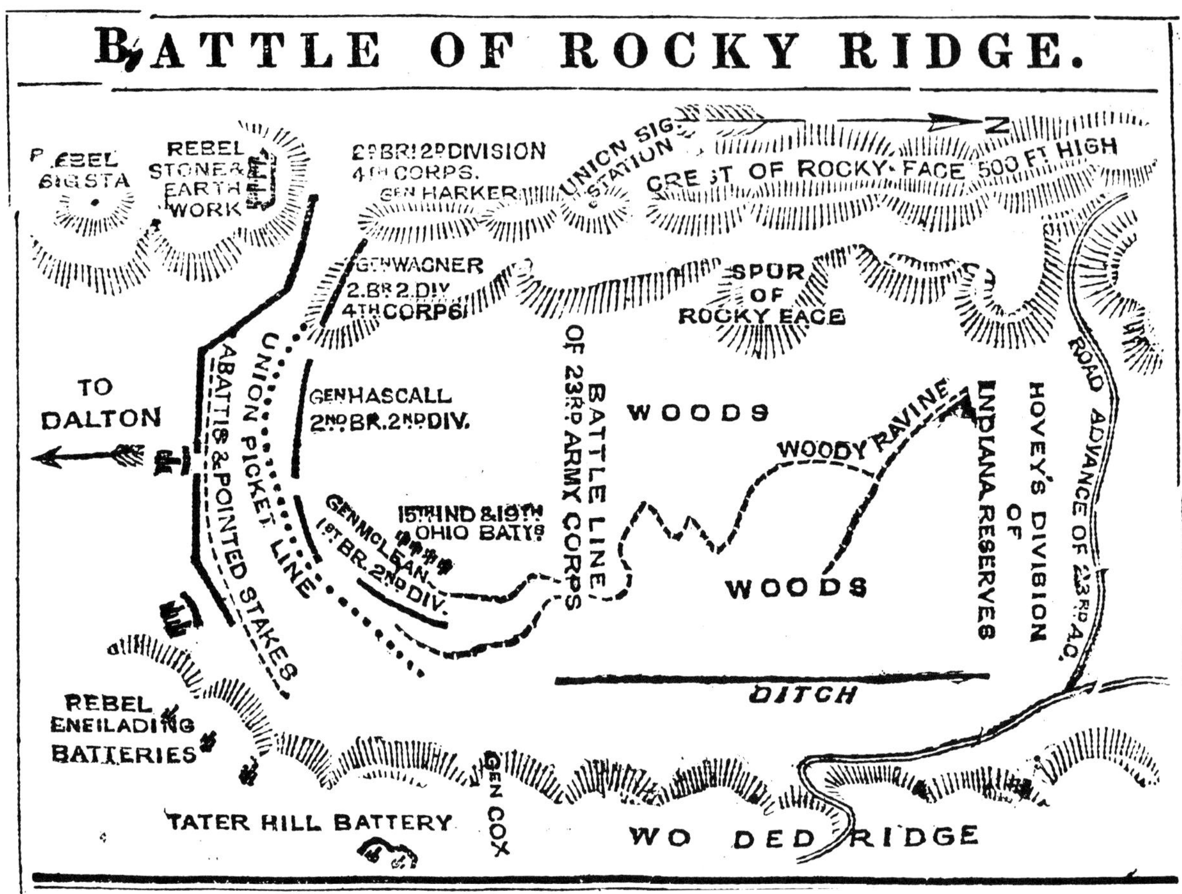
BATTLE OF ROCKY RIDGE.
REBEL STONE & EARTH WORK
2ND BR. 2ND DIVISION 4TH CORPS.
GEN HARKER
UNION SIG. STATION
CREST OF ROCKY FACE 500 FT HIGH
GEN WAGNER 2. BR 2. DIV 4TH CORPS
SPUR OF ROCKY FACE
TO DALTON
ABATTIS & POINTED STAKES
UNION PICKET LINE
GEN HASCALL 2ND BR. 2ND DIV.
BATTLE LINE OF 23RD ARMY CORPS
WOODS
WOODY RAVINE
15TH IND & 19TH OHIO BATYS
GEN MCLEAN 1ST BR. 2ND DIV.
WOODS
INDIANA RESERVES
HOVEY'S DIVISION OF
ROAD ADVANCE OF 23RD A.C.
DITCH
REBEL ENFILADING BATTERIES
TATER HILL BATTERY
GEN COX
WO DED RIDGE

MAP 37

The Battle of Rocky Face Ridge, Georgia

Published in the *New York Tribune*, May 20, 1864

(Original 10 × 12 cm.)

THIS BATTLE, THE INITIAL ACTION OF THE ATLANTA CAMPAIGN, OCCURRED OVER THE course of five days and encompassed a number of engagements. In order to protect an important railroad junction near Dalton, Joseph E. Johnston's Confederate army constructed strong defensive works on Rocky Face Ridge to the north and west of the town. William T. Sherman's forces advanced against this line in several locations. On May 9, troops of the Army of the Cumberland under Charles Harker and George Wagner moved south along the summit of the ridge to dislodge entrenched Confederates, striking the divisions of Benjamin Cheatham and Carter Stevenson. Troops of the Army of the Ohio moved south through the Crow Valley in a supporting demonstration. Several attacks tested this section of the Confederate line, and all met with repulse. Two days later, realizing that continuing the engagement would be futile, Sherman ordered his army to march around Johnston in a flanking movement.

Elias Smith, the *Tribune*'s correspondent and the apparent author of this map, observed the fighting from Rocky Face Ridge and stated that the country stretched before him like a map. Oriented with north to the right, the map portrays the Union probe along the northern wing of the extensive Confederate position. Johnston's defensive line ("abattis and pointed stakes," *left*) continued at a right angle along Rocky Face Ridge in the direction of Dalton. At the top of the map the brigades of Harker and Wagner (Army of the Cumberland), the Union signal station established on May 8, and the Confederate defenses are shown. Twenty-third Army Corps (Army of the Ohio) brigades of Milo Hascall and Nathaniel McClean, and Alvin Hovey's division (*right*) operated in the Crow Valley (not labeled). The map gives the impression that the major action took place in the valley, but the battle was largely restricted to the ridge top, a fact recorded by Smith in his account. Smith, however, errs in marking what appears to be a gap between the opposing forces on the ridge.

Reports in U.S. War Department, *War of the Rebellion*: ser. 1, vol. 38, pt. 4.
Maps in U.S. War Department, *Atlas*: pl. 55, no. 6.
Other newspaper maps: None.

SHERMAN'S FLANK MOVEMENT.

The Route Taken by the Commander of the Union Army in the Southwest to Outflank Atlanta— Why Hood Had to Leave His Defences, &c.

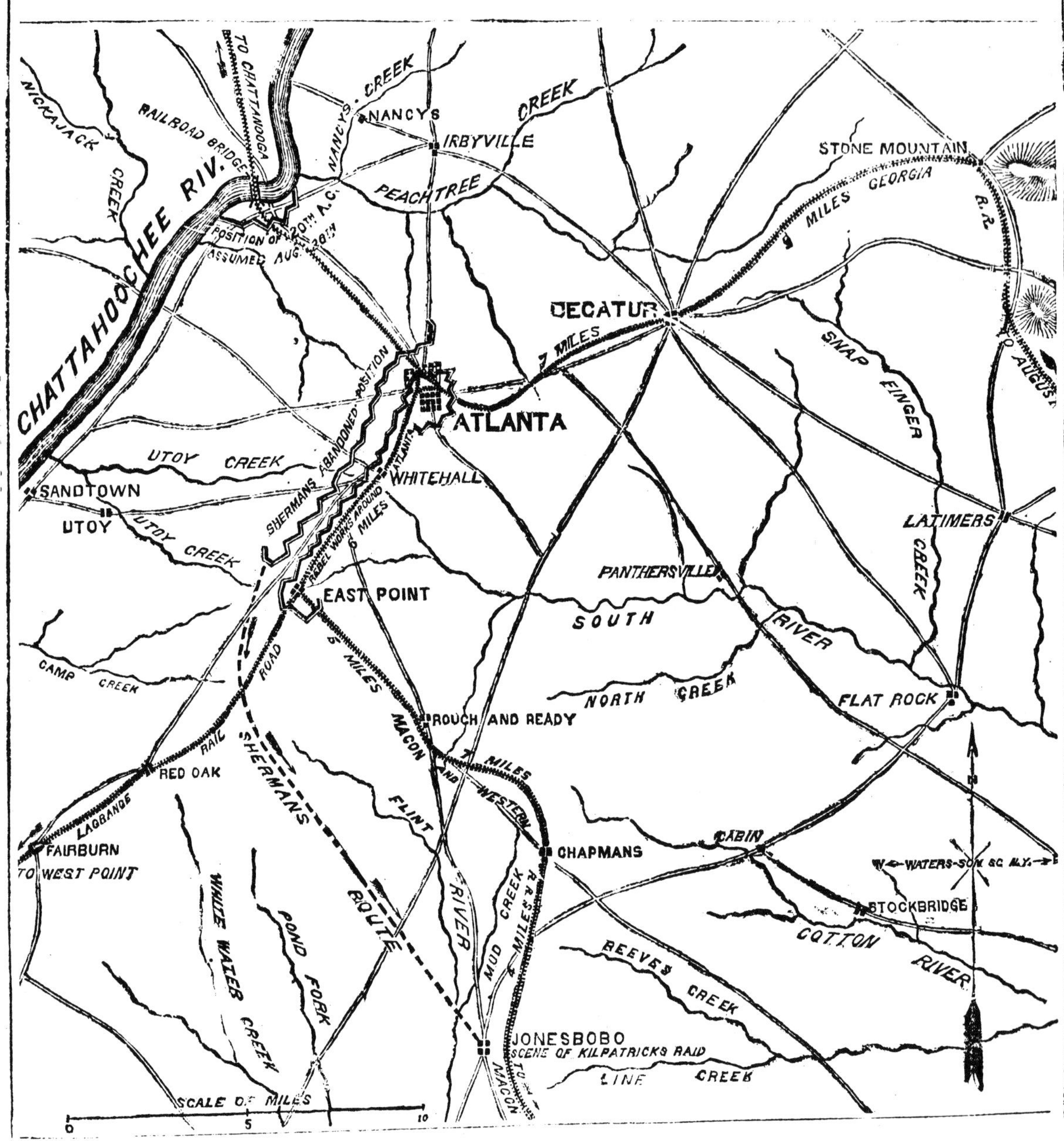

MAP 38

The Campaign around Atlanta, Georgia

Published in the *New York Herald*, September 4, 1864

(Original 24 × 24 cm.)

IN A SERIES OF MANEUVERS AND BATTLES DURING THE SPRING AND SUMMER OF 1864, William T. Sherman's army steadily progressed toward Atlanta. After Joseph E. Johnston failed to halt Sherman's progress, John B. Hood replaced him as overall Confederate commander. On July 20, the aggressive Hood attacked the Union army as it crossed Peach Tree Creek, but the Confederates suffered heavy losses and withdrew into the defenses of Atlanta. Two days later Hood struck the Union left flank but was again repulsed, in the Battle of Atlanta. Sherman established a strong U-shaped line around the city from the north. During August he shifted his lines southwest to cut the railroad. Hood countered these moves by extending his left and blocking Union advances at Ezra Church and Utoy Creek. On August 26, Sherman mobilized his army and finally turned Hood's flank by getting to Jonesboro first and driving off a Confederate attack. With the railroad severed, Hood had to evacuate Atlanta. Union troops occupied the city on September 1.

The lack of cartographic coverage of the Atlanta campaign resulted largely from Sherman's ban on correspondents and his restrictions on what news was admissible. Few detailed newspaper maps of the various engagements exist. The *Herald*'s map accurately depicts the position of roads, railroads, towns, and rivers but only vaguely represents military information. Confederate lines are shown stretching from Atlanta to East Point; they actually continued, parallel to the Macon & Western Railroad, to the vicinity of Rough and Ready. The flanking movement marked "Sherman's route" represents the general operations of the Union army, but in fact three separate columns moved against Hood's line, severing his railroad connections several places between Rough and Ready and Jonesboro. At the bottom of the map is noted Hugh Kilpatrick's cavalry raid (August 18–22) against Hood's line of communications, but there is no indication of Hood's attempt to recover Jonesboro. To the north, the Twentieth Corps's position south of the Chattahoochee River should read July, not August, 26th.

Reports in U.S. War Department, *War of the Rebellion*: ser. 1, vol. 38, pts. 1–3, with eleven maps.
Maps in U.S. War Department, *Atlas*: pl. 56, no. 7; pl. 59, no. 7; pl. 61, no. 15; pl. 62, no. 9; pl. 87, no. 6; pl. 88, no. 1.
Other newspaper maps: *Cincinnati Daily Times* (9/3/64), *New York Tribune* (9/19/64), *Philadelphia Inquirer* (9/6/64).

THE BATTLE OF FRANKLIN.

Scene of the Signal Repulse of Hood's Army on the 30th Ultimo.

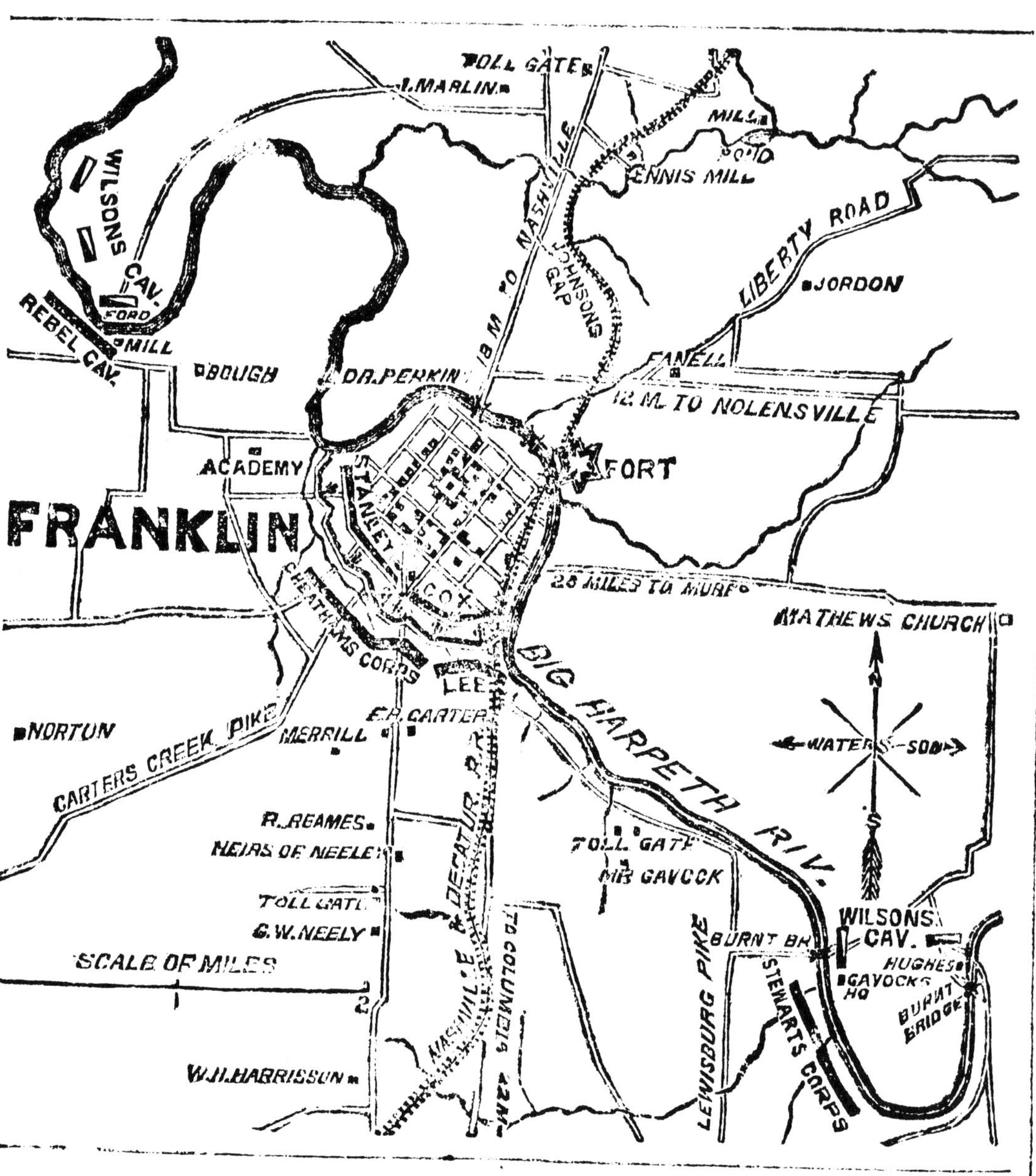

MAP 39

The Battle of Franklin, Tennessee

Published in the *New York Herald*, December 3, 1864

(Original 12 × 12 cm.)

WITH THE FALL OF ATLANTA, JOHN B. HOOD INITIATED A MOVEMENT TO DRAW THE Union army northward by threatening its lines of supply and communications. William T. Sherman countered by detaching troops under John Schofield to join George Thomas in opposing Hood. Considerable maneuvering followed as Hood unsuccessfully tried to impose his army between Schofield and the Union base at Nashville. After three days of skirmishing, Schofield's two corps reached Franklin at dawn on November 30 and entrenched, with their left and right wings resting on the Harpeth River. Hood opened the battle in the afternoon with a general frontal assault. This attack carried some of the outer works and Confederate troops temporarily breached the Union line where it crossed the Columbia Pike, but reserves repulsed Hood's army, which continued to attack all along the Union line until night. In the middle of the night, Schofield crossed the river unmolested and continued toward Nashville.

The *Herald*'s map, printed in New York less than three days after the event, accurately depicts the area and much of the action. The Union position extended farther south of Franklin than is shown, with the line passing just outside the E. H. Carter house. The main Confederate attack moved up the Columbia Pike (the unlabeled road running north-south, west of the railroad), and much of the fighting took place around the Carter house. The map indicates the corps of Stephen D. Lee, Benjamin Cheatham, and Alexander Stewart (*lower right corner*). Despite the locations shown, it was Stewart who attacked the Union left, while Lee's late-arriving corps formed to his rear. The division of Jacob Cox on the Union left and David Stanley's corps on the Union right are noted in the correct locations. James H. Wilson's cavalry operated on the left flank (*lower right*), as shown, where they participated in a heated skirmish with Nathan B. Forrest's cavalry, not Stewart's corps, north of the river. The map errs in showing cavalry units northwest of Franklin and neglects to show the advanced position of George Wagner's division on the Columbia Pike, where they were overrun by Confederates at the beginning of the battle. On December 5, the *Herald* printed a revised version of this map with corrected Confederate troop locations.

Reports in U.S. War Department, *War of the Rebellion*: ser. 1, vol. 45, pt. 1, with one map.
Maps in U.S. War Department, *Atlas*: pl. 72, no. 1; pl. 73, nos. 3, 4, 5; pl. 105, no. 9.
Other newspaper maps: *New York Herald* (12/5/64), *Philadelphia Inquirer* (12/6/64).

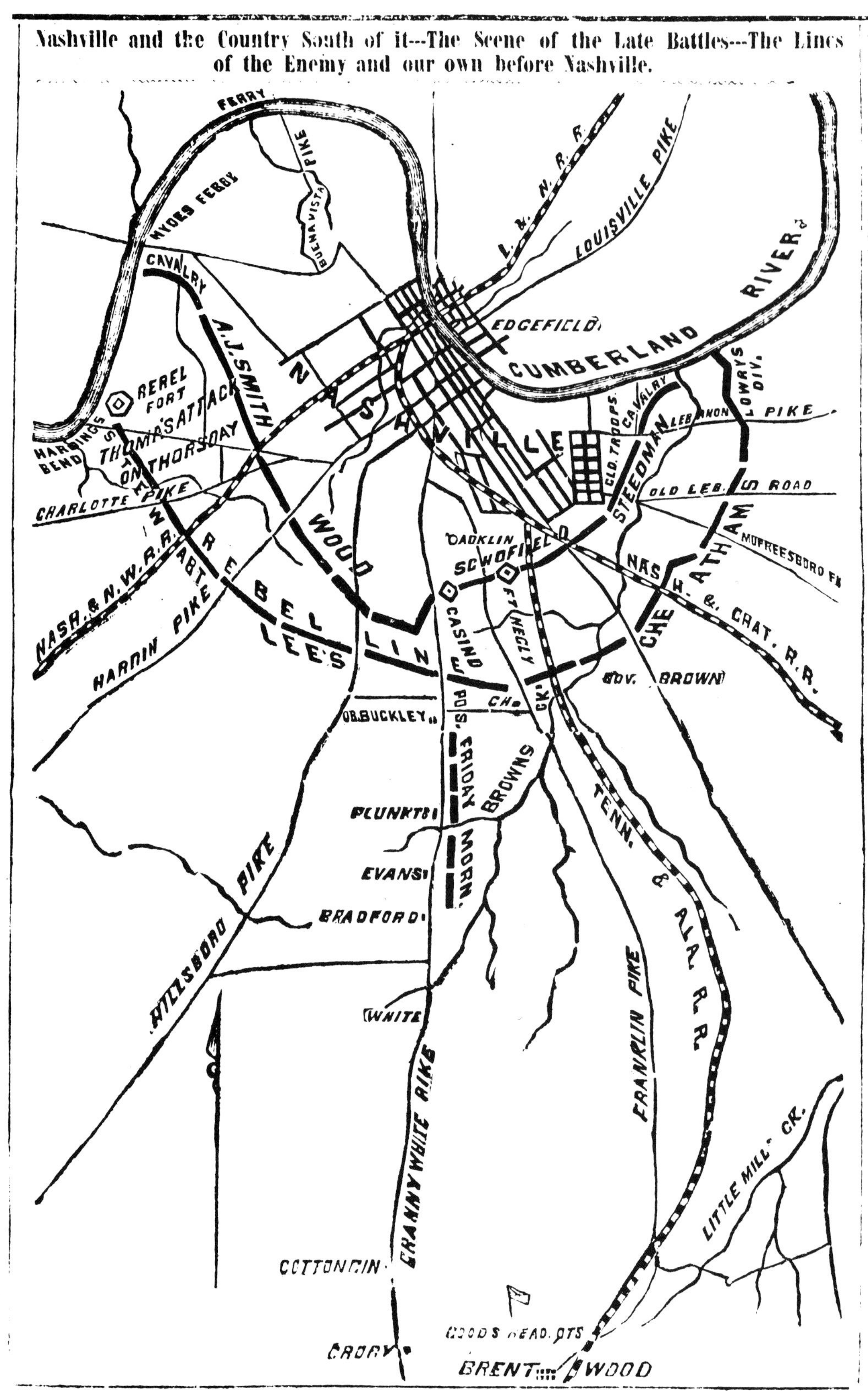

Nashville and the Country South of it—The Scene of the Late Battles—The Lines of the Enemy and our own before Nashville.

M A P 40

The Battle of Nashville, Tennessee

Published in the *Cincinnati Daily Commercial*, December 19, 1864

(Original 25 × 17 cm.)

DESPITE ITS DEFEAT AT FRANKLIN, JOHN B. HOOD'S CONFEDERATE ARMY MOVED ON Nashville. Unable to mount an offensive against George Thomas's strong position, Hood deployed opposite the Union works and hoped for reinforcements. On December 15, after two weeks of preparations, Thomas initiated a well-coordinated movement against Hood. The day began with a diversionary attack on the Confederate right along the Nashville & Chattanooga Railroad by James Steedman's division. Moving parallel to the Hillsboro Pike, troops under A. J. Smith and Thomas Wood then struck the left of the Confederate line while James Wilson's cavalry turned its flank. Confederates commanded by Alexander Stewart slowly gave ground and retired to the Granny White Pike. Hood shifted Benjamin Cheatham's corps to bolster the left of his line, and Steedman forced back the weakened Confederate right. Nightfall allowed Hood to reorganize his lines, but the following day his badly outnumbered army was driven from the field.

The map, drawn by Hugh Allen, depicts the Union lines, including Wood's salient, west of the Granny White Pike, and the Black brigades, under Steedman ("cld. troops," east of Nashville), as they appeared before the attack of the 15th. The Confederate positions are portrayed considerably less accurately. The corps of Stewart, Cheatham, and Stephen D. Lee are properly aligned (semicircle south of Nashville) but did not extend as far as shown. The Confederate right began just beyond the Nashville & Chattanooga Railroad, from there running to the Hillsboro Pike, where it angled sharply to the south parallel to the road. Confederate cavalry temporarily acted as a wing on the far left, establishing near the river a battery that the mapmaker apparently interpreted as a continuation of the line and a terminal fort. This confusion over the extent of the Confederate line accounts for the note indicating the point of the Union attack ("Thomas attack on Thursday"), which struck the Confederate flank along Hillsboro Pike. The position of part of the Union line on the 16th appears along the Granny White Pike ("pos. Friday morn."). Wood's corps occupied this position on the night of the 15th, but the locations of other Union troops on the second day are not shown. On the 15th, Hood made his headquarters, farther north than shown (bottom of map), east of the Granny White house (*lower center*).

Reports in U.S. War Department, *War of the Rebellion*: ser. 1, vol. 45, pt. 1, with one map.
Maps in U.S. War Department, *Atlas*: pl. 72, no. 2; pl. 73, nos. 1, 2.
Other newspaper maps: *New York Herald* (12/18/64).

Appendix

The following is a list of all daily Northern newspapers known to have published Civil War maps and the total number of maps they published each year between April 1, 1861, and April 30, 1865.

	1861	*1862*	*1863*	*1864*	*1865*	*Totals*
Baltimore American & Commercial Advertiser	4	4	0	0	0	8
Boston Daily Journal	5	8	3	4	0	20
Chicago Daily Tribune	1	98	92	27	0	218
Chicago Evening Journal	0	0	2	0	0	2
Chicago Post	23	9*	5	4	0**	41
Chicago Times	0	47	17	11	1	76
Cincinnati Daily Commercial	4	2	1	3	2	12
Cincinnati Daily Enquirer	2	0	0	0	0	2
Cincinnati Daily Gazette	4	14	16	5	0	39
Cincinnati Daily Times	36	76	31	19	8	170
Daily Missouri Democrat	0	2	3	0	0	5
Daily Missouri Republican	10	12	4	0	0	26
Daily Ohio State Journal (Columbus)	1	5	1	0	0	7
New York Herald	115	257	199	104	33	708
New York Times	35	72	5	4	0	116
New York Tribune	27	98	35	16	4	180
Philadelphia Inquirer	63	115	52	42	13	285
The Press (Philadelphia)	2	0	0	0	0	2
The Sun (New York)	18	37*	11	9	3	78
The World (New York)	19	20	4	4	4	51
Totals	369	876	481	252	68	2046

*No issues located for July–December.
**No issues located.

Select Bibliography

Manuscript Sources

James Gordon Bennett Papers, Library of Congress.

James Gordon Bennett Papers, New York Public Library.

Albert H. Bodman Papers, Chicago Historical Society.

Sylvanus Cadwallader Papers, Library of Congress.

Sydney Howard Gay Papers, Rare Book and Manuscript Library, Columbia University.

Horace Greeley Papers, Library of Congress.

Horace Greeley Papers, New York Public Library.

Harper & Row Archives, Rare Book and Manuscript Library, Columbia University.

Frederic Hudson Papers, Concord Public Library.

Henry J. Raymond Papers, New York Public Library.

Whitelaw Reid Papers, Library of Congress.

George Hay Stuart Papers, Library of Congress.

George Alfred Townsend Papers, Maryland State Archives.

Henry Villard Papers, Widener Library, Harvard University.

Printed Sources

Cartography and Maps

Ager, John. "Maps and Propaganda," *Bulletin of the Society of University Cartographers* 11 (1977): 1–15.

Bechler, Gustavus. *Atlas Showing Battles, Engagements, and Important Localities Connected With the Campaigns in Virginia*. Philadelphia: G. R. Bechler, 1864.

Blakemore, M. J., and J. Brian Harley. "Concepts in the History of Cartography, A Review and Perspective," *Cartographica* 17 (1980).

Bosse, David. *Civil War Newspaper Maps of the Northern Daily Press: A Cartobibliography*. Westport, Conn.: Greenwood Press, 1993.

Canan, H. V. "Maps for the Civil War," *Armor* 65 (1956): 34–42.

Commager, Henry S. Introduction to *The Official Atlas of the Civil War*. New York: Thomas Yoseloff, 1958.

Gilmartin, Patricia. "The Design of Journalistic Maps: Purposes, Parameters, and Prospects," *Cartographica* 22 (1985): 1–18.

Gulley, Harold, and Louis DeVorsey. "Lost in Battle," *The Geographical Magazine* 28 (1986): 288–93.

Karrow, Robert W., and Ronald Grim. "Two Examples of Thematic Maps: Civil War and Fire

Insurance Maps," in David Buisseret, ed., *From Sea Charts to Satellite Images: Interpreting North American History through Maps*. Chicago: University of Chicago Press, 1990: 213–37.

Lilley, David A. "Anticipating the Atlas to Accompany the Official Records," *Lincoln Herald* 84 (1982): 37–42.

McMurtrie, Douglas. *Printing Geographic Maps with Movable Type*. New York: privately printed, 1925.

Monmonier, Mark. "Maps in the New York Times, 1860–1980: A Study in the History of Journalistic Cartography," *Proceedings of the Pennsylvania Academy of Science* 58 (1984): 79–83.

———. *Maps with the News: The Development of American Journalistic Cartography*. Chicago: University of Chicago Press, 1989.

Muntz, A. Philip. "Union Mapping in the American Civil War," *Imago Mundi* 17 (1963): 90–94.

O'Reilly, Noel, David Bosse, and Robert W. Karrow. *Civil War Maps: A Graphic Index to the* Atlas to Accompany the Official Records of the Union and Confederate Armies. Chicago: Newberry Library, 1987.

Rhoads, James B. "Civil War Maps and Mapping," *The Military Engineer* 49 (1957): 38–43.

Ristow, Walter. "Journalistic Cartography," *Surveying and Mapping* 17 (1957): 369–90.

Robinson, Arthur. *The Look of Maps*. Madison: University of Wisconsin Press, 1985.

Stephenson, Richard W. *Civil War Maps: An Annotated List of Maps and Atlases in the Library of Congress*. Washington: Library of Congress, 1989.

U.S. Military Academy. *The West Point Atlas of the Civil War*. New York: Frederick A. Praeger, 1962.

U.S. National Archives. *A Guide to Civil War Maps in the National Archives*. Washington, D.C.: National Archives Trust Fund Board, 1986.

U.S. War Department. *Atlas to Accompany the Official Records of the Union and Confederate Armies*. Washington, D.C.: Government Printing Office, 1891–95.

Woodward, David. *The All American Map: Wax Engraving and Its Influence on Cartography*. Chicago: University of Chicago Press, 1977.

———, ed. *Five Centuries of Map Printing*. Chicago: University of Chicago Press, 1975.

Civil War

Barrett, John G. *The Civil War in North Carolina*. Chapel Hill: University of North Carolina Press, 1963.

Baxter, William. *Pea Ridge and Prairie Grove, or Scenes and Incidents of the War in Arkansas*. Cincinnati: Poe & Hitchcock, 1866.

Blackford, Susan L., comp. *Letters from Lee's Army, or Memoirs of Life In and Out of the Army in Virginia During the War Between the States*. New York: Charles Scribner's Sons, 1947.

Boatner, Mark M. *The Civil War Dictionary*. New York: David McKay, 1988.

Cadwallader, Sylvanus. *Three Years with General Grant*. Edited by Benjamin P. Thomas. New York: Alfred Knopf, 1956.

Carter, Robert G. *Four Brothers in Blue, or Sunshine and Shadows of the War of the Rebellion*. Austin: University of Texas Press, 1978.

Carter, Samuel. *The Final Fortress: The Campaign for Vicksburg, 1862–1863*. New York: St. Martin's, 1980.

Chickamauga and Chattanooga National Park Commission. *Atlas of the Battlefields of Chickamauga, Chattanooga, and Vicinity.* Washington, D.C.: Government Printing Office, 1901.

Connelly, Thomas L. *Civil War Tennessee: Battles and Leaders.* Knoxville: University of Tennessee Press, 1979.

Cooling, Benjamin F. *Forts Henry and Donelson: The Key to the Confederate Heartland.* Knoxville: University of Tennessee Press, 1987.

Davis, William C. *Battle at Bull Run.* Baton Rouge: Louisiana State University Press, 1977.

Doubleday, Abner. *Chancellorsville and Gettysburg.* New York: Charles Scribner's Sons, 1882.

Dowdey, Clifford. *The Seven Days: The Emergence of Robert E. Lee.* Boston: Little, Brown, 1964.

Fite, Emerson D. *Social and Industrial Conditions in the North during the Civil War.* New York: Peter Smith, 1930.

Freeman, Douglas S. *Lee's Lieutenants: A Study in Command.* New York: Charles Scribner's Sons, 1942–44.

Grant, Ulysses S. *Personal Memoirs of U. S. Grant.* New York: C. L. Webster, 1885–86.

Harrison, Lowell. *The Civil War in Kentucky.* Lexington: University Press of Kentucky, 1975.

Henderson, G. F. R. *Stonewall Jackson and the American Civil War.* London: Longmans, Green, 1898.

Howe, M. A. DeWolfe, ed. *Marching with Sherman: Passages from the Letters and Campaign Diaries of Henry Hitchcock.* New Haven: Yale University Press, 1927.

Hughes, Nathaniel C., Jr. *The Battle of Belmont: Grant Strikes South.* Chapel Hill: University of North Carolina Press, 1991.

Humphries, Andrew A. *The Virginia Campaign of '64 and '65: The Army of the Potomac and the Army of the James.* New York: Charles Scribner's Sons, 1883.

Johnson, Robert U., and Clarence Buell, eds. *Battles and Leaders of the Civil War,* 4 vols. New York: Century, 1887–88.

Jones, Virgil. *The Civil War at Sea: March 1862–July 1863, the River War.* New York: Holt, Rinehart and Winston, 1961.

Kennedy, Frances, ed. *The Civil War Battlefield Guide.* Boston: Houghton Mifflin, 1990.

Krick, Robert. *Stonewall Jackson at Cedar Mountain.* Chapel Hill: University of North Carolina Press, 1990.

Leech, Margaret. *Reveille in Washington, 1860–1865.* New York: Harper & Bros., 1941.

Livermore, Thomas. *Numbers and Losses in the Civil War in America: 1861–65.* Bloomington: Indiana University Press, 1957.

Longstreet, James. *From Manassas to Appomattox: Memories of the Civil War in America.* Philadelphia: J. P. Lippincott, 1896.

Luvas, Jay, and Harold Nelson. *The U.S. Army War College Guide to the Battles of Chancellorsville and Fredericksburg.* Carlisle, Pa.: South Mountain Press, 1988.

McClellan, George B. *McClellan's Own Story, the War for the Union.* New York: Charles Webster, 1887.

McDonough, James L. *Chattanooga: A Death Grip on the Confederacy.* Knoxville: University of Tennessee Press, 1984.

———. *Five Tragic Hours: The Battle of Franklin.* Knoxville: University of Tennessee Press, 1983.

Monaghan, Jay. *Civil War on the Western Border, 1854–1865.* Boston: Little, Brown, 1955.

Moore, Frank, ed. *The Rebellion Record, A Diary of American Events, With Documents, Narratives, Illustrative Incidents, Poetry, Etc.,* 12 vols. New York: D. Appleton, 1861–1873.

Patch, Joseph. *The Battle of Ball's Bluff*. Leesburg, Va.: Potomac Press, 1958.

Pfanz, Harry W. *Gettysburg: The Second Day*. Chapel Hill: University of North Carolina Press, 1987.

Phillips, Christopher. *Damned Yankee: The Life of General Nathaniel Lyon*. Columbia: University of Missouri Press, 1990.

Quaife, Milo, ed. *From the Cannon's Mouth: The Civil War Letters of General Alpheus S. Williams*. Detroit: Wayne State University Press, 1959.

Sears, Stephen. *Landscape Turned Red: The Battle of Antietam*. New Haven: Ticknor & Fields, 1983.

Sherman, William T. *Memoirs of General William T. Sherman*. New York: D. Appleton, 1875.

Shiloh National Military Park Commission. *The Battle of Shiloh and the Organizations Engaged*. Washington, D.C.: Government Printing Office, 1903.

Sullivan, James R. *Chickamauga and Chattanooga Battlefields*. Washington, D.C.: National Park Service, 1956.

Trudeau, Noah A. *Bloody Roads South: The Wilderness to Cold Harbor, May–June 1864*. Boston: Little, Brown, 1989.

U.S. National Park Service. *Pea Ridge National Military Park, Arkansas*. Washington, D.C.: National Park Service, 1974.

U.S. Naval War Records Office. *Official Records of the Union and Confederate Navies in the War of the Rebellion*. Washington, D.C.: Government Printing Office, 1894–1922.

U.S. War Department. *Report of the Secretary of War, 1864; 1865*. Washington, D.C.: Government Printing Office, 1865; 1866.

———. *The War of the Rebellion: A Compilation of the Official Records of the Union and Confederate Armies*. Washington, D.C.: Government Printing Office, 1880–91.

Van Horne, Thomas. *History of the Army of the Cumberland, Its Organization, Campaigns, and Battles* (with atlas by Edward Ruger). Cincinnati: R. Clarke, 1875.

Webb, Alexander. *The Peninsula: McClellan's Campaign of 1862*. New York: Charles Scribner's Sons, 1881.

Weld, Stephen M. *War Diary and Letters of Stephen Minot Weld, 1861–1865*. Boston: Massachusetts Historical Society, 1979.

Williams, T. Harry. *Lincoln and His Generals*. New York: Grosset & Dunlap, 1952.

Engraving and Printing

Beam, Philip. *Winslow Homer's Magazine Engravings*. New York: Harper & Row, 1979.

Byrn, Edward. *The Progress of Invention in the Nineteenth Century*. New York: Munn, 1900.

Carpenter, J. "Concerning the Graphotype," *Once A Week* (1867): 181–84.

Chatto, William. *A Treatise on Wood Engraving, Historical and Practical*. London: Charles Knight, 1861.

Comparto, Frank. *Chronicles of Genius and Folly: R. Hoe & Company and the Printing Press as a Service to Democracy*. Culver City, Calif.: Labyrinthos, 1979.

"Desultory Thoughts on Wood-Engraving and Wood-Cut Printing," *The Knickerbocker or New York Monthly Magazine* 41 (1853): 51–57.

Emerson, William A. *Practical Instruction in the Art of Wood Engraving*. East Douglas, Mass.: Charles Batcheller, 1876.

Everett, George. "Printing Technology as a Barrier to Multi-Column Headlines, 1850–1895," *Journalism Quarterly* 53 (1976): 528–32.

Fuller, Samuel E. *A Manual of Instruction in the Art of Wood Engraving*. Boston: J. Watson, 1867.

Gambee, Budd L. "American Book and Magazine Illustration of the Later Nineteenth Century," in Frances Brewer, ed., *Book Illustration: Papers Presented at the Third Rare Book Conference of the American Library Association*. Berlin: Gebr. Mann Verlag, 1963: 45–55.

———. *Frank Leslie and His Illustrated Newspaper*. Ann Arbor: Department of Library Science, University of Michigan, 1964.

Gilks, Thomas. *The Art of Wood Engraving*. London: Winsor & Newton, 1867.

Griffin, Gillett. "The Development of Woodcut Printing in America," *Princeton University Library Chronicle* 20 (1958): 7–18.

Hamilton, Sinclair. *Early American Book Illustrators and Engravers, 1670–1870*. Princeton: Princeton University Press, 1968.

Hind, Arthur M. *A History of Engraving and Etching from the Fifteenth Century to the Year 1914*. New York: Dover Publications, 1963.

"How Our Pictures Are Made," *The Child At Home*, vol. 2 (1860): 19.

Hunter, Dard. *Papermaking: The History and Technique of an Ancient Craft*. New York: Alfred Knopf, 1947.

Kainen, Jacob. "Why Bewick Succeeded," in *Contributions from the Museum of History and Technology, Bulletin 218*. Washington, D.C.: U.S. National Museum, 1959: 186–201.

Kubler, George A. *A New History of Stereotyping*. New York: privately printed, 1941.

Lossing, Benson. *A Memorial of Alexander Anderson, M.D., the First Engraver on Wood in America*. New York: privately printed, 1872.

Mackellar, Thomas. *The American Printer*. Philadelphia: L. Johnson, 1866.

Moran, James. *Printing Presses: History and Development from the Fifteenth Century to Modern Times*. London: Faber & Faber, 1973.

Munsell, Joel. *Chronology of the Origin and Progress of Paper and Papermaking*. Albany: J. Munsell, 1876.

Penny, Virginia. *The Employments of Women: A Cyclopedia of Woman's Work*. Boston: Walker, Wise, 1863.

Rainey, Sue. "Wood Engraving in America," in Mildred Abraham, ed., *Embellished with Numerous Engravings: The Works of American Illustrators and Wood Engravers, 1670–1880*. Charlottesville: University of Virginia Library, 1986: 7–29.

Reiner, Imre. *Woodcut/Wood Engraving: A Contribution to the History of the Art*. London: Publix Publishing, 1947.

Ringwalt, J. Luther. *American Encyclopedia of Printing*. Philadelphia: Menamin & Ringwalt, 1871.

Tebbel, John. *A History of Book Publishing in the United States*. New York: R. R. Bowker, 1972.

Tucker, Stephen D. "History of R. Hoe & Company, 1834–1885," *Proceedings of the American Antiquarian Society* 28 (1973): 351–453.

Weitenkampf, Frank. *The Illustrated Book*. Cambridge: Harvard University Press, 1938.

Winship, Michael. "Printing with Plates in the Nineteenth-Century United States," *Printing History* 5 (1983): 15–26.

Woodward, David. "The Decline of Commercial Wood-Engraving in Nineteenth-Century America," *Journal of the Printing Historical Society* 10 (1974): 57–83.

Journalism

Andrews, J. Cutler. *The North Reports the Civil War.* Pittsburgh: University of Pittsburgh Press, 1955.

———. *The South Reports the Civil War.* Princeton: Princeton University Press, 1970.

Babcock, Havilah. "The Press and the Civil War," *Journalism Quarterly* 6 (1929): 1–5.

Bleyer, Willard G. *Main Currents in the History of American Journalism.* Boston: Houghton Mifflin, 1927.

Brown, Francis. *Raymond of the "Times."* New York: W. W. Norton, 1951.

Browne, Junius. *Four Years in Secessia.* Hartford, Conn.: American Publishing, 1865.

———. *The Great Metropolis: A Mirror of New York.* Hartford, Conn.: American Publishing, 1869.

Bullard, Frederic. *Famous War Correspondents.* Boston: Little, Brown, 1914.

Carlson, Oliver. *The Man Who Made News: James Gordon Bennett.* New York: Duell, Sloan & Pearce, 1942.

Cortissoz, Royal. *The Life of Whitelaw Reid.* New York: Charles Scribner's Sons, 1921.

Crozier, Emmet. *Yankee Reporters, 1861–65.* New York: Oxford University Press, 1956.

Davis, Elmer. *History of the* New York Times, *1851–1921.* New York: New York Times, 1921.

Dill, William A. *Growth of Newspapers in the United States.* Lawrence: Department of Journalism, University of Kansas, 1928.

Emery, Edwin, and Michael Emery. *The Press and America: An Interpretative History of the Mass Media.* Englewood Cliffs, N.J.: Prentice-Hall, 1978.

Exman, Eugene. *The House of Harper: One Hundred and Fifty Years of Publishing.* New York: Harper & Row, 1967.

Fahrney, Ralph. *Horace Greeley and the "Tribune" in the Civil War.* Cedar Rapids, Iowa: Torch Press, 1936.

Fermer, Douglas. *James Gordon Bennett and the* New York Herald. Woodbridge, U.K.: Boydell Press, 1986.

Fiske, Stephen R. "Gentlemen of the Press," *Harper's New Monthly Magazine* 26 (1863): 361–67.

Goldsmith, Adolph. "Reporting the Civil War, Union Army Press Relations," *Journalism Quarterly* 33 (1956): 478–87.

Griffis, William E. *Charles Carleton Coffin, War Correspondent, Traveller, Author and Statesman.* Boston: Estes & Lauriat, 1898.

Harper, Joseph Henry. *The House of Harper.* New York: Harper & Bros., 1912.

Hudson, Frederic. *Journalism in the United States from 1690 to 1872.* New York: Harper & Bros., 1873.

Hutt, Allen. *The Changing Newspaper.* London: Gordon Frazer, 1973.

Jackson, Mason. *The Pictorial Press, Its Origins and Progress.* London: Hurst & Blackett, 1885.

Kenny, Daniel J. *American Newspaper Directory and Record of the Press.* New York: Watson, 1861.

Kinsley, Philip. *The* Chicago Tribune: *Its First Hundred Years.* New York: Alfred Knopf, 1943.

Knox, Thomas. *Camp-Fire and Cotton-Field: Southern Adventure in the Time of War.* Philadelphia: Jones Bros., 1865.

Langley, Peter. "Pessimism-Optimism of Civil War Military News, June, 1863–March, 1865," *Journalism Quarterly* 49 (1972): 74–78.

Lee, Alfred M. *The Daily Newspaper in America.* New York: Macmillan, 1937.

Lee, James M. *History of American Journalism.* Boston: Houghton Mifflin, 1923.
Marszalek, John. *Sherman's Other War: The General and the Civil War Press.* Memphis: Memphis State University Press, 1981.
Mathews, Joseph. *Reporting the Wars.* Minneapolis: University of Minnesota Press, 1957.
Maverick, Augustus. *Henry J. Raymond and the New York Press.* Hartford, Conn.: A. S. Hals, 1870.
Mott, Frank Luther. *American Journalism: A History of Newspapers in the United States through 260 Years.* New York: Macmillan, 1953.
———. *A History of American Magazines, 1850–1865.* Cambridge: Harvard University Press, 1938.
Newell, Robert H. *The Orpheus C. Kerr Papers.* New York: Blakeman & Mason, 1862.
North, S. N. D. *History and Present Condition of the Newspaper and Periodical Press in the United States.* Washington, D.C.: Government Printing Office, 1884.
O'Brien, Frank. *The Story of "The Sun."* New York: George H. Doran, 1918.
Randall, James G. "The Newspaper Problem and Its Bearing upon Military Secrecy during the Civil War," *American Historical Review* 23 (1918): 303–23.
Rosewater, Victor. *History of Cooperative News-Gathering in the United States.* New York: D. Appleton, 1930.
Rutland, Robert. *The Newsmongers: Journalism in the Life of the Nation, 1690–1972.* New York: Dial, 1973.
Salmon, Lucy M. *The Newspaper and the Historian.* New York: Oxford University Press, 1923.
Shanks, William F. G. "How We Get Our News," *Harper's New Monthly Magazine* 34 (1867): 511–22.
Starr, Louis M. *Bohemian Brigade: Civil War Newsmen in Action.* New York: Alfred Knopf, 1954.
Thompson, W. Fletcher. *The Image of War: Pictorial Reporting of the American Civil War.* New York: Thomas Yoseloff, 1960.
Townsend, George Alfred. "Campaigning With General Pope," *Cornhill Magazine* 6 (1862): 758–70.
———. *Campaigns of a Non-Combatant.* New York: Blelock, 1866.
Villard, Henry. "Army Correspondence," *Nation* 1 (1865): 79–81; 114–16; 144–46.
———. *Memoirs of Henry Villard, Journalist and Financier, 1835–1900.* Boston: Houghton Mifflin, 1904.
Weisberger, Bernard. *Reporters for the Union.* Boston: Little, Brown, 1953.
Wendt, Lloyd. *Chicago Tribune: The Rise of a Great American Newspaper.* Chicago: Rand McNally, 1979.
Wilkie, Franc. *Pen and Powder.* Boston: Ticknor, 1888.
Wilson, Quintus C. "Voluntary Press Censorship during the Civil War," *Journalism Quarterly* 19 (1942): 251–61.

Index

Designed by Martha Farlow

Composed by The Composing Room of Michigan, Inc., in Bodoni

Printed by The Maple Press Company on 80-lb. Glatco Matte Smooth
and bound in Holliston Roxite A with Multicolor Antique endsheets

ILLINOIS
INDIANA
OHIO
MISSOURI
Ohio R.
23
KENTUCKY
3
5
7
11
Cumberland R.
10
9
40
39
ARKANSAS
34
Arkansas R.
13
TENNESSEE
Mississippi R.
12
33
31
Tennessee R.
37
26
MISSISSIPPI
38
25
30
28
ALABAMA
GEORGIA
LOUISIANA
FLORIDA
15